Perrier,
c'est fou !

Perrier, c'est fou !

150 years of history

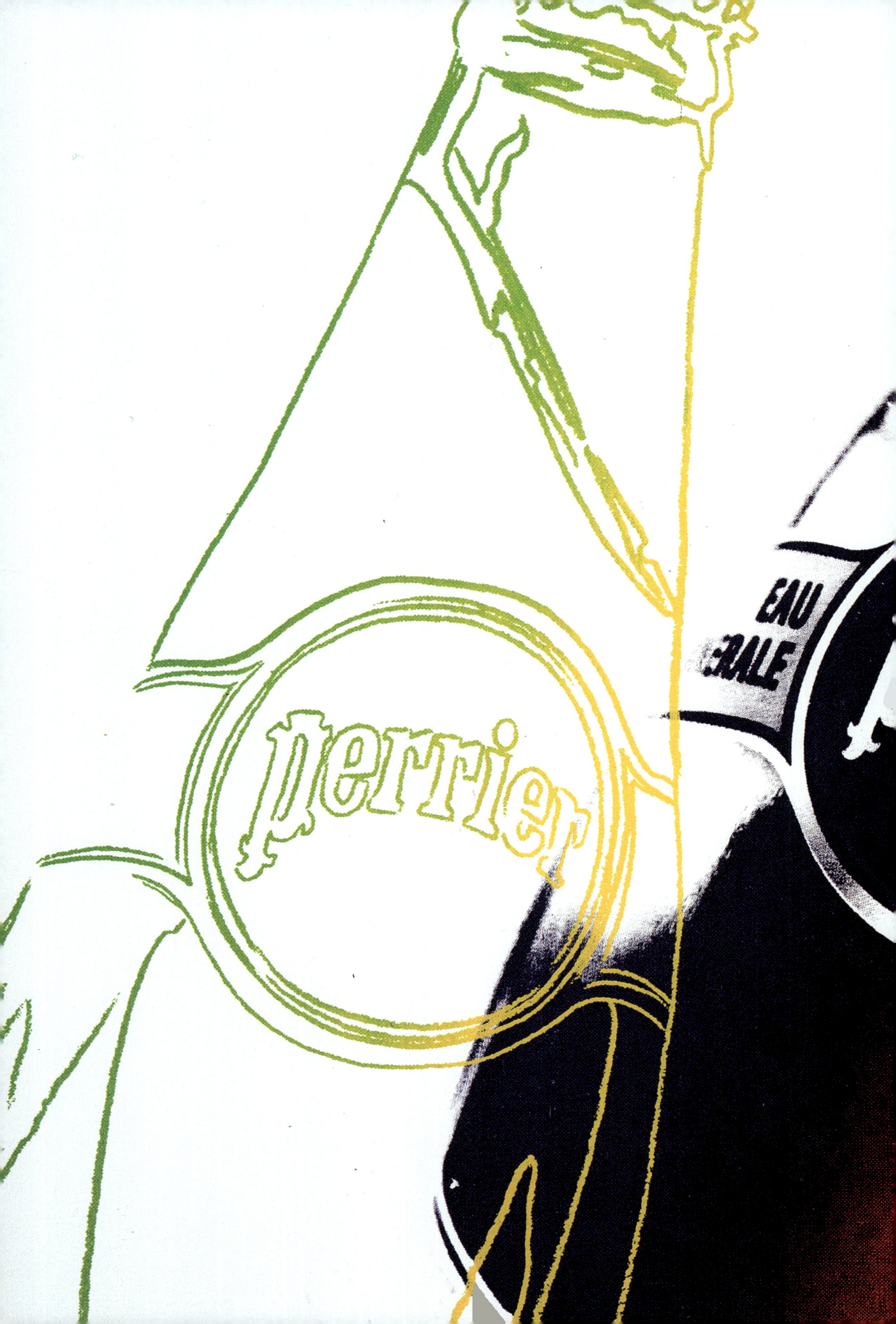
perrier
EAU

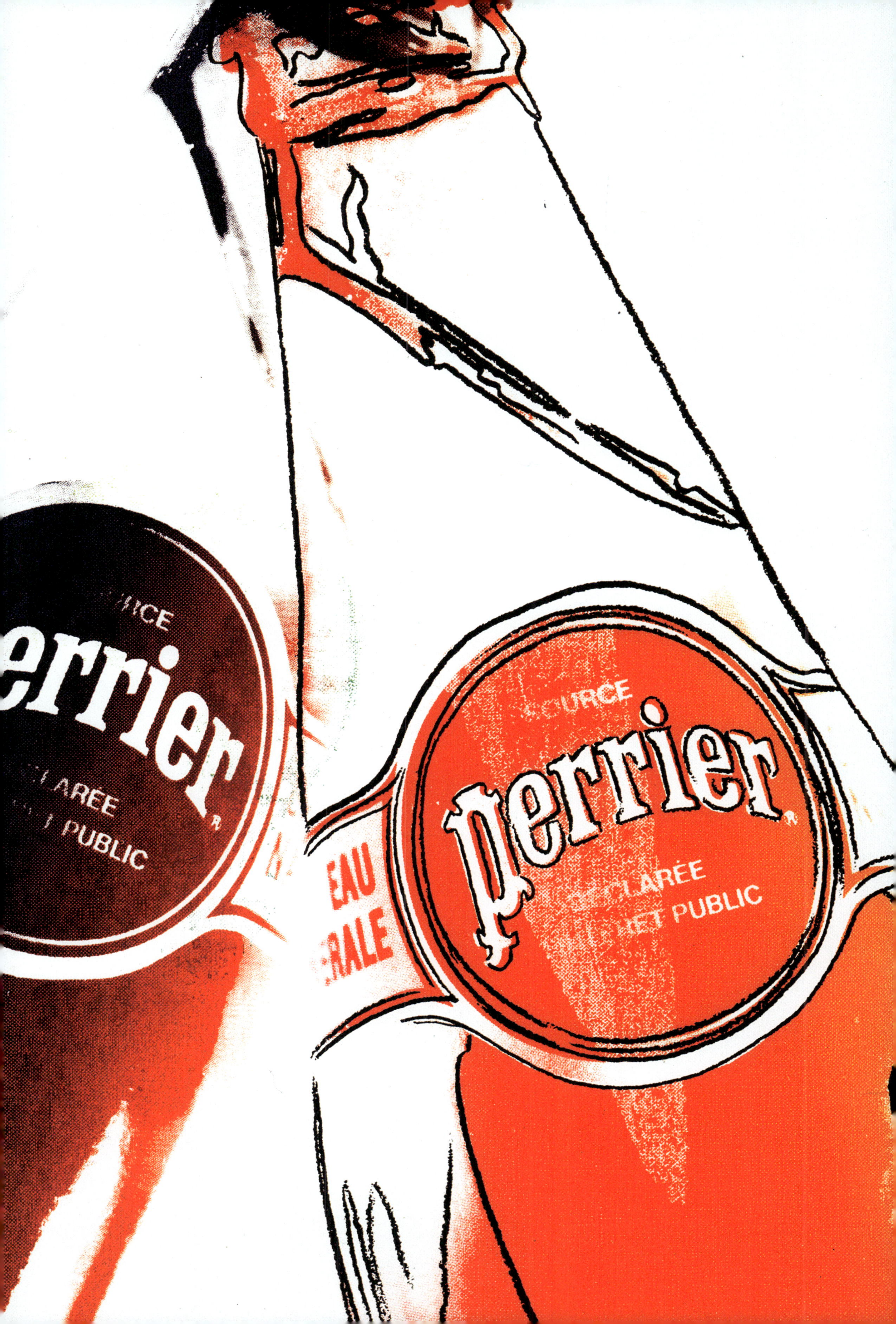
perrier
PUBLIC
perrier
EAU
PUBLIC

Design and production
Les Éditions Textuel, 2013
4 impasse de Conti
75006 Paris
www.editionstextuel.com

Author: Fabienne Waks
Picture researcher: Hélène Orizet
Graphic design: Agnès Boulmer
Translation: Marianne Chalmers

Preceding double-page spread:
Silkscreen print by Andy Warhol,
1983

Publisher's note:
PERRIER® is a trademark of the
Nestlé Group. For ease of reading,
all references to Perrier henceforth
imply PERRIER®.

contents

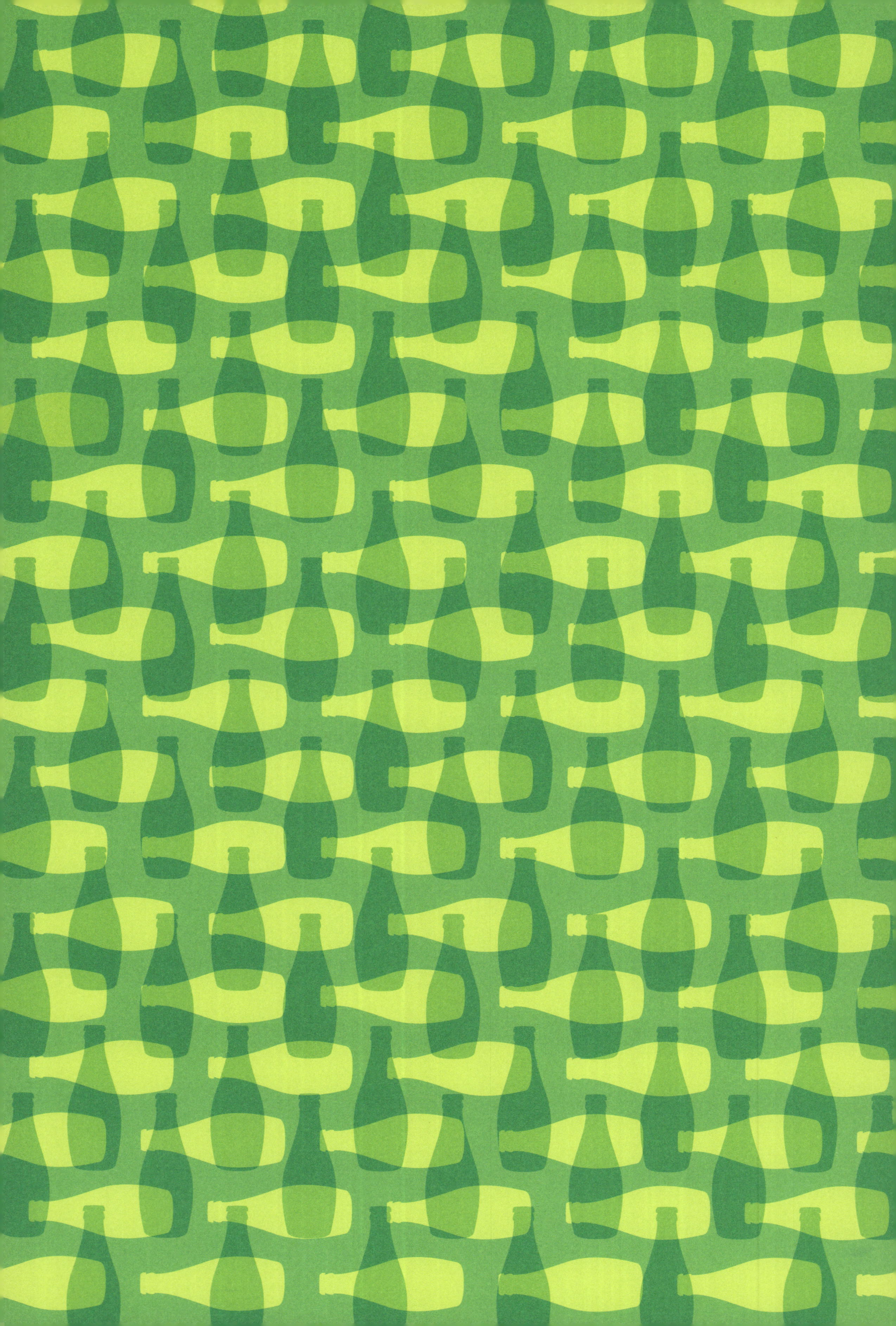

natural history lessons

The history of a water known worldwide as Perrier has its roots in prehistoric times in a spring formed millions of years ago by the vagaries of nature. It already had its aficionados in the ancient world. The Carthaginian general Hannibal stopped off in Vergèze in 218 BC on his march to Rome while his enemies, the Romans, built the first baths there to relax in the bubbling waters.

Perrier before Perrier

1863

On June 23, in the reign of Emperor Napoleon III, a decree is signed authorizing the exploitation of the spring at Les Bouillens in Vergèze in the Gard département, which has been known since Roman times. Alphonse Granier, the owner of the site, builds a spa resort.

1868

A spa company known as the Société de l'Etablissement Thermal des Eaux Minérales de Vergèze is founded, offering spa clients a variety of types of baths and the opportunity to sample the water from Les Bouillens.

1870

The Hôtel des Baigneurs is built to replace the timber facilities devastated by fire. Keen to spread the word about the beneficial properties of water from Les Bouillens, Alphonse Granier dubs it "the princess of table waters" in an advertisement.

1888

The spa, which has changed its name to the Société Anonyme des Eaux de Vergèze ou des Bouillens, goes bankrupt. It is taken over by Louis Rouvière, a wine grower, but lies dormant for several years.

1894

Louis Rouvière invites Louis-Eugène Perrier, a physician and director of the spa at Euzet-les-Bains, to take on the task of revitalizing Les Bouillens.

1898

Doctor Perrier single-handedly takes over the helm of the new company, the Société Anonyme des Eaux Minérales, Boissons et Produits Hygiéniques de Vergèze. He perfects techniques for water and gas capture, establishes the optimum blend and designs the very first bottle. Les Bouillens water "to go" is born.

1903

Doctor Perrier's efforts to attract funding for his spa in Vergèze pique the interest of St. John Harmsworth, brother of the British press magnates, who buys shares in the company.

think British, drink global

1906

As a tribute to the Doctor during his lifetime, St. John Harmsworth calls both his company and his water "Perrier" and thus the Compagnie de la Source Perrier is born. It has already established its credentials with a Royal Warrant "By Appointment to His Majesty the King of England" and is exported primarily to the British Isles and its colonies, in particular India. The unusual shape of the bottle is inspired by an Indian club. St. John Harmsworth is paralyzed in an automobile accident.

1907

7.5 million bottles are produced in 1907, of which 7 million are exported mainly to London, with a small number going to New York.

1910

Production assumes an industrial scale with the construction of a new factory and the introduction of a cutting-edge production process. There are now almost 300 employees.

1928

The Vergèze bottling plant is reorganized and doubles in size in preparation for entry into the French market. Advertisements present Perrier as the "champagne of table waters".

1933

When the Perrier spring is declared to be of "public interest", work is carried out to reinforce the protected area around it. Over 18 million bottles are sold throughout the world and in France, where Perrier is gaining devotees. St. John Harmsworth is succeeded after his death by a group of British investors.

1936

The Perrier Girl, designed by Jean-Gabriel Domergue, is born. Advertisements for Perrier proliferate in magazines. A campaign offering variations on "the champagne of table waters" theme is particularly eye-catching as it draws on the talents of some of the best writers of the era. The company merges with a subsidiary and becomes Source Perrier SA.

1940

The British shareholder-owned Perrier company is requisitioned by the Germans during the Occupation to supply the German navy, the Kriegsmarine.

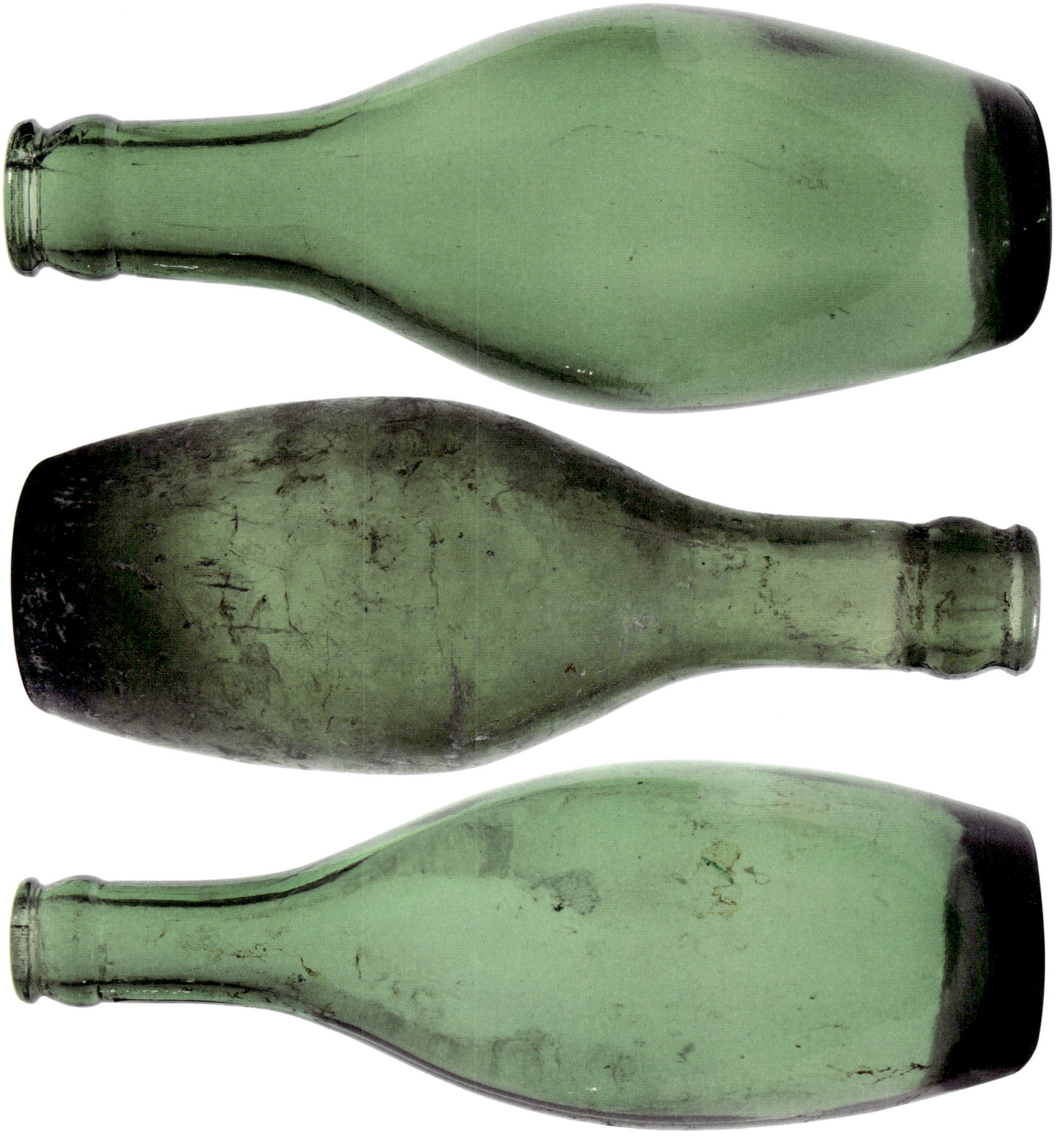

Perrier goes "Pschitt"

1947

Gustave Leven, a young stockbroker, buys the Source Perrier public company from its British shareholders, who are struggling to relaunch production in the post-war period. 34 million bottles are marketed. The new CEO, a true captain of industry, is firmly committed to modernizing Perrier as an industry and in terms of advertising.

1949

Advertising executive Jean Davray invents the slogan "Perrier, l'eau qui fait Pschitt", referring to the sound made when the bottle is opened, and commissions top poster designers to illustrate the slogan, with Carlu being the first. The company Société Source Perrier SA is listed on the Paris Stock Exchange.

1950

A new industrial plant is built in Vergèze. In the early 1950s, sales rise to 131 million bottles, of which over 100 million are for the French market.

1954

Gustave Leven buys up other mineral water springs and embarks on a huge diversification program. Pschitt orange and Pschitt lemon sodas are launched onto the market.

1959

After the quarter liter, half liter and large format, Perrier is also available as a magnum and axes its advertisements against the high cost of living.

1960

Perrier commercials by top directors, including Georges Lautner and François Reichenbach, are a huge hit at movie theaters.

1967

Comic strip capers: Forest, creator of the legendary 1964 *Barbarella* comic strip, lends his curvaceous creation to Perrier.

1969

Painter Salvador Dali brings a splash of color to the French daily newspapers *France-Soir* and Le *Figaro* on November 19 with a full-page drawing as a gift from Perrier to their readers.

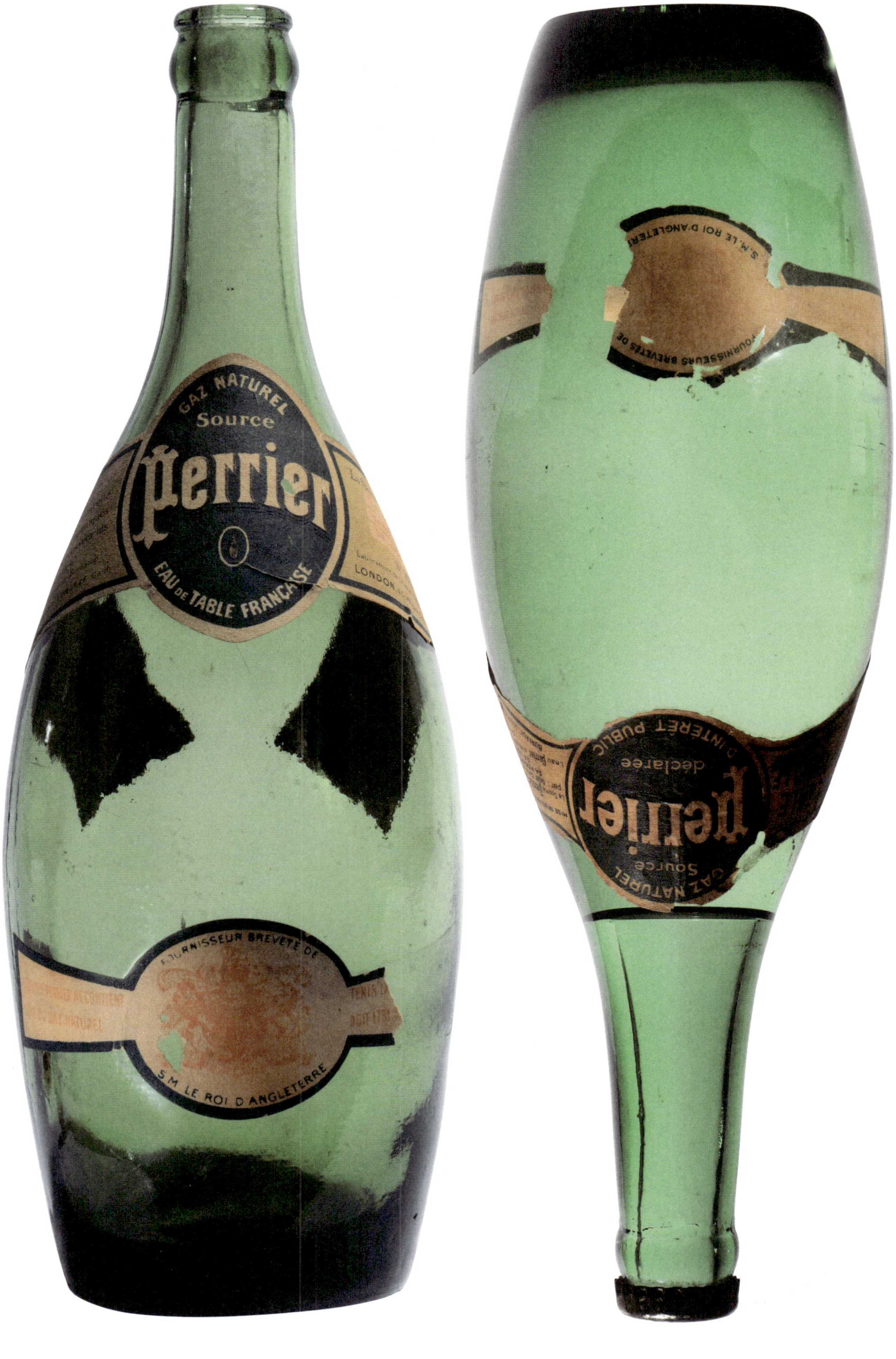
GAZ NATUREL
Source
Perrier
EAU DE TABLE FRANÇAISE
FOURNISSEUR BREVETÉ DE
S.M. LE ROI D'ANGLETERRE

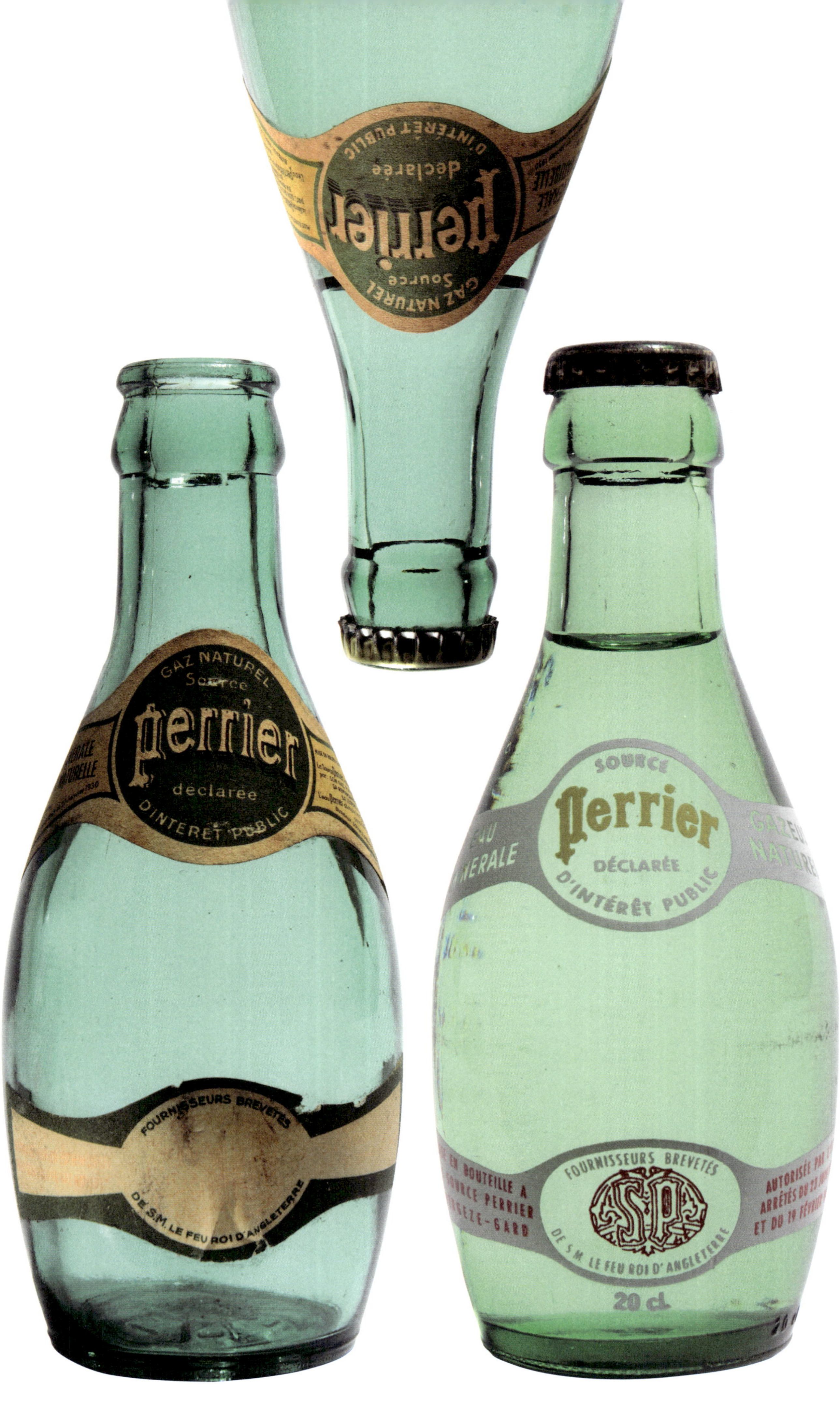
GAZ NATUREL
Source
Perrier
declarée
D'INTERET PUBLIC
FOURNISSEURS BREVETÉS
DE S.M. LE FEU ROI D'ANGLETERRE
SOURCE
Perrier
DÉCLARÉE
D'INTÉRÊT PUBLIC
FOURNISSEURS BREVETÉS
DE S.M. LE FEU ROI D'ANGLETERRE
20 cl

the boom years

1970

Jean Davray invents a new landmark slogan: "Perrier, c'est fou!" (Perrier is zany!). The bottle is decorated for the first time with a tuxedo to celebrate New Year's Eve 1970.

1972

Source Perrier SA, now the fifth-largest food-processing group in France, buys shares in Italian, Brazilian and Spanish springs.

1973

The factory expands with the addition of a bottle manufacturing plant (Verrerie du Languedoc) and a new bottling unit is built.

1976

Perrier tries to crack the US market. The famous movie director and actor Orson Wells praises the natural properties and health benefits of sparkling mineral water from the south of France. *La Main*, a film shot by Serge Gainsbourg, is yet another daring move.

1979

Flavored Perrier water is given an exclusive launch in the United States.

1983

Andy Warhol, the king of Pop Art, travels to Paris at the request of Jean Davray. The American artist with a colorful and fertile imagination designs a series of silkscreen prints of Perrier bottles intertwining in a Pop Art ballet and wins the French national poster prize in 1983.

1987

The Perrier commercial by Georges Lautner is a winner at the "7 d'or" French television awards.

1988

Perrier is now sold in 119 countries. In excess of one billion bottles are produced annually and the factory expands with the addition of a third plant.

1990

Minute traces of benzene, presenting no health risks, are detected in a batch of bottles by a laboratory in Atlanta, Georgia. Gustave Leven issues a worldwide recall of bottles to protect Perrier's unblemished reputation.

1991

Perrier roars back with the *Water, Air, Life* campaign and Jean-Paul Goude's film *The Lion* wins a clutch of awards including the top prize at the prestigious Cannes International Advertising Festival. Ridley Scott makes planets dance and transports tennis champion John McEnroe into the future in the film *The Mirage*, which was also a Cannes prize-winner in 1991.

entering the Nestlé fold

1992

Nestlé, the world's top food-processing group and owner of other prestigious springs, buys Source Perrier SA, a key step to becoming the biggest global player in the bottled water market.

1993

La Madelon, the last part of the *Water, Air, Life* opus, wins many of the year's advertising awards.

1996

Following in the footsteps of the iconic Perrier bottles, a glass designed by Martin Szekely now appears on the scene and becomes a must-have item on café tables. St. John Harmsworth's house at the Vergèze site becomes a museum of the history of Perrier.

1997

The film initially called *Le Bar* and then *Piaf*, directed for Perrier by Bruno Aveillon, makes a big impact.

1998

Perrier goes back to its poster roots and is awarded the Grand Prix de l'Affichage advertising poster award for its "T-shirt" campaign.

2001

Perrier also goes into portable mode with new PET (polyethylene terephthalate) plastic bottles which are easy to carry, keeping pace with the new habit of drinking on the move.

2003

Lightly sparkling Perrier water makes an appearance and adopts the name Perrier fines bulles in 2012.

2006

Launch of an ambitious investment program lasting several years to modernize the production facility. Three new bottling lines are created. The Verrerie du Languedoc glassworks is sold in order to refocus on the core mineral water business.

2009

The world is melting in the heat and Perrier is the ultimate refreshment in the film *Melting*, which won several awards, in particular a Bronze Lion at the Cannes Lions International Festival of Creativity.

2013

The one-billion-bottle barrier is broken with ten bottling lines. Perrier celebrates its 150th anniversary in style under the Pop Art banner, featuring Warhol designs. Suspense is in the air with Perrier Secret Place, an interactive game full of surprises.

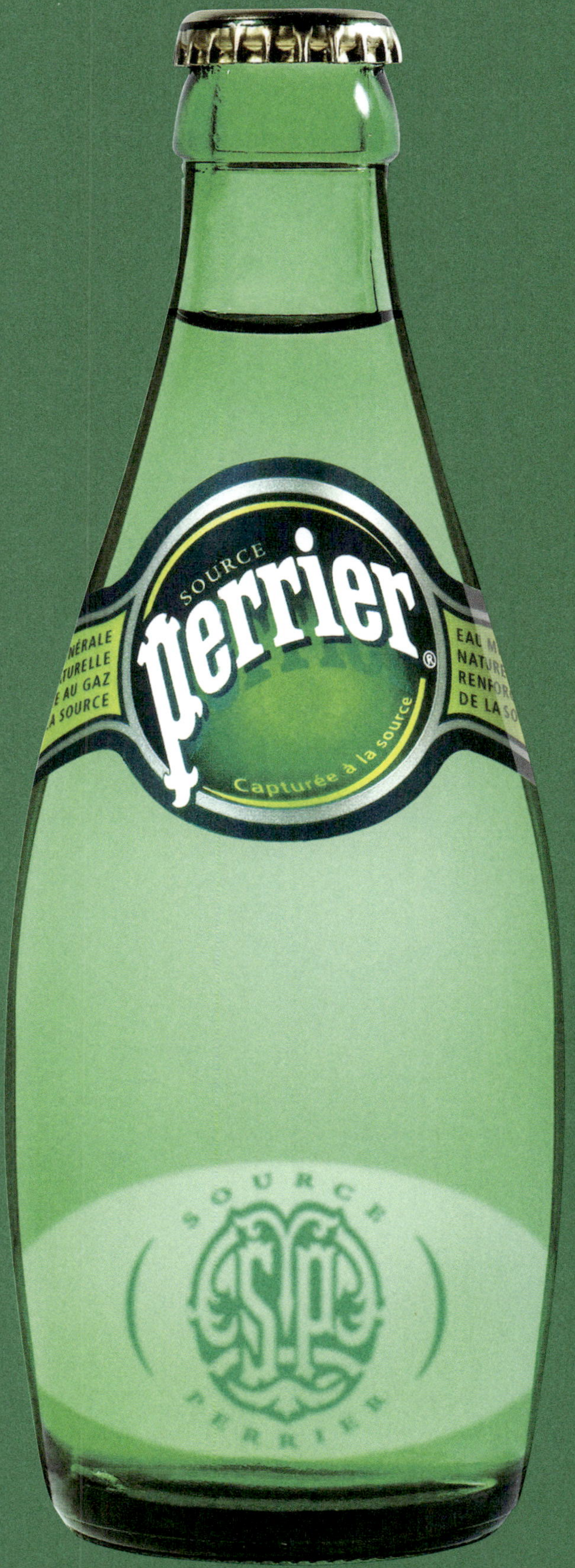
SOURCE
Perrier®
Capturée à la source
SOURCE
PERRIER

the miracle of Les Bouillens

Something wondrous bubbles up from the ground just a few miles from Nîmes, in the heart of the Provencal garrigue in the South of France. This unique miracle is the product of a series of natural events. The waters of Les Bouillens, dubbed Perrier in the 20th century, came to the surface of the earth as the result of a series of eruptions, the first of which created the Nîmes fault 120 million years ago. A subsequent collapse along this fault line 30 million years ago separated the garrigue from the Vistrenque plain where Les Bouillens water rises to the surface. Extensive flooding in the late Tertiary Period then deposited chalk, sand and clay sediment. When the waters receded from the plain 25 million years later, they left behind a thick layer of impermeable marl which protected the Les Bouillens water reservoir. For millions of years, rainwater slowly penetrated the ground mingling with gas of volcanic origin and traveling along fissures in the limestone rocks. Slowly but surely, the water eventually emerged above ground, bubbling as carbon dioxide gas was released.

the Romans bathed in the bubbling waters of Les Bouillens

The waters of Les Bouillens, an enduring wonder, then entered the annals of Ancient History. Hannibal, the commander of a huge army with some ten thousand animals in tow, including a herd of 37 elephants, is said to have broken his journey in Vergèze. In 218 BC, the hawkish Carthaginian general set out to conquer Rome, crossing the Alps en route. History records both this great feat and his eventual defeat, as Hannibal failed to capture this city which ruled over the western Mediterranean. Legend has it that the warrior slaked his thirst with water from Les Bouillens. By contrast, it is a proven fact that the Romans used to relax in the bubbling waters as Vergèze was a major staging post on the Domitian Way (*Via Domitia*), the 300-mile route begun in 118 BC to link Rome to the Iberian Peninsula via the territory of Narbonne in Gaul. Roman garrisons marched along this route to Vergèze from the Gate of Augustus in Nîmes (*Nemausis*, conquered in 120 BC). To enhance the relaxation and restorative facilities there, the Romans built a pool where they could plunge into the bubbling Les Bouillens waters and the Vergèze thermal baths were born. In the 19th century, the Granier family, who owned Les Bouillens, uncovered traces of the original Roman dressed-stone pool and many medals bearing the images of Julius Caesar and Augustus.

a health-giving spring

Over the centuries, the waters of Les Bouillens, which were a bathing spot and local attraction, acquired a reputation for their health-giving properties. According to a dissertation submitted to the Académie de Nîmes in 1810 by Dr. Dax, best remembered as a pioneer of the theory of the dominance of the left hemisphere of the human brain in language production: "Every year, from late July to early September, people suffering from partial or total non-febrile rheumatism, with or without gout, headaches, false ankylosis, pain following a fracture, sprain or bruising, chronic tremor caused by muscular deficiency, paralysis of one side of the body and skin diseases, go there to bathe, or rather to wallow in the mud. All of the aforementioned ailments can be cured at Les Bouillens (this is the local name for the pool as the waters appear to bubble)." The release of carbonated water was followed with keen interest by major names in 19th century science. Thus in 1867, Antoine Béchamp, Professor of Chemistry and Pharmacy at the Faculty of Medicine at Montpellier, who was well-known for his animosity towards Louis Pasteur, investigated Les Bouillens. "In this natural pool, cold, cloudy acidic water, which is soapy to the touch, bubbles continuously. The sight of this large expanse of water, seething and bubbling constantly as carbon dioxide is released, is a geological feature which is as surprising as it is astonishing for anyone seeing the natural phenomenon for the first time. Les Bouillens owes its name to this and it is difficult to conceive of a more colorful yet fitting expression for this geological feature". The reputation of this natural wonder extended far beyond Vergèze.

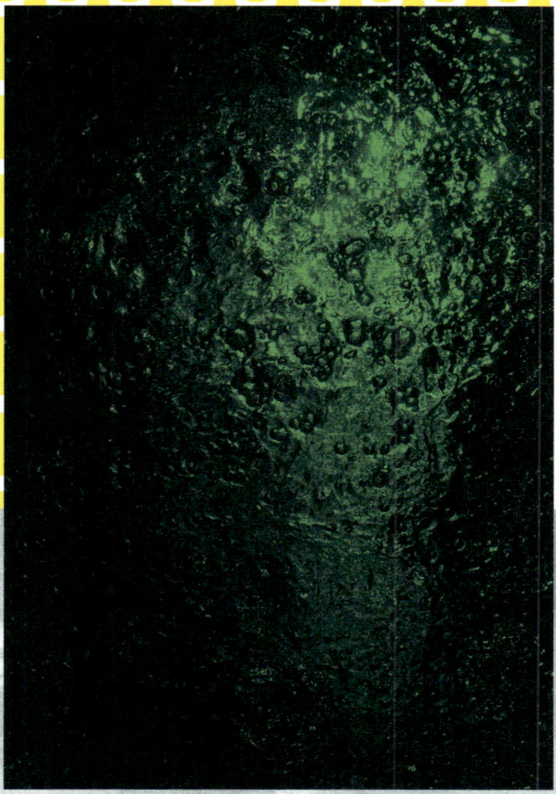

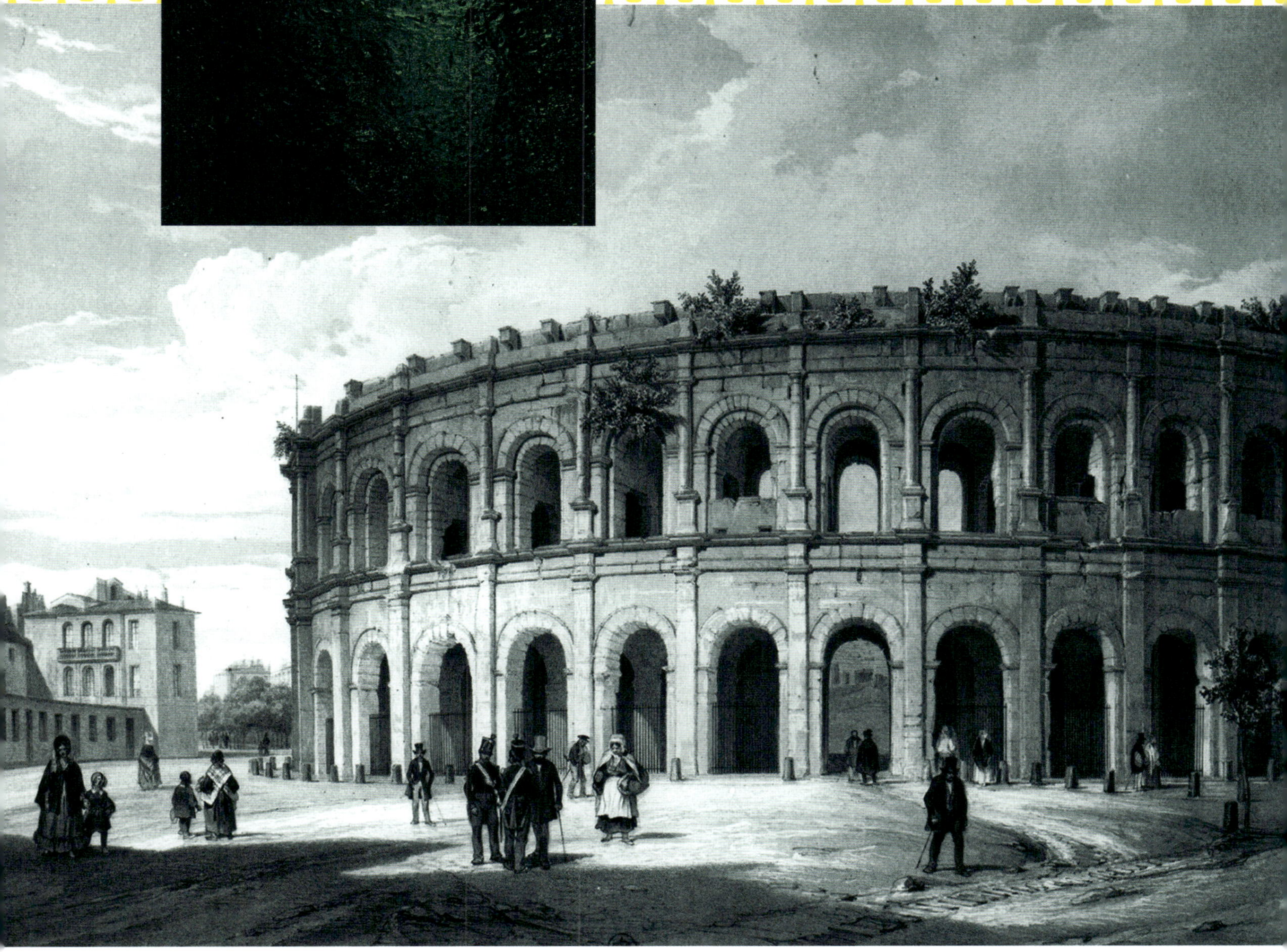

Top: View of the Perrier spring.
Bottom: View of the amphitheater in Nîmes, 19th century engraving by Arnout.

the health-giving waters of the Vergèze spa

What better cure for skin diseases or rheumatism than the waters of Les Bouillens? Site owner Alphonse Granier was determined to capitalize on this natural wonder and to transform the pond at Vergèze into an ultra-fashionable spa resort. There was stiff competition as the fashion for spa towns was at its peak. There was even talk of "spa fever", fueled by Emperor Napoleon III, a passionate devotee of spa treatments. A system of regulation was quickly introduced to maintain standards; the French Academy of Medicine monitored the various spa treatments and a Mineral Water Commission was created in 1854. Health inspections were carried out in spa establishments, the largest of which employed specialist physicians.

spa clients were surprised by the booming noise of the waters

Alphonse Granier inherited Les Bouillens, which had been in the family since 1762, before which it belonged to an Ursuline order from Montpellier. He was full of drive and ambition and even became Mayor of Vergèze. For the launch of his spa resort in 1857, Alphonse Granier fenced off the spring, erected wooden barriers and charged an admission fee, much to the outrage of local residents. This had been a freely accessible summer meeting place for the local population since the Middle Ages. After several court hearings, Alphonse Granier was granted permission to operate the spring commercially on June 23, 1863. He created the Société de l'Etablissement Thermal des Eaux Minérales de Vergèze, offering a range of hot, cold or mud baths. He also sold sparkling mineral water, emphasizing the fact that it did not share its provenance with the water supplying the baths. He bored several new wells to provide water for the spa clients to drink. The former pond found a new lease on life as a pool devoted entirely to bathing.
Spa clients were sometimes surprised by the booming noise of the bubbling waters and admired the large natural bubbles. Alphonse Granier called in scientists who made detailed studies of the beneficial properties of the waters of Les Bouillens. It was a daring move to stake his future on water in an area devoted to vine growing. However, spa facilities proliferated there, even though very few of them ultimately stood the test of time. The acidic springs of Vergèze were on a par with the sulfurous springs of Fonsanges, Les Fumades, Cauvalat, Saint-Jean-de-Ceyrargues, and the bituminous springs at Euzet. According to Doctor Edouard Tribes in an address to the Académie du Gard in 1868: "You are all aware, Gentleman, of the growing importance of mineral waters these days and the increasing popularity of these health-giving springs where people come to seek relief from pain or an improvement in their health. While offering new and powerful therapeutic treatments for the sick, they also contribute to the wealth of the areas in which they are located."

the "princess of table waters"

Unfortunately, some of the facilities were destroyed by fire in 1869. Alphonse Granier did not lose heart and began to build the Hôtel des Baigneurs, with a high-quality restaurant, to provide accommodation for his spa clientele. He invested in advertising to spread the word about the novelty and quality of the waters in Vergèze.
They established their credentials in 1870 as "the princess of table waters", claiming to be easy to digest and refreshing, with tonic properties, especially "when drunk with wine, cordial or absinthe". The waters of Les Bouillens were already known in distant climes as they could be found in Egypt, in particular in Alexandria. Despite this phenomenally successful first foray into advertising, the company, which now traded as the Société Anonyme des Eaux Minérales de Vergèze ou des Bouillens, was wound up in 1887 with substantial debts.
Louis Rouvière, a landowner and wine merchant in Vergèze, bought the Les Bouillens estate a year later. In 1894, he leased the company with the option of a sale to a physician from Nîmes by the name of Doctor Perrier.

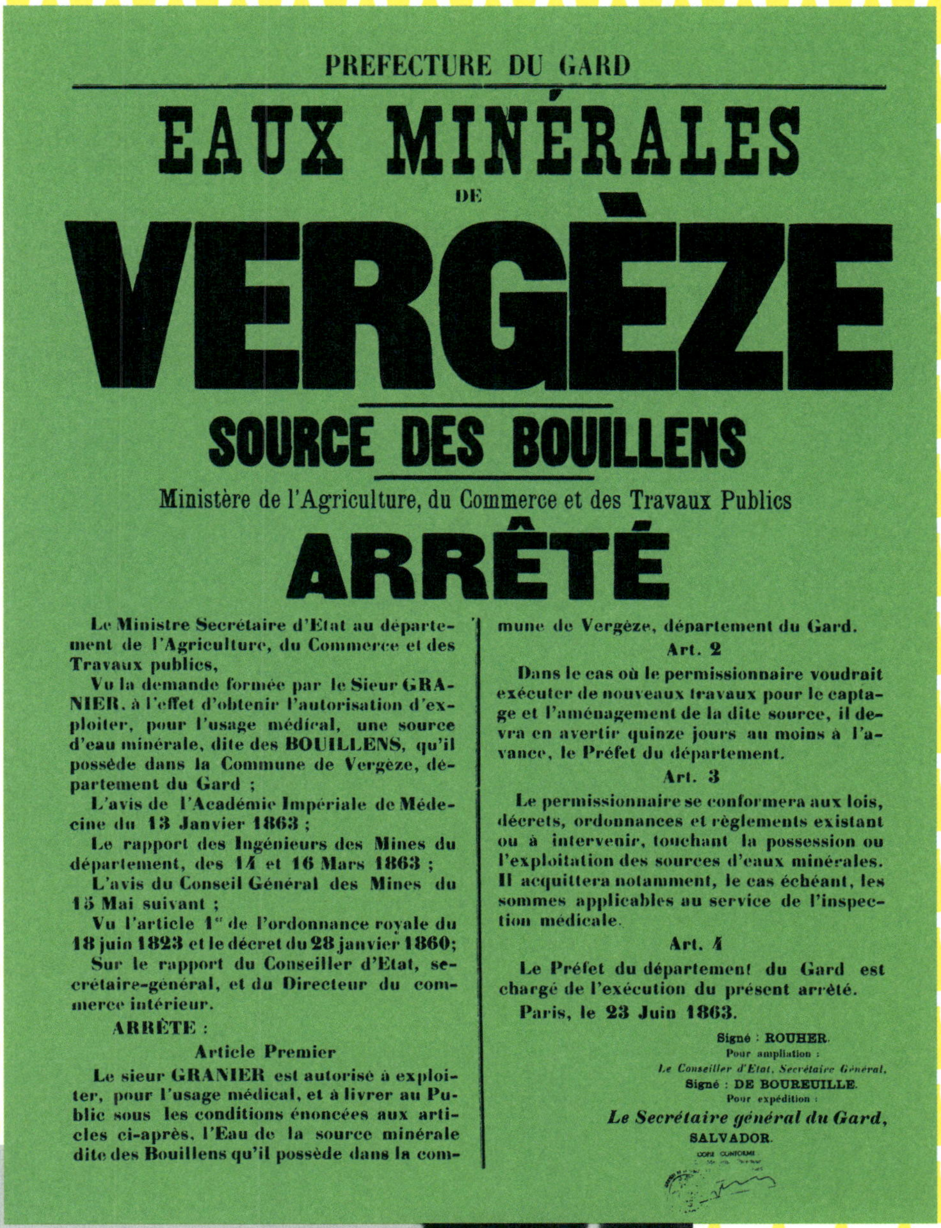

PREFECTURE DU GARD

EAUX MINÉRALES

DE

VERGÈZE

SOURCE DES BOUILLENS

Ministère de l'Agriculture, du Commerce et des Travaux Publics

ARRÊTÉ

Le Ministre Secrétaire d'Etat au département de l'Agriculture, du Commerce et des Travaux publics,

Vu la demande formée par le Sieur GRANIER, à l'effet d'obtenir l'autorisation d'exploiter, pour l'usage médical, une source d'eau minérale, dite des BOUILLENS, qu'il possède dans la Commune de Vergèze, département du Gard ;

L'avis de l'Académie Impériale de Médecine du 13 Janvier 1863 ;

Le rapport des Ingénieurs des Mines du département, des 14 et 16 Mars 1863 ;

L'avis du Conseil Général des Mines du 15 Mai suivant ;

Vu l'article 1er de l'ordonnance royale du 18 juin 1823 et le décret du 28 janvier 1860;

Sur le rapport du Conseiller d'Etat, secrétaire-général, et du Directeur du commerce intérieur.

ARRÊTE :

Article Premier

Le sieur GRANIER est autorisé à exploiter, pour l'usage médical, et à livrer au Public sous les conditions énoncées aux articles ci-après, l'Eau de la source minérale dite des Bouillens qu'il possède dans la commune de Vergèze, département du Gard.

Art. 2

Dans le cas où le permissionnaire voudrait exécuter de nouveaux travaux pour le captage et l'aménagement de la dite source, il devra en avertir quinze jours au moins à l'avance, le Préfet du département.

Art. 3

Le permissionnaire se conformera aux lois, décrets, ordonnances et règlements existant ou à intervenir, touchant la possession ou l'exploitation des sources d'eaux minérales. Il acquittera notamment, le cas échéant, les sommes applicables au service de l'inspection médicale.

Art. 4

Le Préfet du département du Gard est chargé de l'exécution du présent arrêté.

Paris, le 23 Juin 1863.

Signé : ROUHER.
Pour ampliation :
Le Conseiller d'Etat, Secrétaire Général,
Signé : DE BOUREUILLE.
Pour expédition :
Le Secrétaire général du Gard,
SALVADOR.

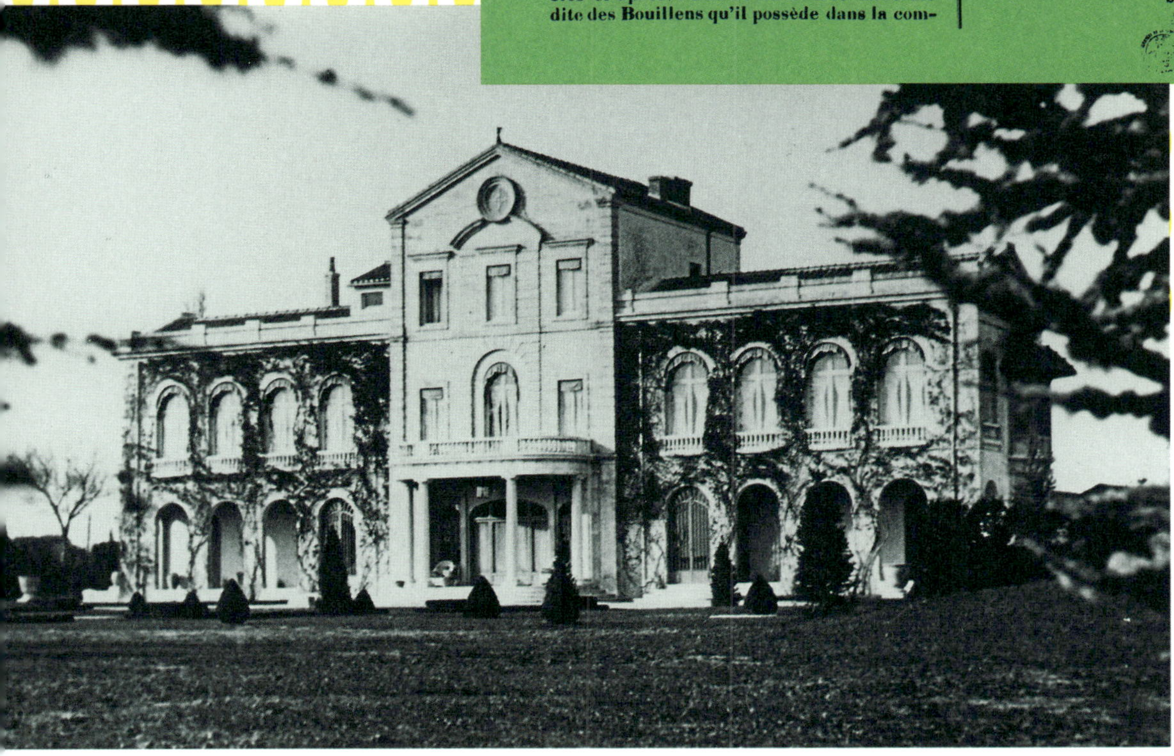

Top: Ministerial decree of June 23, 1863 authorizing Alphonse Granier to exploit the Les Bouillens spring. Bottom: View of the Perrier 'Castle' in Vergèze.

Doctor Perrier bottles water

Is there a future in the waters of Les Bouillens? This was doubtless the question preying on the mind of medical physician Doctor Louis-Eugène Perrier when he was asked in 1894 by the spring owner Louis Rouvière to take up the post of Medical Director. The spa resort was yet to make a profit and Louis Rouvière, a wealthy wine merchant, realized that he was unlikely to be more successful than his predecessor unless he harnessed the potential of science. The spa resort could never flourish without a doctor who was famous or at the very least inspired confidence in the spa clients. Louis Rouvière set his sights on the undisputed regional expert on spa treatments, who was also a major political figure. Doctor Perrier had been Medical Director since 1875 at the Euzet-les-Bains springs in the Gard département, about 10 miles from Uzès, and would retain this position until his death in 1912.
He also worked at the Les Fumades spa, but gave up this role when he took over Les Bouillens.

the ideal blend of water and gas

Doctor Perrier was in his element with water as he had written his thesis on osteophytic arthritis for which he prescribed steam baths and hydrotherapy. He was also a born inventor who filed a number of patents, and a model of committed citizenship who was elected Deputy Mayor of Nîmes in 1870 at the end of the Empire, and served as Acting Mayor in 1871 and then Republican Departmental Councilor for the canton of Saint-Mamert.
Although he was intrigued by the potential of Les Bouillens, Doctor Perrier was a cautious man by nature and opted for a trial period. He rented the spa establishment with the option to buy the whole property. He exercised this option four years later, becoming chief administrator of the Société Anonyme des Eaux Minérales, Boissons et Produits Hygiéniques de Vergèze.
Given his location in the heart of one of the finest French wine-producing areas, Doctor Perrier decided to play the local card. He launched a sparkling wine made with water from Les Bouillens claiming that it was healthier than distilled drinks. "The gas from the spring offers calming and digestive benefits to supplement the comforting properties of the wine".
He also produced a lemonade and considered manufacturing tablets and effervescent salts.
Doctor Perrier is remembered less for his wine than for identifying the ideal blend of gas and water and then bottling it. In fact, the doctor modernized the facilities by separating water and gas capture.
He collected water at a new well and gas in bell jars placed over the major CO_2 vents. The naturally occurring water and gas were then mixed into a pure sparkling mineral water without additives of any sort, in accordance with the proportions defined by Doctor Perrier: 3.5 parts gas to one part water.
He then designed a bottle with an airtight seal. He wrote to the Cusenier company, with which he was trying to set up a partnership to produce his sparkling wines: "A workman fills 300 bottles per hour with our equipment". Water from Les Bouillens was presented on the bottle labels as natural and aseptic, providing therapeutic benefits absent from artificial sparkling waters. It was also a safe drink as it offered protection from infectious diseases.
Doctor Perrier was brimming with ideas but short on funds. In 1903, he found himself a sponsor in the figure of St. John Harmsworth, who was visiting France to improve his French on completion of his studies. How did an aging physician approaching his seventieth year and a young British man of 27 go into business together? Perhaps the youngest brother wanted to carve out a path for himself away from the shadow of his two domineering press magnate brothers, recently elevated to the peerage.
It is certain that his visit to Les Bouillens represented a watershed. He was not convinced by the merits of spa treatments but by the bottled mineral water, dubbing both the water and the new company founded in 1906 "Perrier". The Compagnie de la Source Perrier was born. Doctor Perrier retained the title of Director of Health and of the Technical Medical Department until his death in 1912, and his name, which had become a commercial brand, is still found on every bottle to this day.

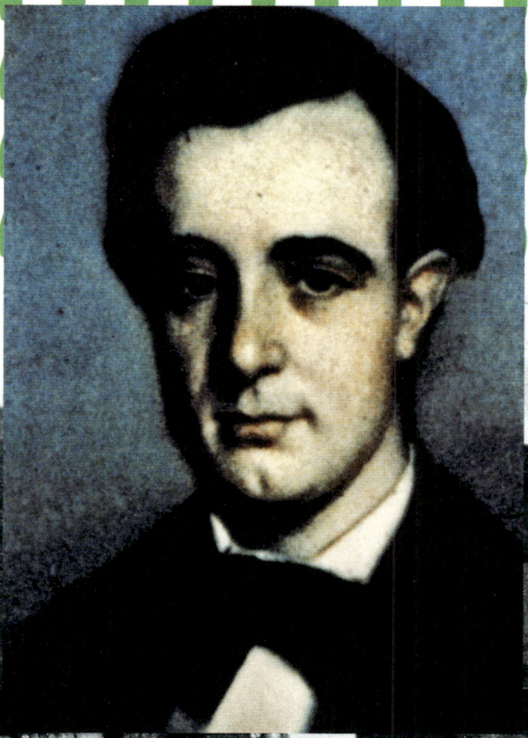

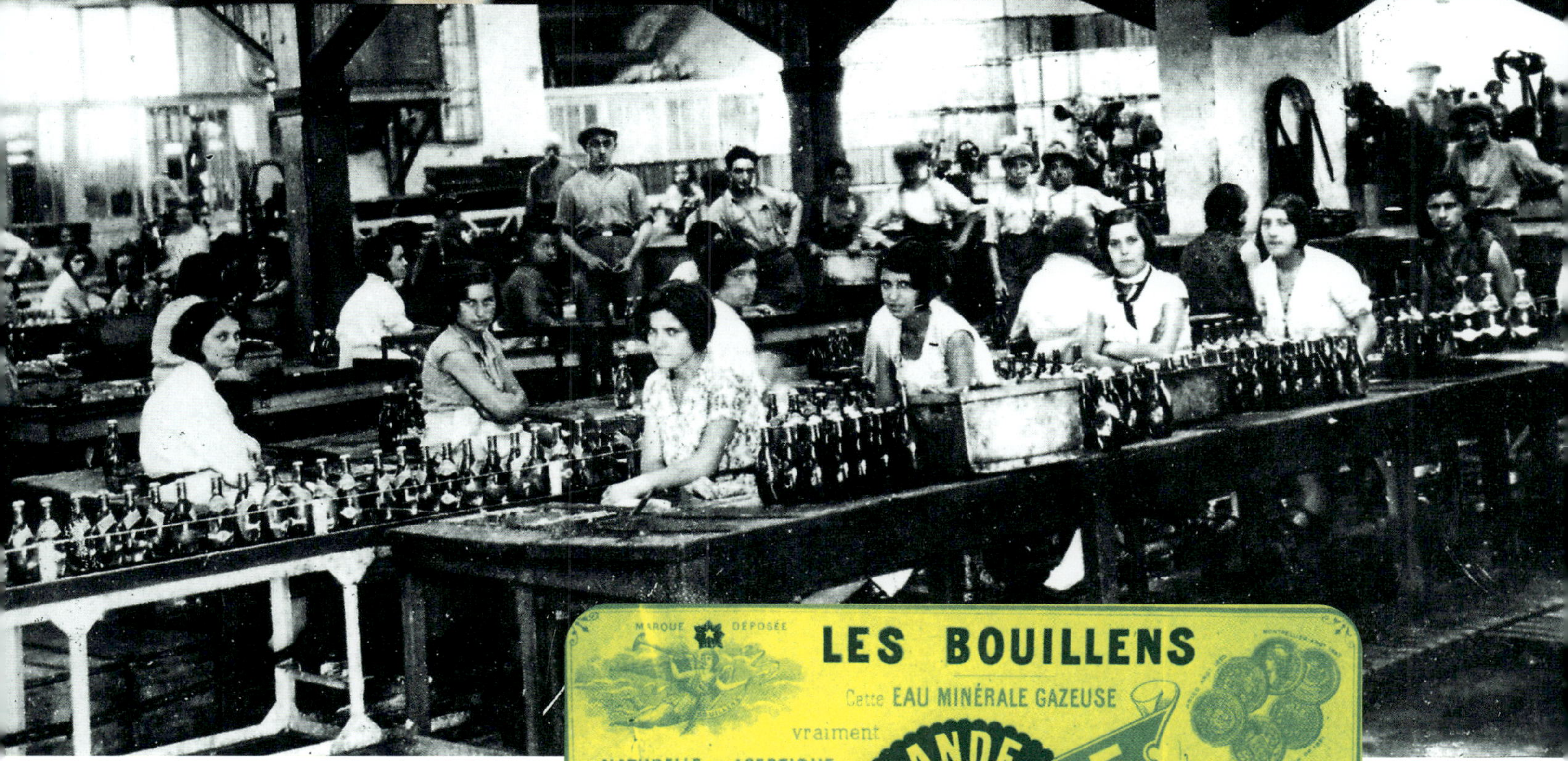

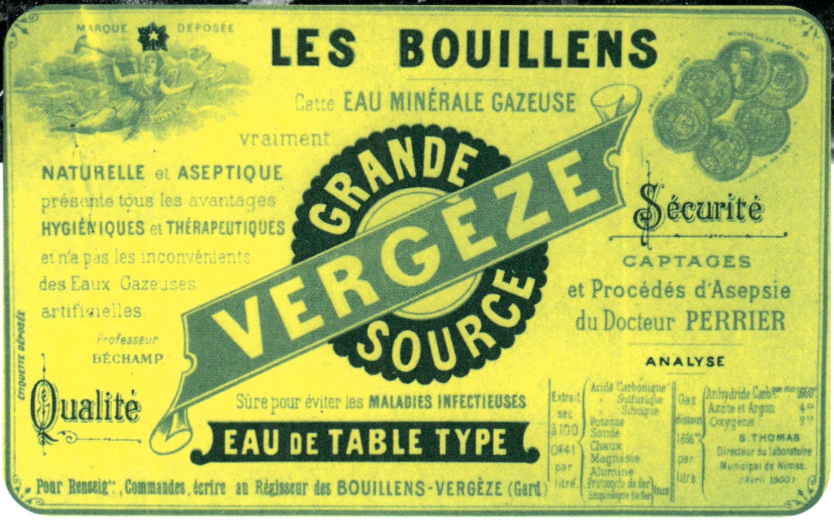

Top: Portrait of Louis Perrier. Center: View of the Perrier bottling plant circa 1927. Bottom: Bottle label.

the club-shaped bottle turns globetrotter

France and England had never been closer. In 1903, St. John Harmsworth settled in Vergèze and Edward VII made a state visit to Paris. The French were thrilled to hear the British monarch announce: "I can assure you that I am delighted to be back with you again, as I always feel at home here". This was the era of the Entente Cordiale. This Entente was displayed in all its glory in May 1908 in London at the Franco-British Exhibition, where some thirty pavilions devoted to fine art, food, industry and health filled eight million visitors with wonder over a six-month period. The Perrier pavilion, a symbol of Franco-British unity, vaunted the merits of its mineral water with a reconstruction of the spring. Perrier was now an international player. As a holder of a Royal Warrant "By Appointment to His Majesty the King" since 1905, it had joined the august ranks of companies such as Fortnum and Mason, Twinings and Lipton. Sir Thomas Lipton is said to have introduced King Edward VII to Perrier. Several years later, Perrier was also made an approved purveyor to the Spanish royal family.

the birth of the "champagne of table waters"

Under the aegis of St. John Harmsworth, the sparkling water from Les Bouillens left the spa and therapeutic environment behind and became synonymous with an elite product, elegant sparkle and the British market, since Perrier was virtually unknown in France.
The young entrepreneur realized that mineral water was now going to be drunk more widely and not in specialist establishments. The only legacy of the spa was St. John Harmsworth's personal recourse to the bubbling baths when he was paralyzed in an automobile accident in 1906.
The new owner of Les Bouillens named this water after Doctor Perrier. By way of celebration, the "princess of table waters" became the "champagne of table waters". St. John Harmsworth designed an unusually-shaped bottle reminiscent of the Indian clubs he used as part of his fitness regime.
The name and the bottle would remain unchanged for the rest of the century. He brought the very best engineers from England and introduced the most sophisticated machinery available to perfect an industrial bottling process. His brothers' wealth as founders of a newspaper empire, which counted the *Daily Mail* and *Daily Mirror* among its prime assets, had considerable advantages and the family's newspapers carried advertising for the water. However, the young St. John Harmsworth was not satisfied with newspaper advertising and invited the young British illustrator Chas Crombie to create a picture book on the rules of golf in 1904. On the back of each illustration was an advertisement for Perrier.
In 1908, the year of the Franco-British Exhibition, the Perrier production facilities were connected via their own branch line to Vergèze railroad station, from which over seven million bottles were dispatched annually to Britain and its colonies. Perrier water was a boon for soldiers and civil servants stationed in hot climes and offered a fitting accompaniment to whisky. Whisky and Perrier were a marriage made in heaven, promoted by the advertising strapline "Ask for a Whis-Per", which mimicked the sound of the water being poured into a glass.
To cater for the British thirst, employee numbers rose sharply from 80 in 1906 to 300 in 1914 and nearly 400 in the 1920s. The plant underwent further modernization and doubled in size between 1926 and 1928 to try to corner the local French market, as the British management had decided to end its splendid isolation and to take an interest in France, which it had neglected up to this point. The Perrier spring was declared to be of "public interest" on May 19, 1933 which meant that a protective area could be established around it, banning all underground excavations without prior authorization. This official recognition was also an asset in exporting to some countries and for marketing purposes in France. St. John Harmsworth died in this same year and Perrier sold over 18 million bottles, including a small number in France.
The ashes of the founder of La Source Perrier were scattered in the English Channel. His last wishes remained true to the motto which he printed on the company letterhead: "Every man has two countries: his own and France". St. John Harmsworth built his life and company on these two cultures, two languages which were an integral part of the early advertising for the company and two affinities.

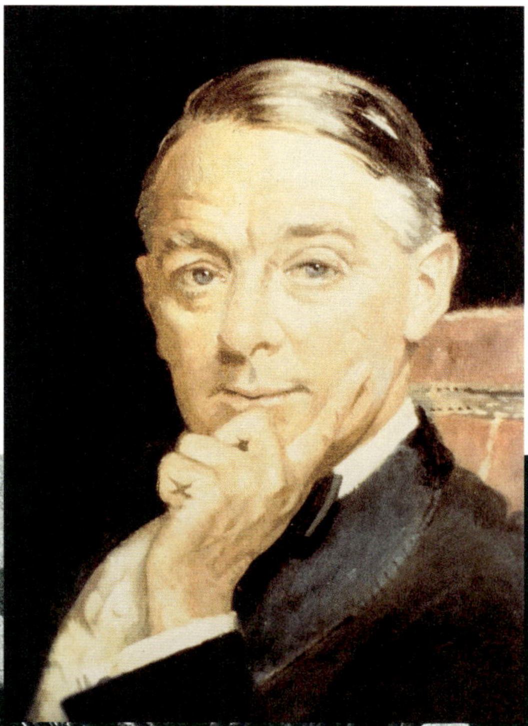

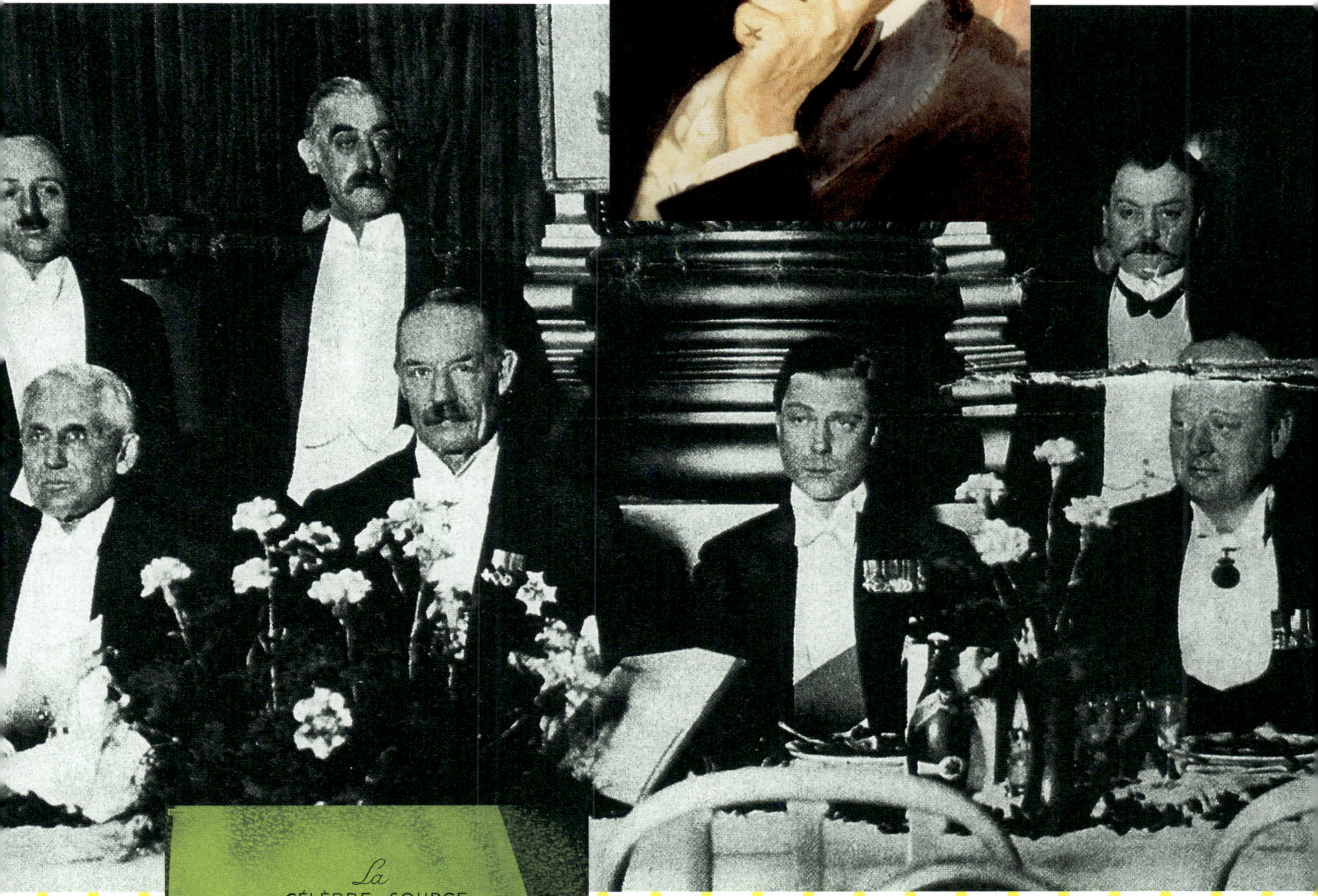

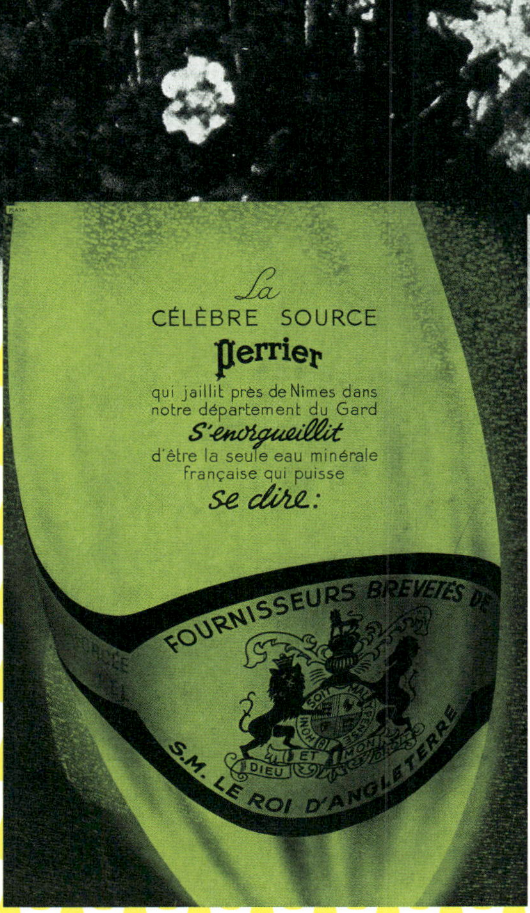

Top: Portrait of St. John Harmsworth. Center: State visit to Paris by King Edward VII accompanied by Sir Winston Churchill, 1903. Bottom: In 1905, the Perrier spring is granted the Royal Warrant "By Appointment to His Majesty the King of England".

eau so chic, so French, so literary

This water from the south of France had captivated Britain and its colonies. The champagne of table waters also wanted to win the hearts of the French. Bottle labels reminiscent of medical prescriptions were consigned to oblivion. Perrier was synonymous with celebration, pleasure, relaxation and now also with French good taste. After traveling the world, Perrier was set to target French polite society represented by wearers of formal hats rather than devotees of the working man's beret. Only a small minority of the French population were mineral water drinkers at the time and the British shareholders on the board of La Source Perrier SA who had succeeded St. John Harmsworth were determined that the sparkling water should put down roots on home turf. The champagne of table waters needed to develop a following among socialites who were habitués of bars and luxury hotels, distinguished sportsmen, tennis, golf and skiing enthusiasts, and especially those pioneering women who had no qualms about wearing pants, a brief skirt or shorts to play sports which were previously an all-male preserve.

artists pair up for Perrier

In order to conquer France, Perrier engaged with the intellectual and artistic ferment of the era. From 1937, major authors and illustrators whose work is still revered today penned a prestigious series known as the "Variation on the champagne of table waters". Colette, the author of *Claudine* and *Le Blé en herbe*, with her myriad identities, voracious appetite for lovers of both genders and passion for cats, was sketched by her friend Luc-Albert Moreau at La Treille Muscate, her home in Saint-Tropez. She drew inspiration from Provence to write an ode to Perrier: "I like water as soon as I wake up, in the afternoon, and at midnight for refreshment after the theatre or the cinema, holiday water, cheerful picnic water on the Provence coast. These are all one and the same water, nice and cold and bright with bubbles so full of natural gas that it moistens the nostrils and eyelashes as you drink it..." Other high-profile pairings were formed, setting their unique stamp on the champagne of table waters. The writer and songwriter Francis Carco, a close friend of Colette, and regular at the Lapin Agile cabaret in Montmartre, joined forces with his great friend Dignimont to conjure up the delightful illusion of sampling champagne when he drank his first glass of Perrier as a 13-year old boy. This artistic series was continued by Carco's close friend Mac Orlan, with a drawing by Vertès. This prolific author who inspired two of the most memorable films of the 1930s, *La Bandera* and *Quai des Brumes* (with the legendary line addressed to Jean Gabin by Michèle Morgan: "You have beautiful eyes, you know"), defined the spirit of water embodied by Perrier in his own inimitable style. In 1937, the food writer and critic Curnonsky celebrated yuletide feasts accompanied by liberal doses of the champagne of table waters in a humorous vein, with a hilarious New Year's Eve party illustrated by Dubout. Pierre Frondaie, the author of *L'homme à l'Hispano*, and a highly respected dramatist, joined forces with Chas Laborde in 1938 and revealed that he called Perrier the "water with springs in it" when he was a child. Another contributor was Elizabeth Lion, who was not a writer but a bona fide pioneer, a flying ace, nicknamed "the Lioness". Her text, illustrated by Louis Ferrand, revealed to readers that Perrier was the pilot's secret weapon, "one of the key components of a successful bombing sortie".

a boxed set illustrated by Salvador Dali

Although the "Variation on the champagne of table waters" series was put on hold, Perrier had acquired a taste for literature. La Source Perrier SA joined forces with Jean Giono to publish a work simply entitled *Provence* in 1939. The author from Manosque described his beloved countryside in this book illustrated by Girieud. Several decades later, in the early 1970s, Perrier returned to its literary and artistic roots: a boxed set illustrated by Dali contained several slim volumes, one of which, *La France des sources*, was penned by the writer Gaston Bonheur and another, *Éloge de Perrier*, was written by the author Françoise Parturier, who had applied to be admitted to the Académie française, an all-male institution at the time.

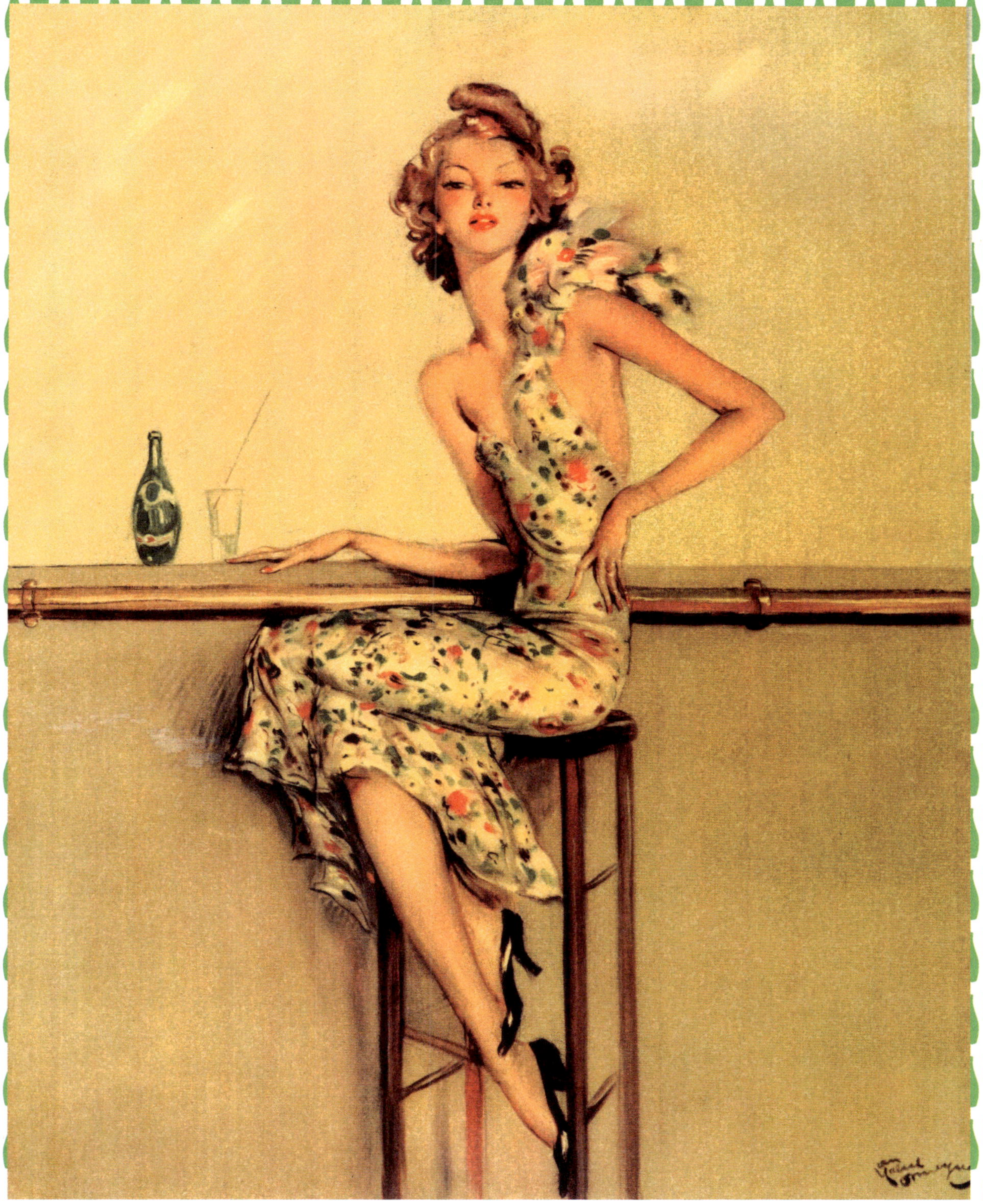

"Perrier Girl" drawn by Jean-Claude Domergue, 1936.

modern, creative, diverse

Named by an Englishman and requisitioned by the Germans during the Occupation, Perrier water became a fully-fledged French brand when 33-year old stockbroker Gustave Leven took over the helm in 1947. He knew no more about mineral water than St. John Harmsworth in the early days. He was initially tasked with finding a buyer, then took on the business himself. He was unable to resist the temptation to pay an impromptu visit to Vergèze, where he spent quite some time wandering around the site, which seemed to have gone into hibernation. He was immediately convinced that he could transform this ailing plant into a highly efficient machine. Production was just ticking over after World War II and Perrier seemed to be a Provençal Sleeping Beauty, but Gustave Leven was the perfect Prince Charming. With his brilliant mind and visionary, intuitive streak, he knew how to create a good impression and to surround himself with the very best talent. Not content with waking Perrier from its slumbers, he would propel the brand into a new industrial and advertising league. Gustave Leven's first move was to build up the potential of the bottling plant by modernizing the facilities. A new vaulted building was erected to improve production flow and it was connected to the railroad branch line. He imported bottling machinery from the United States and, like most French entrepreneurs, he studied the American model and drew inspiration from US soda manufacturing techniques to refresh the industrial process. Between 1948 and 1952, production sky-rocketed from 30 to 150 million bottles to meet the new French appetite for sparkling mineral water. During the 1950s, the mantra for the plant was to concentrate as many operations on site as possible. Bottle tops and crates were manufactured in situ. A paper mill and print works were then added to supply millions of labels. Over the course of the decade, Gustave Leven invented new products and launched the Pschitt Orange and Pschitt Lemon flavored sodas. However it was not sufficient simply to slake thirsts; it was also necessary to whet appetites. In tandem with modernizing facilities at the plant, Gustave Leven revived Perrier's reputation for creativity, taking it to new heights with his high school friend Jean Davray, the Vice President responsible for advertising.

Jean Davray was a published author and playwright with an established reputation in Parisian literary circles. A close friend of Claude Mauriac and the novelist and future Académie française member Henri Troyat, Gustave Leven's right-hand man was also an art collector and enthusiast. He masterminded the renaissance of Perrier's advertising tradition with a succession of original and intelligent campaigns, drawing on the top talent in the field. With his legendary sense of humor, Jean Davray established his credentials for elegant and witty advertising with slogans ranging from "L'eau qui fait Pschitt", imitating the fizz of a bottle being opened, to "Perrier, c'est fou" (Perrier is zany).

A sprawling site

Another major step forward came in 1973, when a second building was constructed and the Verrerie du Languedoc glassworks was built on site to manufacture bottles for the factory. The site now sprawled over tens of thousands of square meters and a third ultra-modern bottling plant was opened in 1988. Production was commensurately high, comfortably exceeding the billion bottle mark. Perrier had cracked the French market, and in 1976, Gustave Leven set himself the task of reconquering the English-speaking world. Within the space of a few years, Perrier was the drink of choice in the United States, where it was prized for its natural, healthy properties. Gustave Leven was now head of the fifth largest French food-processing company, which he had gradually built up by buying a number of mineral water springs since the 1950s and diversifying into other products such as cheese.

In February 1990, minute traces of benzene were detected in a batch of bottles by a laboratory in Atlanta, Georgia. Although it was slightly higher than the permitted level in the United States, it complied with French regulations and presented no health risk. Since Perrier's reputation for perfection and unblemished quality were sacrosanct for Gustave Leven, he issued a worldwide recall of all bottles and replaced them with fresh output.

This grand gesture set the seal on the Leven era, a forty year epic which had elevated Perrier to great heights.

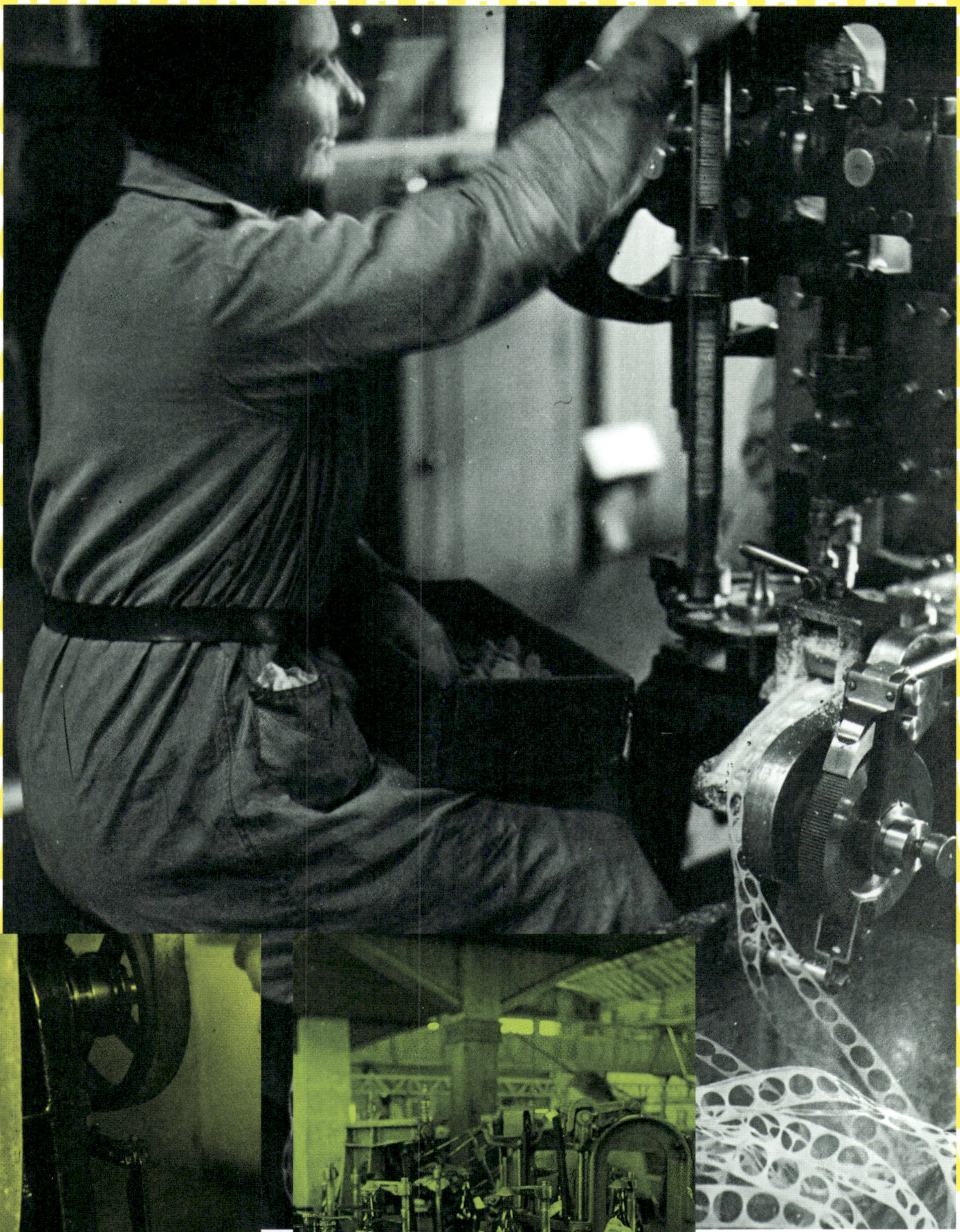

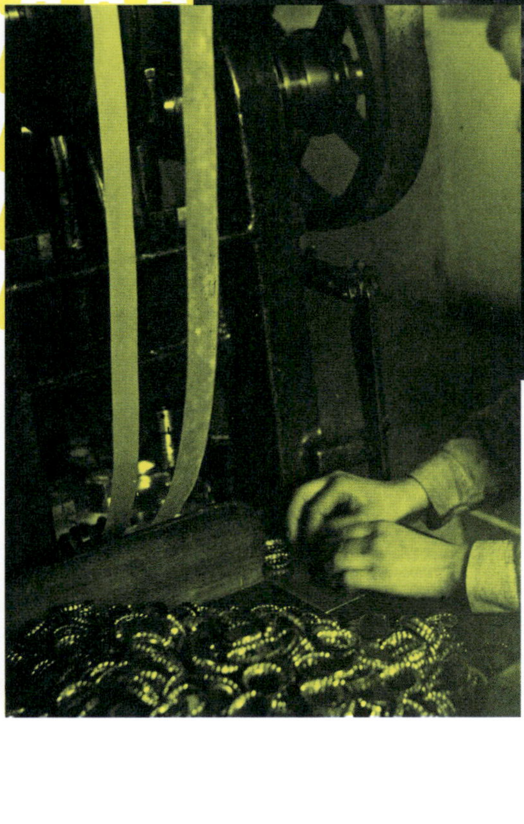

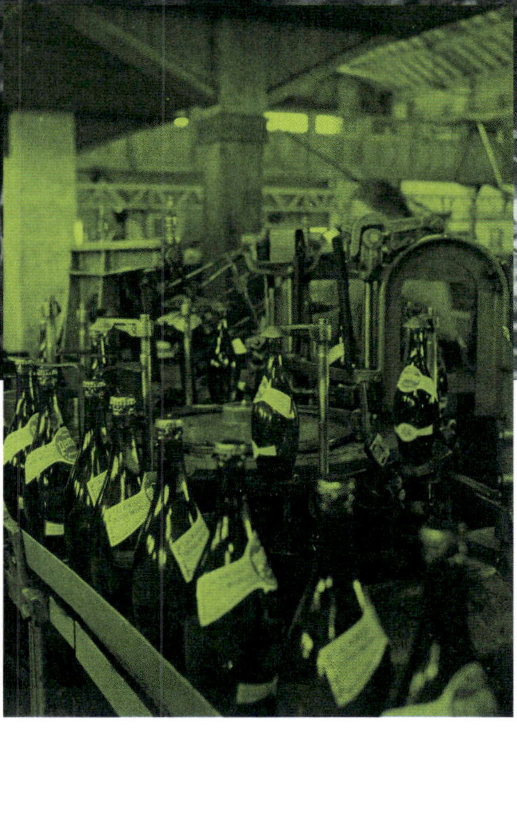

Views of the plant
at Vergèze, 1950.

the Roland Garros French Open Crown

Could it be that the French sent Perrier over to the British to thank them for bringing the game of tennis with them on their summer vacations to the south of France? Irrespective of whether this was truly a quid pro quo, the fact remains that the Brits were the first exponents of this ball game on French soil in the 1880s. The French middle-classes succumbed to the charms of tennis after World War I. Roland Garros was launched in 1928 and hosted the Davis Cup final in which Henri Cochet defeated René Lacoste who, along with their friend Jean Borotra, were the Three Musketeers of French tennis. Perrier demonstrated its natural advertising pedigree with features in the magazine *L'illustration.* The company, which was still in British hands, was delighted at the success of a homegrown sport. It was such a stylish and elegant sport that players featured prominently in advertisements in the 1920s. A decade later, painter Jean-Gabriel Domergue depicted his Perrier Girl as a tennis player relaxing after a set.

sportsmen and women's water of choice

Tennis and Perrier were inseparable and the little bottle had its devotees among sports stars from every discipline, enlisting swimmers, footballers, rugby players and cyclists for its advertisements. The eye-catching Perrier van has been refreshing cyclists on the Tour de France since the 1930s and the winner of each stage from 1960 to 1985 always downed a small bottle of Perrier when he dismounted. The stylish water with a hint of a British accent flexed its muscles at the most popular French sporting event and became familiar to huge audiences watching each stage of the Tour de France with bated breath.
The water of choice of sportsmen and women made a strong comeback on the lawns at Roland Garros when Perrier became the official tournament partner in 1978. Tennis grew in popularity, becoming a sport and an event loved by its exponents, live spectators and television audiences, with club members, rising steadily every year since 1968. As the stadium reaches its 50th anniversary, tournaments are at last being broadcast live on French television in the afternoons with a round-up in the evening. Roland Garros mania has kicked off, crowning its kings and queens, worshipping each year's new idols or its enduring tennis legends. Perrier is part of this frenzy, raising its profile on the courts with each passing year. The brand logo appeared on drinks coolers, then the umpire's chairs and finally the players' benches, chairs and sun umbrellas. In 2011, Perrier became associated with the *Trophée des légendes.* Every year since 1998, this tournament has reunited some thirty world tennis stars and former champions with a distinguished pedigree who played at Roland Garros in their heyday and now return to the courts to relive the past, much to the delight of the spectators. In 2012, Perrier celebrated its 35-year partnership with players and spectators. The Roland Garros tournament is now an unmissable fixture in late May.

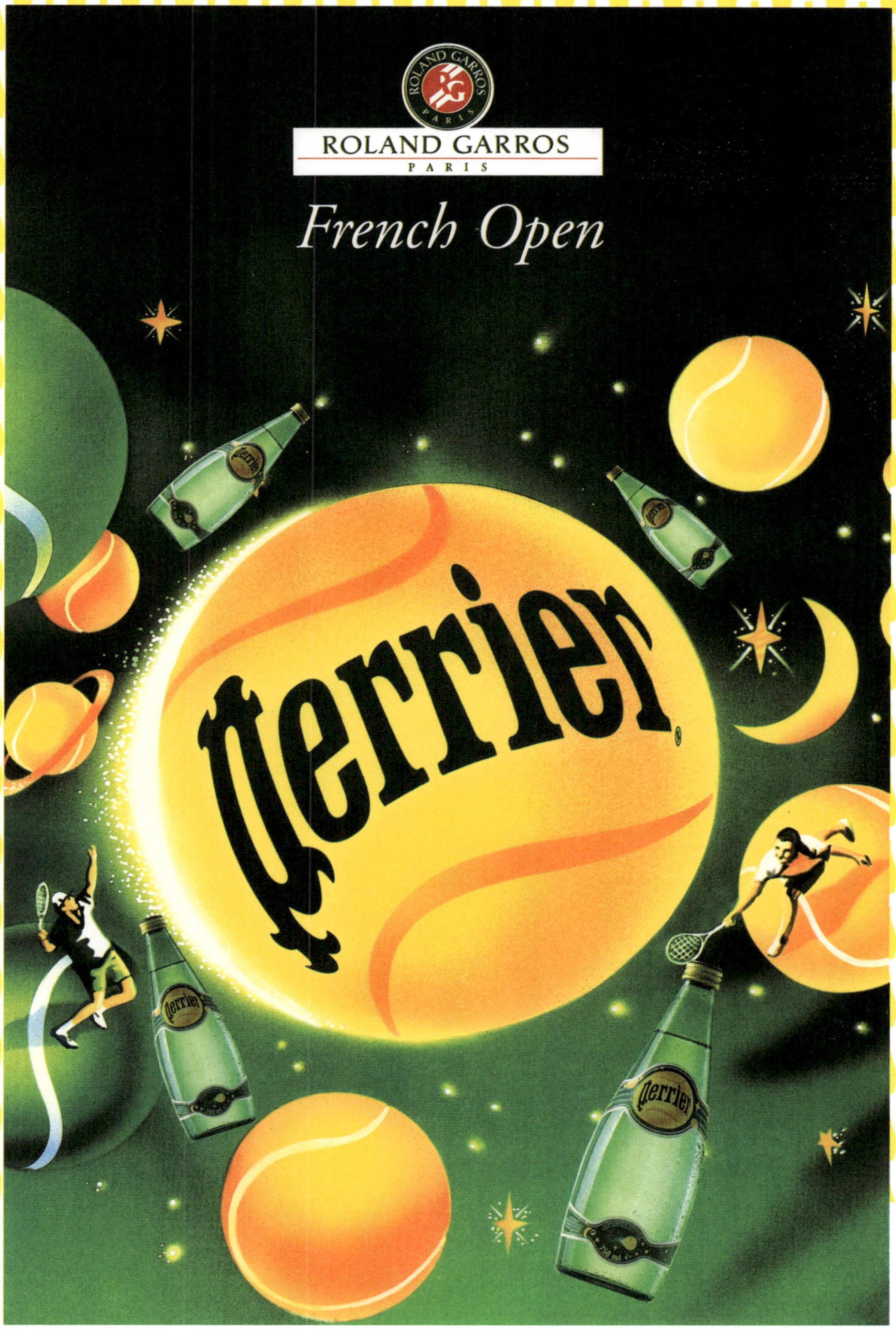

Roland Garros poster.

new age Perrier

Perrier took on a new identity in 1992, as one of the iconic mineral waters in the Nestlé Group stable. Although there were significant changes at a management and organizational level, Perrier retained its irrepressible verve, sticking close to its edgy, avant-garde roots.
As a symbol of continuity with the past, St. John Harmsworth's former home, known as the "château" or castle, became a museum celebrating the Perrier story. It nestles in a lush green oasis, an extraordinary garden stocked with 90 different species, with a harmonious blend of flowerbeds, ponds and topiary sculptures strangely reminiscent of Perrier advertisements.
Huge changes were made at the Vergèze site to comply with the Nestlé approach to production, quality standards and efficiency. When the industrial equipment was completely redesigned, protection of the environment around the spring was also enhanced, affecting almost 3,500 hectares, of which 1,000 hectares is leased to farmers who have signed up to an organic charter. Within the space of a few years, the site was completely redesigned, focusing on bottling. The glassworks were sold off and the plant was equipped with machinery to meet the wide variety of consumer requirements. This is apparent in the explosion of formats and containers since 2001, when the first PET (polyethylene terephthalate) plastic bottles were introduced. Virtually every year brought new innovations and Perrier was now available in glass or plastic bottles and cans.

a globetrotter

The bottling site got a new lease on life symbolized by the launch of a huge investment and modernization program in 2006, with new bottling lines and optimized warehousing and shipping capabilities for France and further afield to support production volumes of approximately one billion bottles.
Perrier water is still a seasoned traveler. Since its earliest days it has packed its Indian club-shaped bottle and airtight lid, crossed the English Channel and traveled to the far-flung reaches of the Empire where the British were staunchly waiting, whisky or gin glass in hand, for their mixer. When Perrier crossed the Atlantic in the 1970s, it won over the East Coast yuppies who could at last refresh themselves with natural sparkling mineral water after a jog.
In trendy nightlife mode, Perrier struck poses at New York's Club 54, a disco hotspot and meeting place for the jet set, performers and the underground scene.
As Perrier celebrates its 150th anniversary, its bottles can be found in 140 countries worldwide. Although it is a bestseller in the United States and Canada, it is also very popular in Russia and South Korea, for example, as well as in Dubai, Mexico, China and Japan, not forgetting Europe. Perrier integrates into different cultures without ever compromising its identity and roots, and raises the temperature all over the world with its intense, refreshing boost. It spans continents, staying ahead of the game, thriving on a heady cultural vibe. This is supported by the Société Perrier cutting-edge web portal, which writes a whole new set of rules for interactive communications. It feeds a new community of highly creative night owls spanning the major cities of the world. Sociétéperrier.com spots trends, shares hotspots, showcases new music and slips its devotees tips about the hottest after-dark venues, the arts, music, culture, fashion, travel and cocktails.

number one for mixology

In this new millennium, Perrier is mixing and matching not just styles but also liquid refreshment in the hands of those cocktail wizards known as mixologists who showcase their skills DJ-style in the hippest bars. Only the best ingredients feature in their cocktails. There would be no mixology without Perrier to provide that sparkling final flourish or take a flavor to new heights.
Bold advertising campaigns helped Perrier to reconquer the market. Perrier left its unique, high-impact and unconventional mark with films, billboard advertising and pioneering digital media. As the brand approaches its 150th anniversary, it has not lost the power to inspire shock and surprise, always staying one trend ahead of the game.

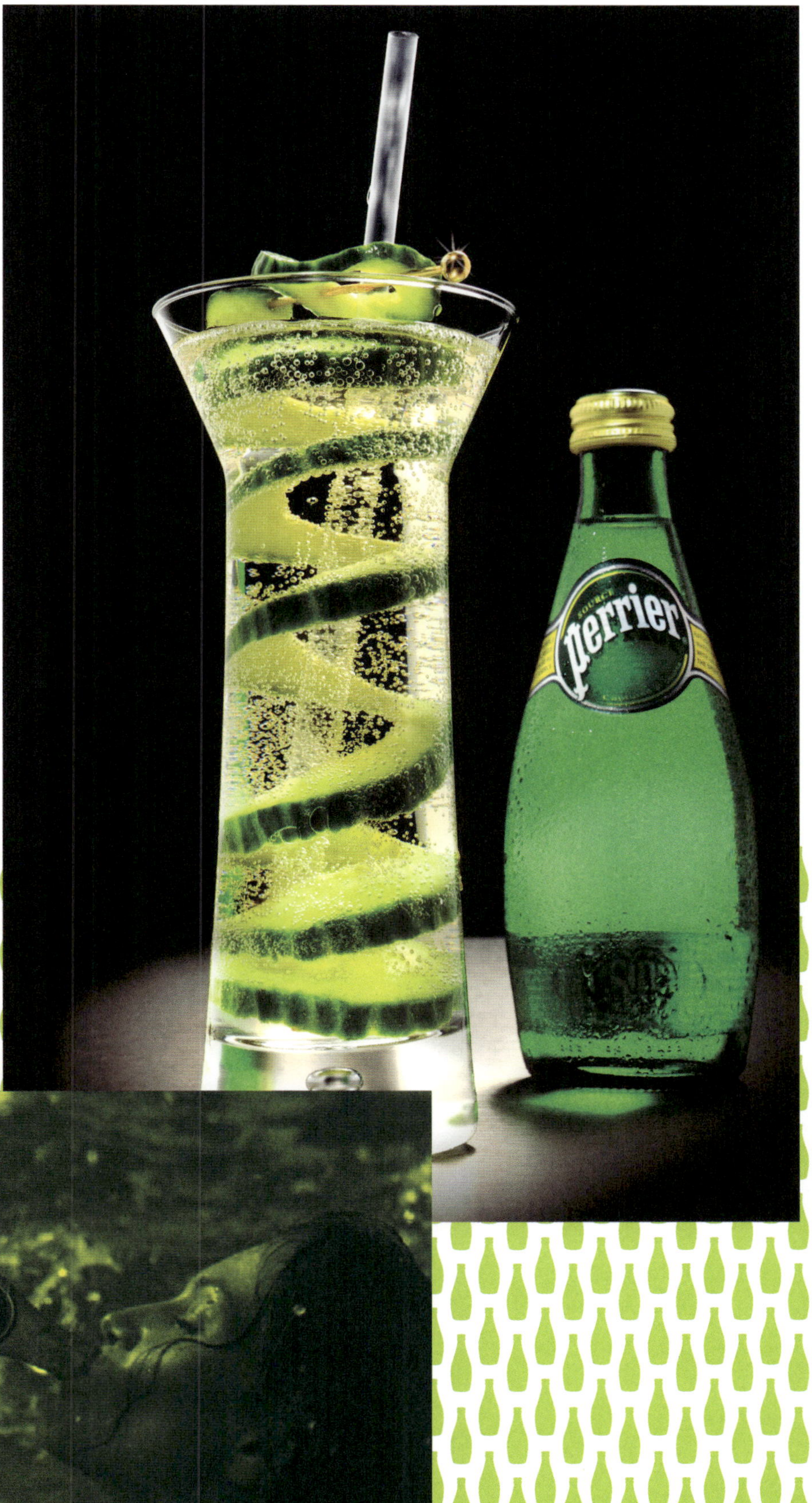

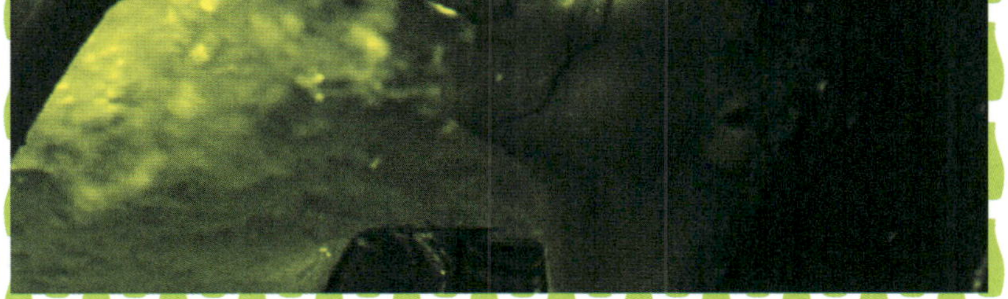

**Top: D-Tox cocktail.
Bottom: Excerpt
from the film *Melting*.**

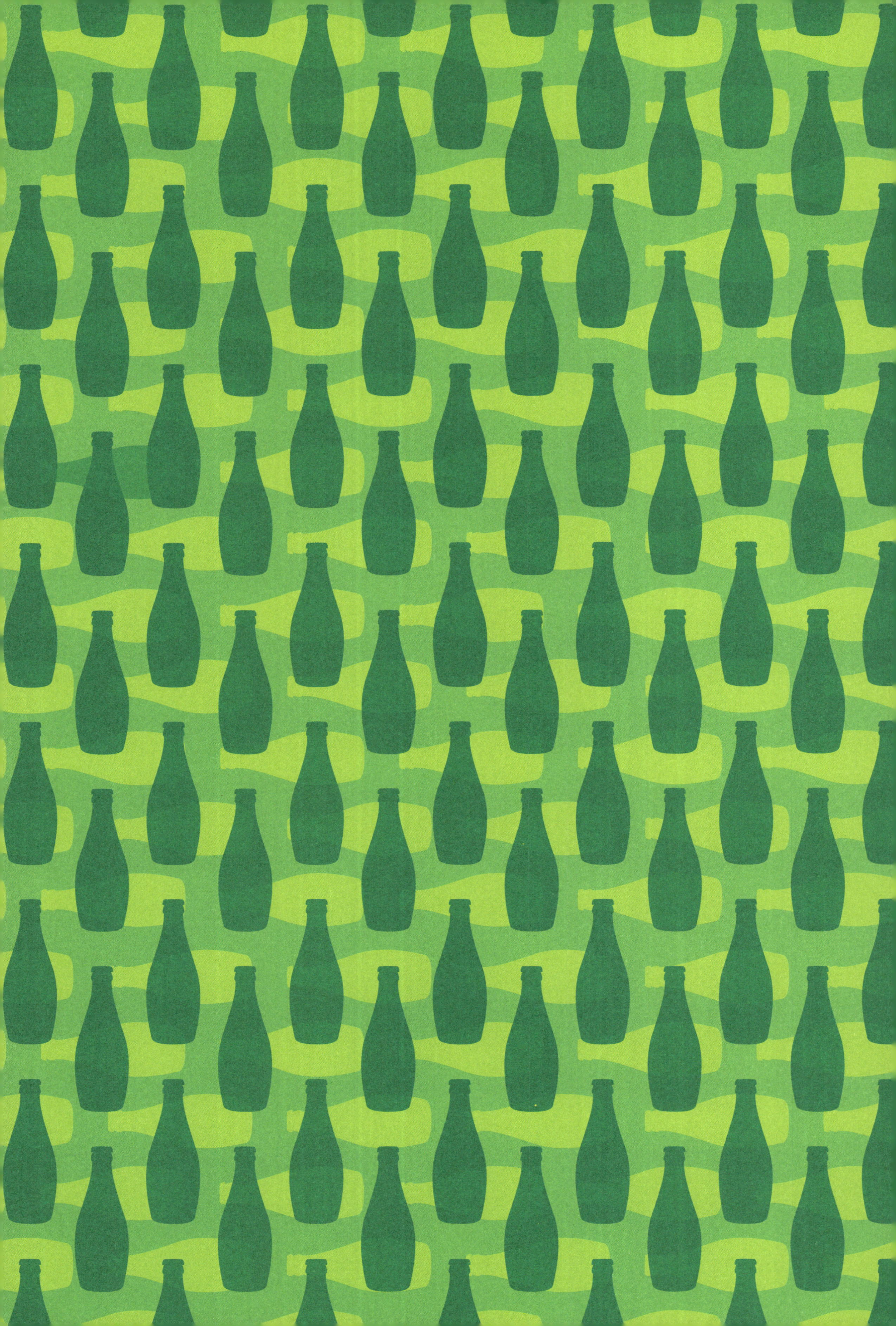

campaign overview

In the very earliest days, before it was even known as Perrier, the water made its first entry in the annals of advertising. The sparkling mineral water made a regal first appearance in the world of advertising as "the princess of table waters". This was the distinguished first title of the water, which would stick for almost three decades. When the little bottle beloved of the British became known as Perrier in the 20th century, it rebranded itself "the champagne of table waters". This festive slogan with its elegant cachet would feature for some forty years in the history of Perrier and in the pages of magazines.

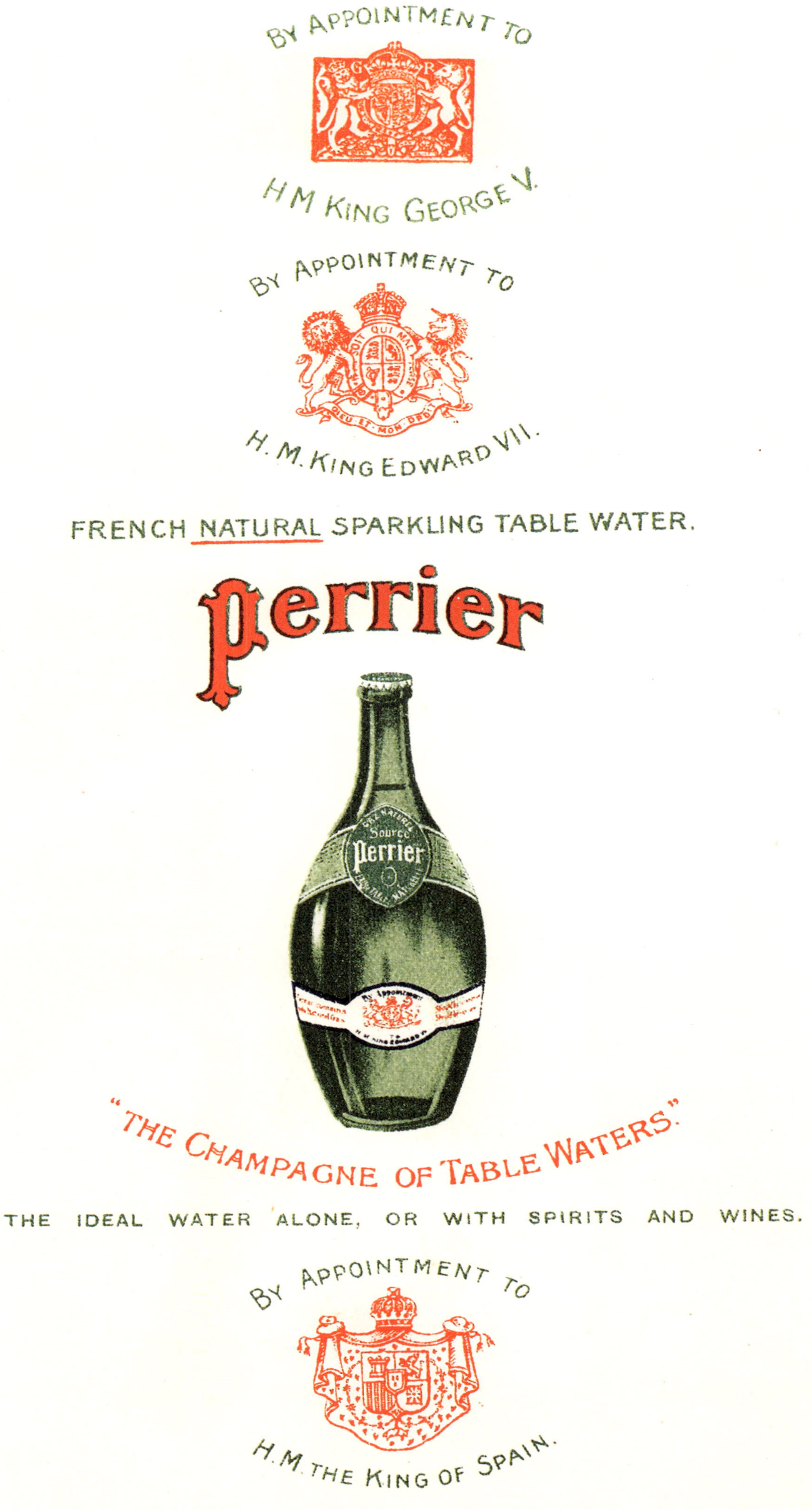
By Appointment to
H M King George V.
By Appointment to
H. M. King Edward VII.
FRENCH NATURAL SPARKLING TABLE WATER.
Perrier
Source
Perrier
"The Champagne of Table Waters."
THE IDEAL WATER ALONE, OR WITH SPIRITS AND WINES.
By Appointment to
H. M. the King of Spain.

variation on the champagne of table waters

In the mid-1930s, Perrier captured the mood of the times and handed over pen and pencil to some of the most famous writers and artists of the age. With the series "Variation on the champagne of table waters", this drink carved out a niche for itself in French intellectual history. Talented pairings were formed and famous writers such as Colette, Francis Carco and Pierre Mac Orlan agreed to be part of the new literary buzz around Perrier in the exalted company of Curnonsky, prince of gastronomes, playwright Pierre Frondaie and aviatrix Elizabeth Lion. They each shared the billing with a top illustrator and the only exception to the couples rule was Jean Effel, who penned both the text and illustrations for his "Variation".

VARIATION SUR LE "CHAMPAGNE DES EAUX DE TABLE"

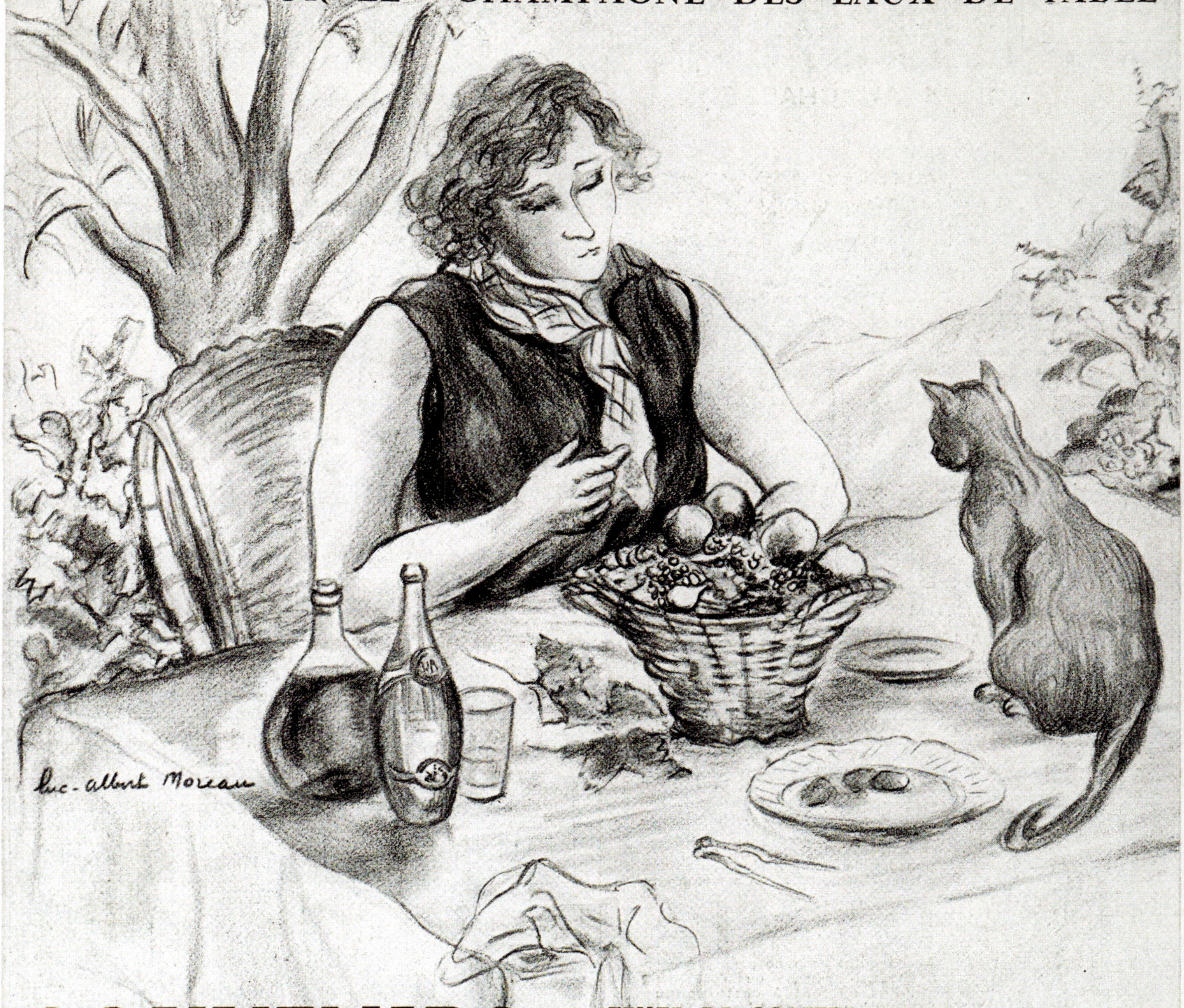

SOUVENIRS

TEXTE DE COLETTE
DESSIN DE LUC-ALBERT MOREAU

Il est moins pénible de boire un verre de vin médiocre que d'avaler une gorgée d'eau fade. C'est à la qualité de l'eau que notre palais réserve ses délicatesses. Loin de m'ôter la subtilité qu'il faut pour apprécier les différents "crus" de l'eau, l'amour que j'ai pour le vin l'a développée.

Nous autres, amis du bon vin, nous savons boire l'eau saine en dehors des repas, et à grands verres. J'aime l'eau du réveil, l'eau d'après-midi, l'eau de minuit qui nous irrigue au sortir du théâtre ou du cinéma, l'eau des vacances, l'eau gaie des pique-nique sur la Côte provençale... Toutes ces eaux ne sont qu'une seule et même eau, bien froide, illuminée de bulles, si chargée de gaz naturel qu'elle humecte, durant qu'on la boit, les narines et les cils...

Du fond d'un grand gobelet bouillonnant montent les souvenirs avec l'effervescence. Mon petit pays d'autrefois, privé d'eau potable, buvait, l'été, l'eau obscure de ses citernes, souvent fétides. Pourtant, à cinq cents pas de là, coulait le trésor inutile des sources non captées, qui sous bois sortaient de terre avec un petit sanglot, se traçaient un lit, se perdaient, reparaissaient à la faveur de quelque usine pierreuse...

L'eau active que j'ai coutume de boire, je ne l'ai connue que bien plus tard. L'ayant goûtée, j'oubliai son nom, et je ne savais le lendemain comment la redemander.

— Enfin, garçon, vous savez bien ce que je veux dire... Une eau qui bondit quand on la débouche... Une eau qui rit. Une eau qui est dans la bouche comme une gorgée de Champagne et une poignée d'aiguilles.

— Ah ! je vois, dis le garçon.

En effet, il ne se trompa pas, et m'apporta une bouteille d'Eau PERRIER.

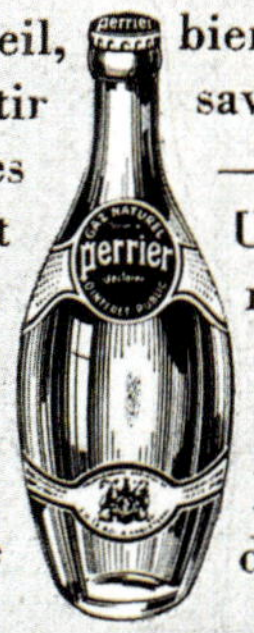

Colette

LE CHAMPAGNE DES EAUX DE TABLE

PLASAL

Colette and Luc-Albert Moreau

Colette was already a major figure on the French literary scene in the 1930s. It was a foregone conclusion that her text would be accompanied by a portrait drawn by Luc-Albert Moreau. This painter, born in Paris in 1882 and deeply affected by World War I, was a marvelous lithographer and illustrated the works of many writers including Montherlant, Colette and Carco.

André Dignimont and Francis Carco

The painter, engraver, illustrator and actor André Dignimont, born in Paris in 1894, shared his love of the nightlife and Montmartre with Francis Carco and illustrated a number of his books. He was also an illustrator for Colette, Jacques Lacretelle, Pierre Louÿs, and even Margaret Mitchell, since he produced the drawings for the French edition of *Gone with the Wind*.

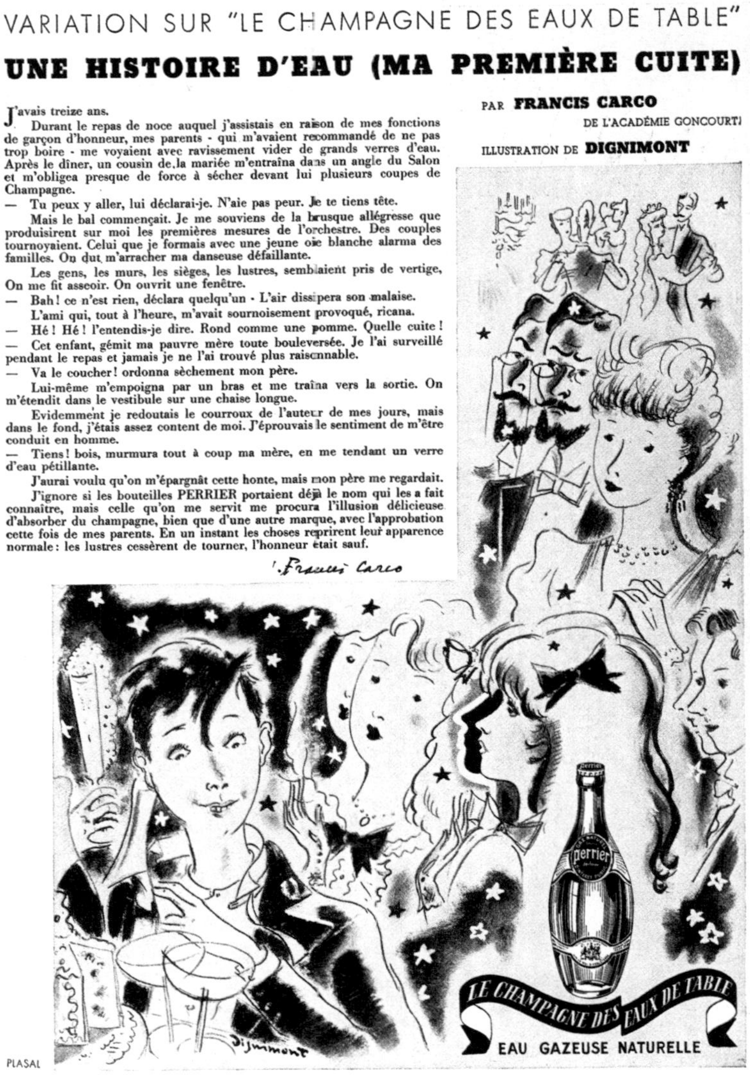

VARIATION SUR "LE CHAMPAGNE DES EAUX DE TABLE"

UNE HISTOIRE D'EAU (MA PREMIÈRE CUITE)

PAR **FRANCIS CARCO**
DE L'ACADÉMIE GONCOURT
ILLUSTRATION DE **DIGNIMONT**

J'avais treize ans.

Durant le repas de noce auquel j'assistais en raison de mes fonctions de garçon d'honneur, mes parents - qui m'avaient recommandé de ne pas trop boire - me voyaient avec ravissement vider de grands verres d'eau. Après le dîner, un cousin de la mariée m'entraîna dans un angle du Salon et m'obligea presque de force à sécher devant lui plusieurs coupes de Champagne.

— Tu peux y aller, lui déclarai-je. N'aie pas peur. Je te tiens tête.

Mais le bal commençait. Je me souviens de la brusque allégresse que produisirent sur moi les premières mesures de l'orchestre. Des couples tournoyaient. Celui que je formais avec une jeune oie blanche alarma des familles. On dut m'arracher ma danseuse défaillante.

Les gens, les murs, les sièges, les lustres, semblaient pris de vertige, On me fit asseoir. On ouvrit une fenêtre.

— Bah! ce n'est rien, déclara quelqu'un - L'air dissipera son malaise.

L'ami qui, tout à l'heure, m'avait sournoisement provoqué, ricana.

— Hé! Hé! l'entendis-je dire. Rond comme une pomme. Quelle cuite!

— Cet enfant, gémit ma pauvre mère toute bouleversée. Je l'ai surveillé pendant le repas et jamais je ne l'ai trouvé plus raisonnable.

— Va le coucher! ordonna sèchement mon père.

Lui-même m'empoigna par un bras et me traîna vers la sortie. On m'étendit dans le vestibule sur une chaise longue.

Evidemment je redoutais le courroux de l'auteur de mes jours, mais dans le fond, j'étais assez content de moi. J'éprouvais le sentiment de m'être conduit en homme.

— Tiens! bois, murmura tout à coup ma mère, en me tendant un verre d'eau pétillante.

J'aurai voulu qu'on m'épargnât cette honte, mais mon père me regardait.

J'ignore si les bouteilles PERRIER portaient déjà le nom qui les a fait connaître, mais celle qu'on me servit me procura l'illusion délicieuse d'absorber du champagne, bien que d'une autre marque, avec l'approbation cette fois de mes parents. En un instant les choses reprirent leur apparence normale: les lustres cessèrent de tourner, l'honneur était sauf.

Francis Carco

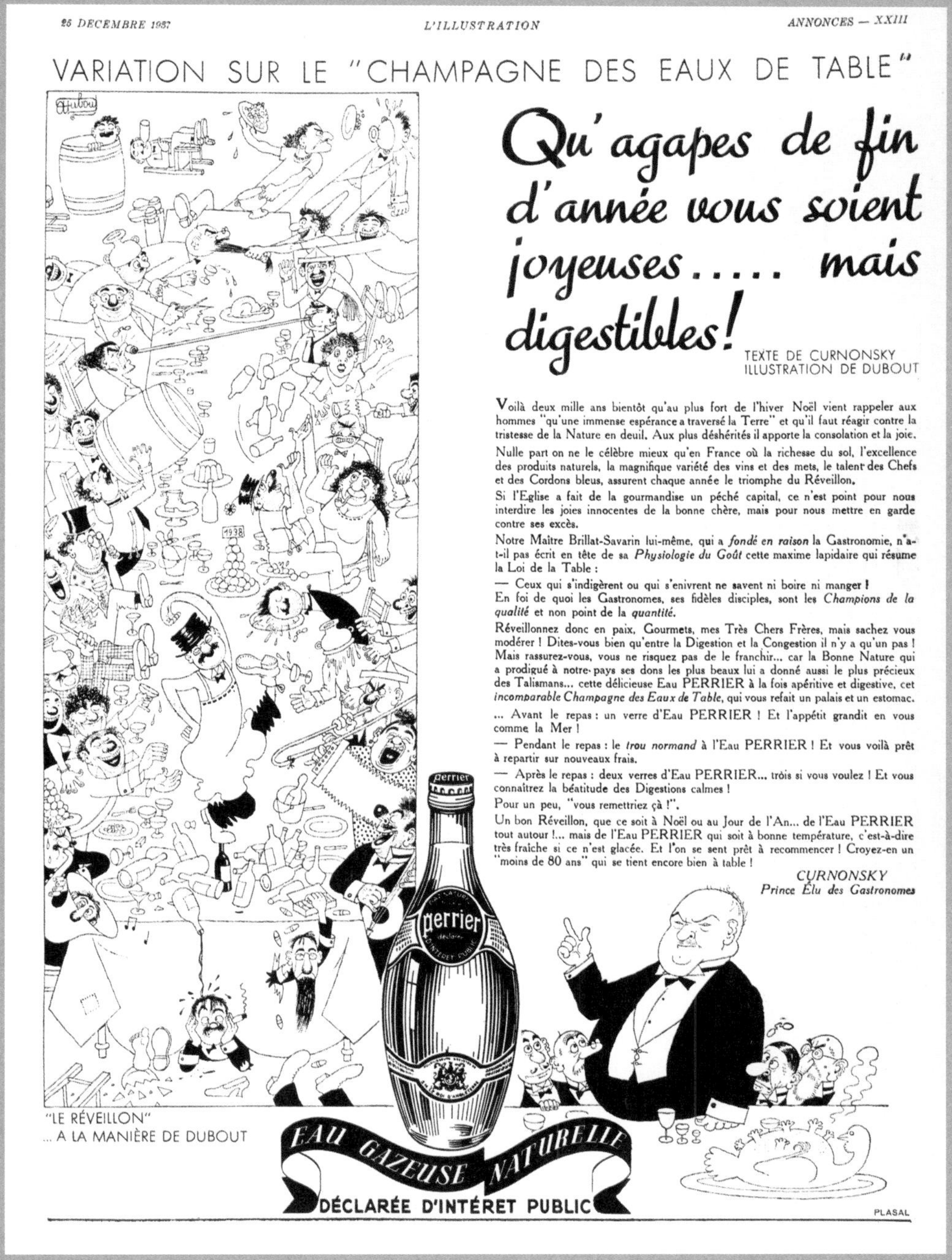

25 DECEMBRE 1937 — L'ILLUSTRATION — ANNONCES — XXIII

VARIATION SUR LE "CHAMPAGNE DES EAUX DE TABLE"

Qu'agapes de fin d'année vous soient joyeuses..... mais digestibles!

TEXTE DE CURNONSKY
ILLUSTRATION DE DUBOUT

Voilà deux mille ans bientôt qu'au plus fort de l'hiver Noël vient rappeler aux hommes "qu'une immense espérance a traversé la Terre" et qu'il faut réagir contre la tristesse de la Nature en deuil. Aux plus déshérités il apporte la consolation et la joie.

Nulle part on ne le célèbre mieux qu'en France où la richesse du sol, l'excellence des produits naturels, la magnifique variété des vins et des mets, le talent des Chefs et des Cordons bleus, assurent chaque année le triomphe du Réveillon.

Si l'Eglise a fait de la gourmandise un péché capital, ce n'est point pour nous interdire les joies innocentes de la bonne chère, mais pour nous mettre en garde contre ses excès.

Notre Maître Brillat-Savarin lui-même, qui a *fondé en raison* la Gastronomie, n'a-t-il pas écrit en tête de sa *Physiologie du Goût* cette maxime lapidaire qui résume la Loi de la Table :

— Ceux qui s'indigèrent ou qui s'enivrent ne savent ni boire ni manger !

En foi de quoi les Gastronomes, ses fidèles disciples, sont les *Champions de la qualité* et non point de la *quantité*.

Réveillonnez donc en paix, Gourmets, mes Très Chers Frères, mais sachez vous modérer ! Dites-vous bien qu'entre la Digestion et la Congestion il n'y a qu'un pas ! Mais rassurez-vous, vous ne risquez pas de le franchir... car la Bonne Nature qui a prodigué à notre pays ses dons les plus beaux lui a donné aussi le plus précieux des Talismans... cette délicieuse Eau PERRIER à la fois apéritive et digestive, cet *incomparable Champagne des Eaux de Table*, qui vous refait un palais et un estomac.

... Avant le repas : un verre d'Eau PERRIER ! Et l'appétit grandit en vous comme la Mer !

— Pendant le repas : le *trou normand* à l'Eau PERRIER ! Et vous voilà prêt à repartir sur nouveaux frais.

— Après le repas : deux verres d'Eau PERRIER... trois si vous voulez ! Et vous connaîtrez la béatitude des Digestions calmes !

Pour un peu, "vous remettriez çà !".

Un bon Réveillon, que ce soit à Noël ou au Jour de l'An... de l'Eau PERRIER tout autour !... mais de l'Eau PERRIER qui soit à bonne température, c'est-à-dire très fraîche si ce n'est glacée. Et l'on se sent prêt à recommencer ! Croyez-en un "moins de 80 ans" qui se tient encore bien à table !

CURNONSKY
Prince Élu des Gastronomes

"LE RÉVEILLON"
... A LA MANIÈRE DE DUBOUT

Albert Dubout and Curnonsky

Meet Albert Dubout, a master of the humorous illustration who delighted several generations with his buxom ladies and little menfolk. Born in Marseille in 1905, he excelled at street and party scenes such as the one he drew to illustrate the text by his partner in humor the writer, critic and prince of gastronomes, Curnonsky.

Perrier girl

When Jean-Gabriel Domergue drew his Perrier Girl,
he was depicting that head-turning image of French womanhood
in all its glory - the embodiment of class, charm
and good taste. In 1936, the famous painter made style
and Perrier synonymous, with his many female
incarnations in evening gowns, day dresses, tennis, ski or bathing
outfits blending elegance with athleticism. The slogan
Perrier "loves modern women" matched their wit and verve.

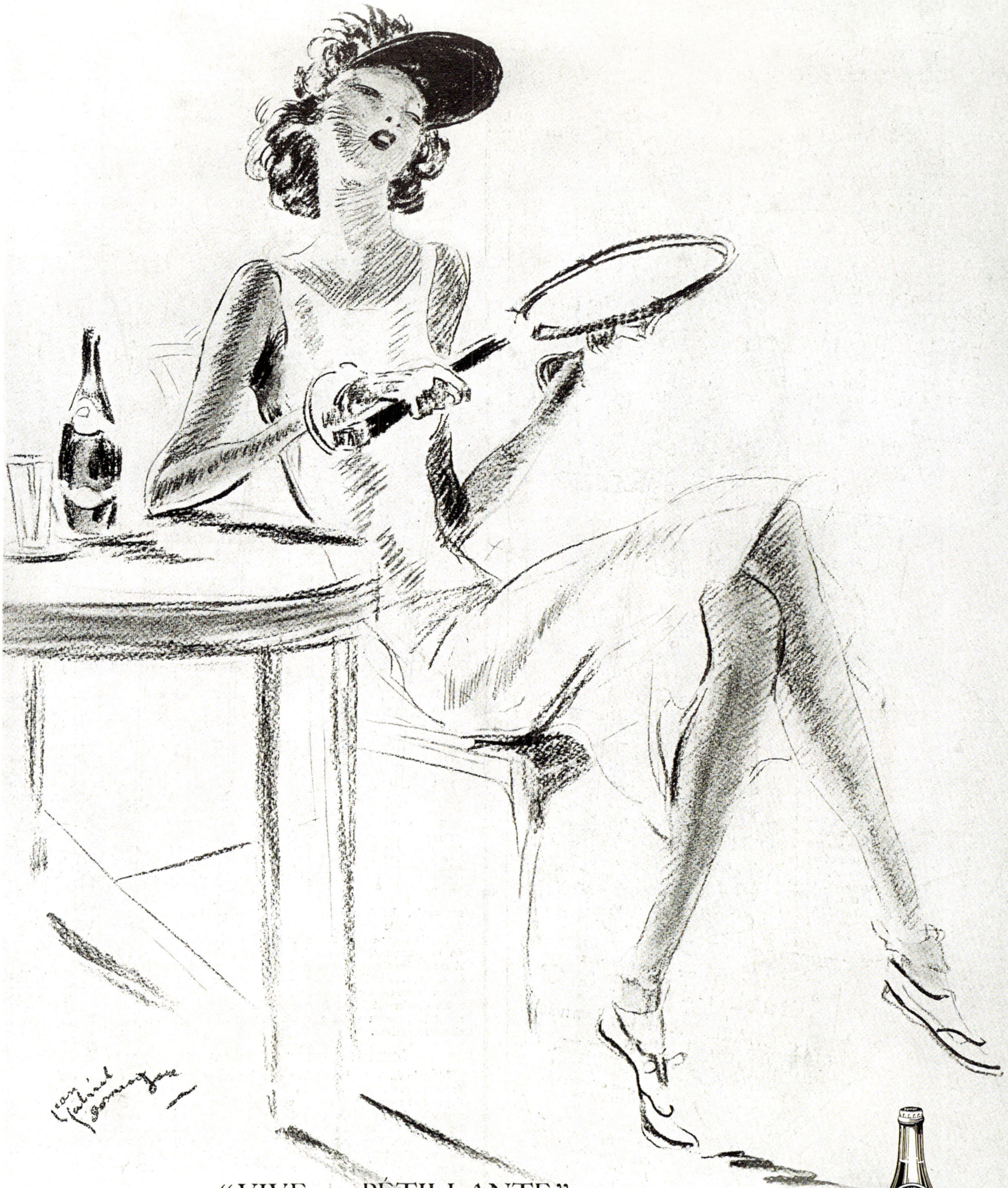

“VIVE et PÉTILLANTE”

En harmonie avec cette joyeuse vitalité qui caractérise la jeunesse sportive, la Source Perrier, eau minérale gazeuse naturelle, pure, légère, digestive, est vraiment la boisson idéale. Rien de plus sain, de plus désaltérant qu'un verre de Perrier très fraîche, avec un rond de citron.

Perrier
LE CHAMPAGNE DES EAUX DE TABLE
DÉCLARÉE D'INTÉRÊT PUBLIC

Envoi de 3 bouchons Perrier brevetés pour reboucher hermétiquement les bouteilles entamées. S'adresser à la Compagnie de la Source Perrier, Vergèze (Gard). Joindre 1 fr. en timbres pour frais d'envoi.

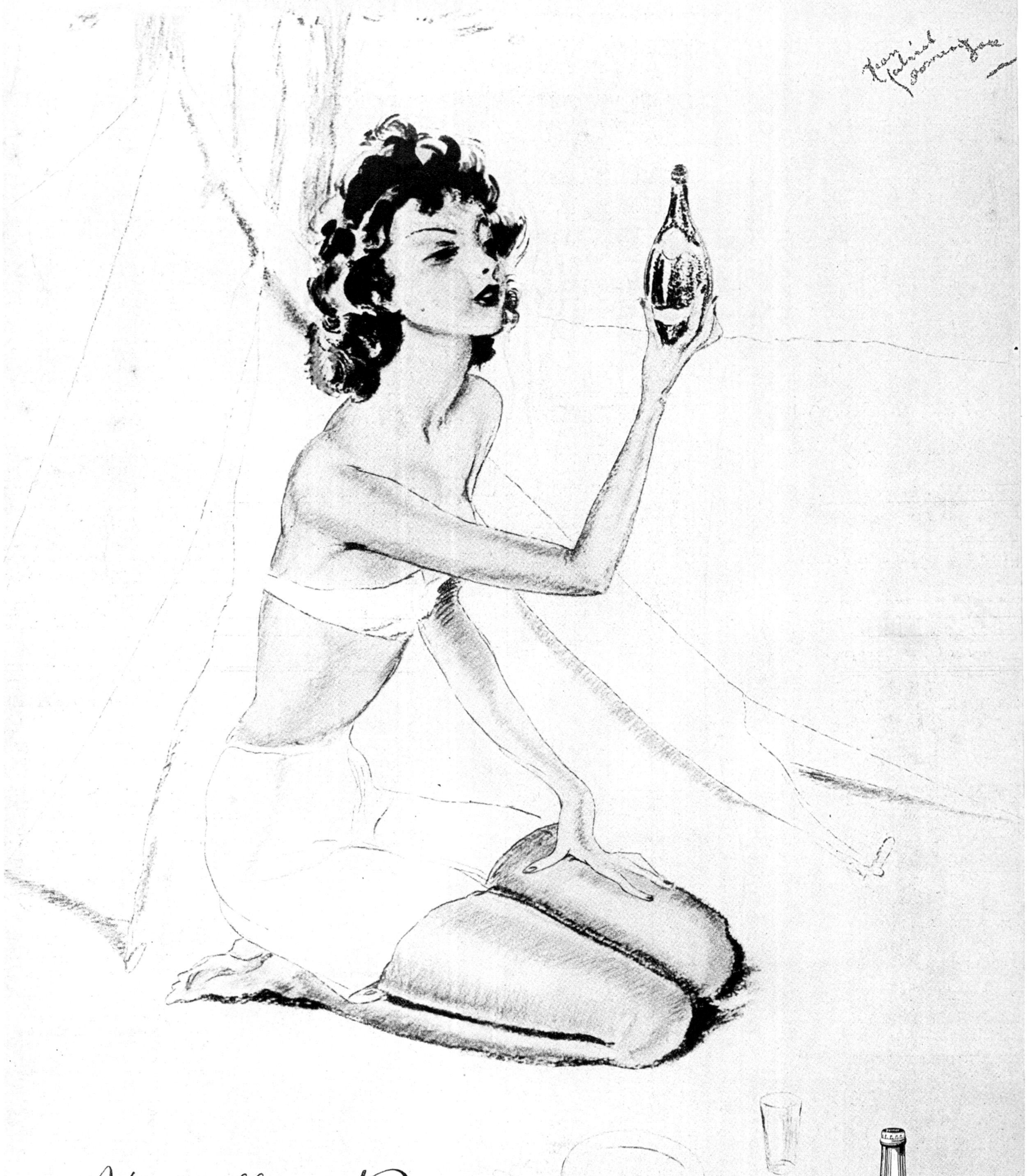

Naturelle et Pure

...comme la joie saine du plein air et du camping, la Source Perrier, pétillante et légère, est partout, en toutes occasions, la boisson préférée de la jeunesse sportive.

Envoi de 3 bouchons Perrier brevetés pour reboucher hermétiquement les bouteilles entamées. S'adresser à la Compagnie de la Source Perrier, Vergèze (Gard). Joindre 1 fr. en timbres pour frais d'envoi.

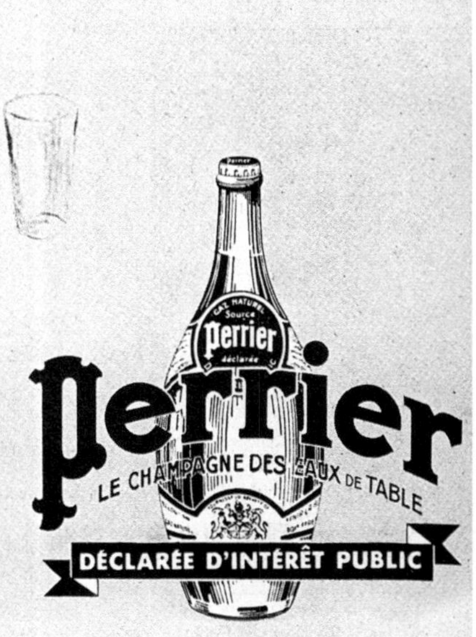

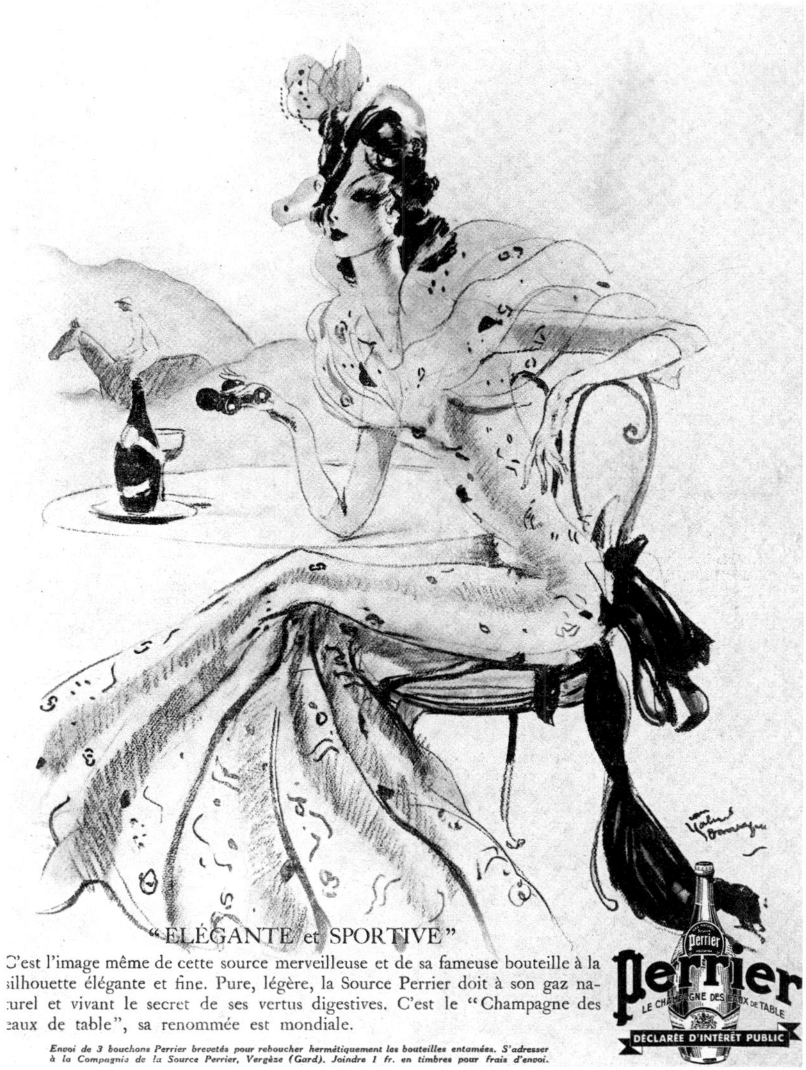

Jean-Gabriel Domergue

Who better than Jean-Gabriel Domergue to bring the Perrier Girl to life? This classically trained artist, who was born in Bordeaux in 1889, earned a reputation as the painter of Parisian women, the inventor of the French pin-up and a sketcher of aristocrats and society ladies. He painted 3,000 portraits and sketched dresses and accessories for the top fashion designers of the era.

two loves

"I have two loves – my country and Paris", sang the voluptuous Josephine Baker in 1931. Perrier picked up on this popular lyric for its 1937 campaign. Every individual loves the most easily digested of table waters presented here, in a manner appropriate to their lifestyle and age. Natural mineral water was now the preserve of every generation and of the country as a whole. Perrier vaunted its virtues for one and all, rehydrating athletes after sport and captivating mothers or well-bred young ladies.

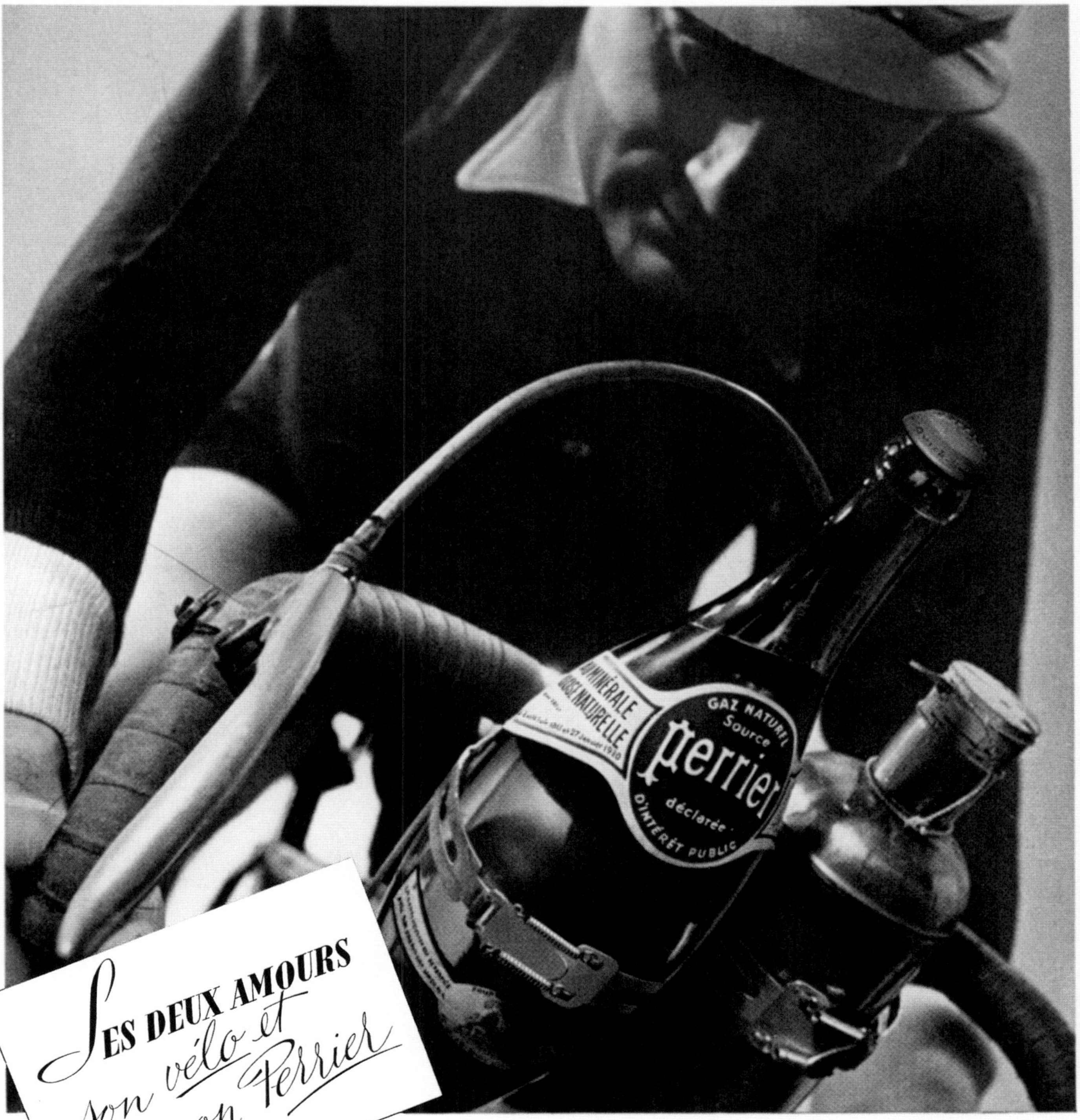

Ses deux amours son vélo et son Perrier

Ses deux amours? Son Vélo, compagnon fidèle, qui lui a procuré les pures joies sportives de la victoire, du triomphe, et... l'eau PERRIER, gazeuse naturelle, compagne fidèle, sur qui il sait pouvoir compter lorsque la lassitude et le découragement s'abattent sur lui, pour lui redonner l'énergie nécessaire qui lui permettra, dans un suprême effort, " d'enlever " l'étape.

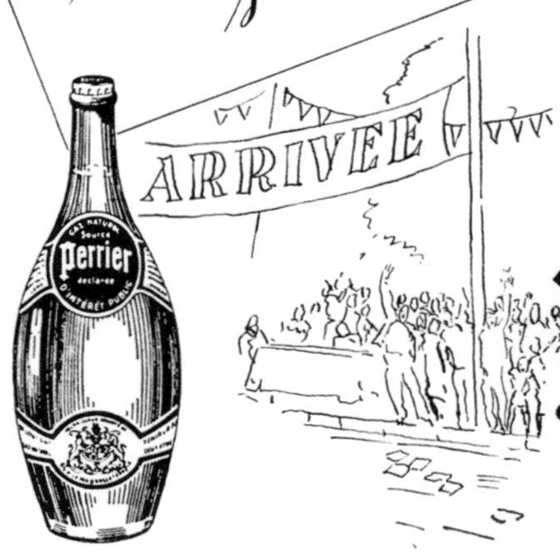

Perrier
LE CHAMPAGNE DES EAUX DE TABLE
DÉCLARÉE D'INTERET PUBLIC

Naturelle

PLASAL

LA PLUS DIGESTIVE DES EAUX MINÉRALES, LA SOURCE PERRIER, JAILLIT A VERGÈZE (GARD)

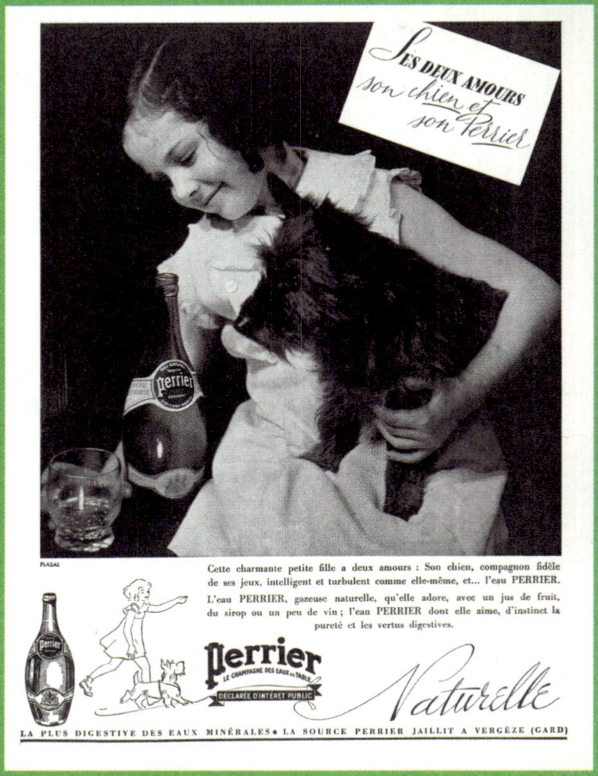

Les deux amours
son chien et
son Perrier
PLASAL
Cette charmante petite fille a deux amours : Son chien, compagnon fidèle de ses jeux, intelligent et turbulent comme elle-même, et... l'eau PERRIER.
L'eau PERRIER, gazeuse naturelle, qu'elle adore, avec un jus de fruit, du sirop ou un peu de vin ; l'eau PERRIER dont elle aime, d'instinct la pureté et les vertus digestives.
Perrier
LE CHAMPAGNE DES EAUX DE TABLE
DECLARÉE D'INTÉRET PUBLIC
Naturelle
LA PLUS DIGESTIVE DES EAUX MINÉRALES • LA SOURCE PERRIER JAILLIT A VERGÈZE (GARD)

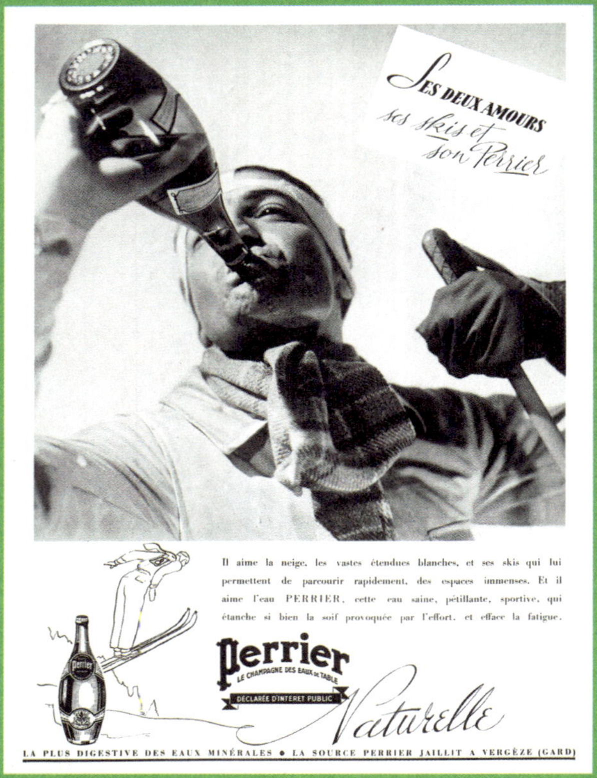

Les deux amours
ses skis et
son Perrier
Il aime la neige, les vastes étendues blanches, et ses skis qui lui permettent de parcourir rapidement, des espaces immenses. Et il aime l'eau PERRIER, cette eau saine, pétillante, sportive, qui étanche si bien la soif provoquée par l'effort, et efface la fatigue.
Perrier
LE CHAMPAGNE DES EAUX DE TABLE
DÉCLARÉE D'INTERET PUBLIC
Naturelle
LA PLUS DIGESTIVE DES EAUX MINÉRALES • LA SOURCE PERRIER JAILLIT A VERGÈZE (GARD)

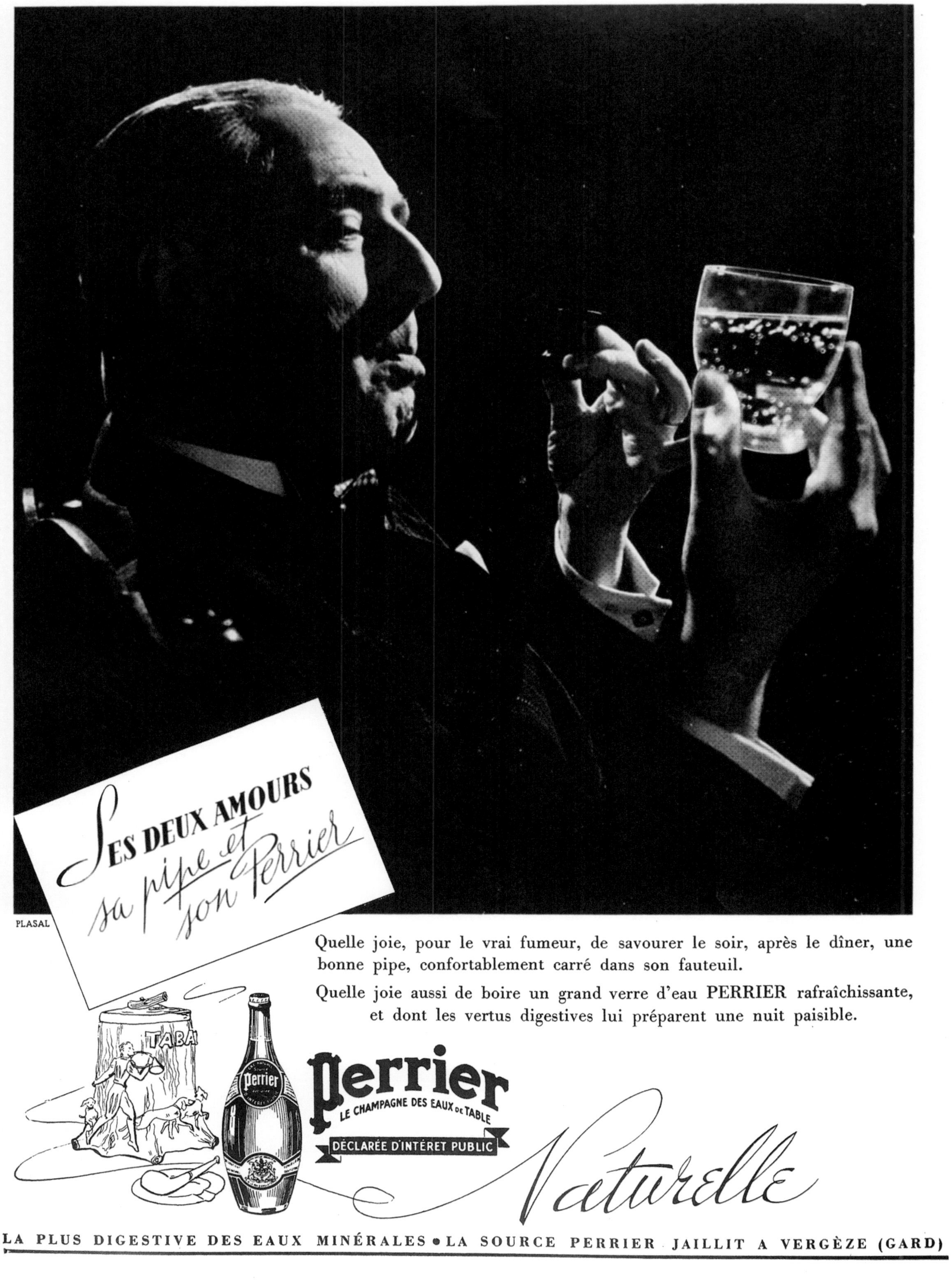
Ses deux amours
sa pipe et son Perrier
PLASAL
Quelle joie, pour le vrai fumeur, de savourer le soir, après le dîner, une bonne pipe, confortablement carré dans son fauteuil.
Quelle joie aussi de boire un grand verre d'eau PERRIER rafraîchissante, et dont les vertus digestives lui préparent une nuit paisible.
TABA
Perrier
Perrier
LE CHAMPAGNE DES EAUX DE TABLE
DÉCLARÉE D'INTÉRET PUBLIC
Naturelle
LA PLUS DIGESTIVE DES EAUX MINÉRALES • LA SOURCE PERRIER JAILLIT A VERGÈZE (GARD)

variations on a comeback

France celebrated its new-found freedom after the war years and wartime shortages. This joy was shared with Perrier which made a comeback as the mood was now one of celebration and happiness, social gatherings and meeting friends in restaurants, at ski resorts, or at home. Sparkling mineral water was described as fostering relaxation and refreshment, and life could get back on an even keel with the well-bred characters drawn by Brenot.

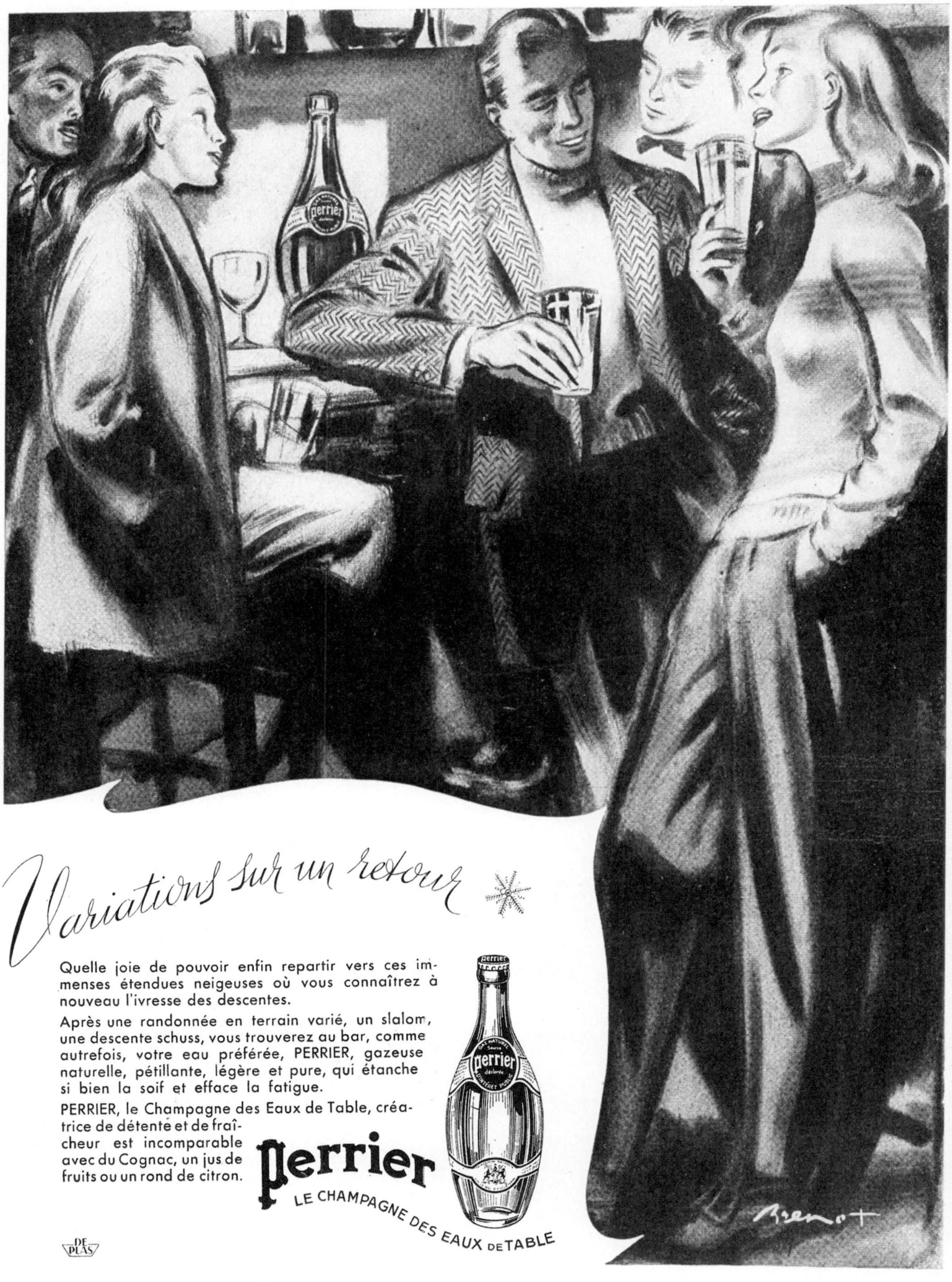

Annonce réalisée pour les publications illustrées en 1947 (Dessinateur : BRENOT)
An advertisement executed for illustrated publications in 1947 (Artist : BRENOT).
Anuncio realizado para publicaciones ilustradas en 1947 (Dibujante : BRENOT).

AGENCE DE PLAS

22, place Vendôme, Paris (Ier). OPÉ : 07-16

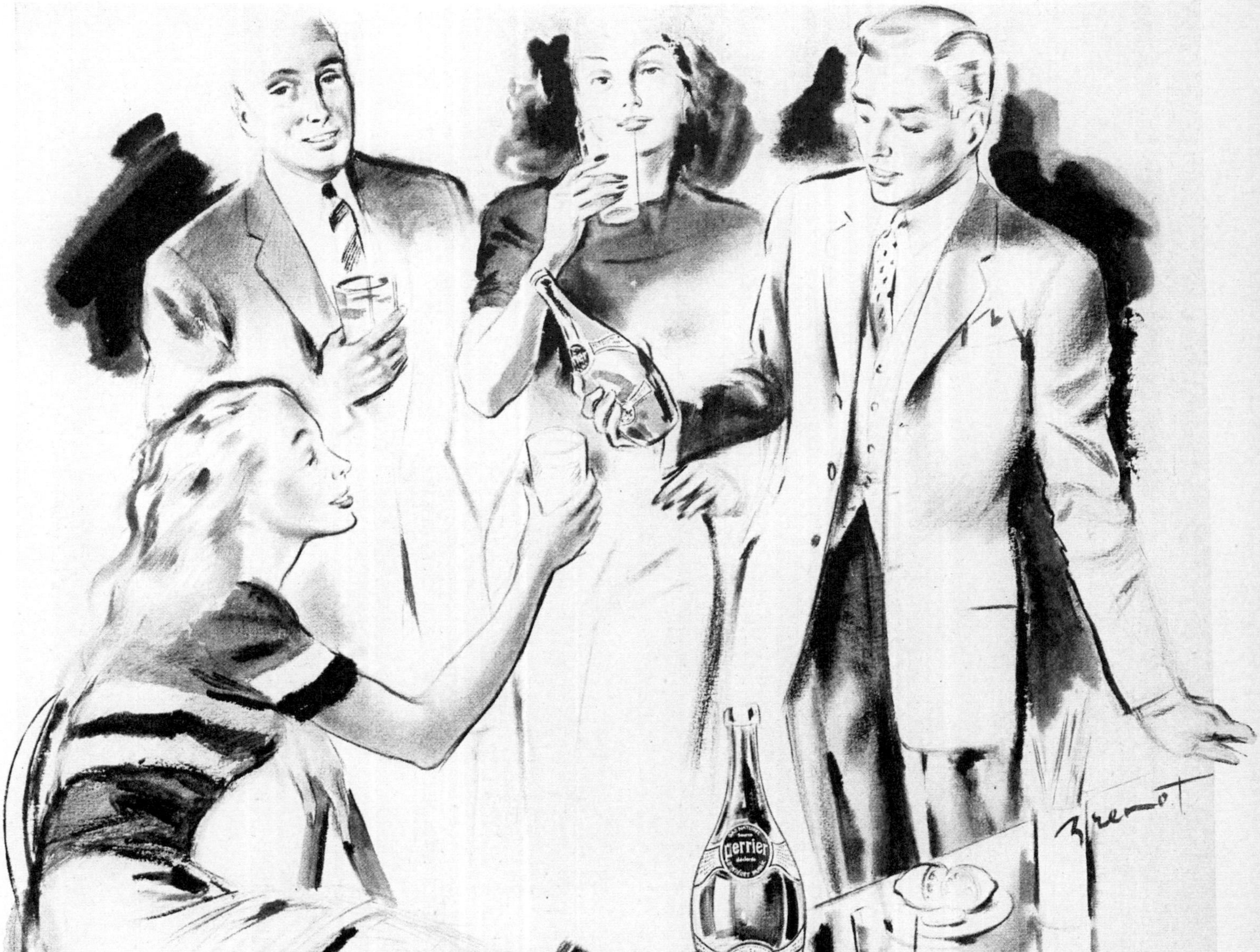
Variations sur un retour...
Réunions mondaines, amicales ou intimes !... Plaisir de recevoir ses amis dans une ambiance de sympathie, de joie et d'élégance.
Compagne pétillante et joyeuse, l'Eau PERRIER, gazeuse naturelle, a retrouvé sa place sur votre table, à votre bar.
Pour vos réceptions, PERRIER, le Champagne des Eaux de Table, incomparable avec un alcool, un jus de fruits ou un rond de citron, est toujours le rafraîchissement le plus apprécié et le plus raffiné dans sa simplicité.
Perrier
LE CHAMPAGNE DES EAUX DE TABLE
DE PLAS

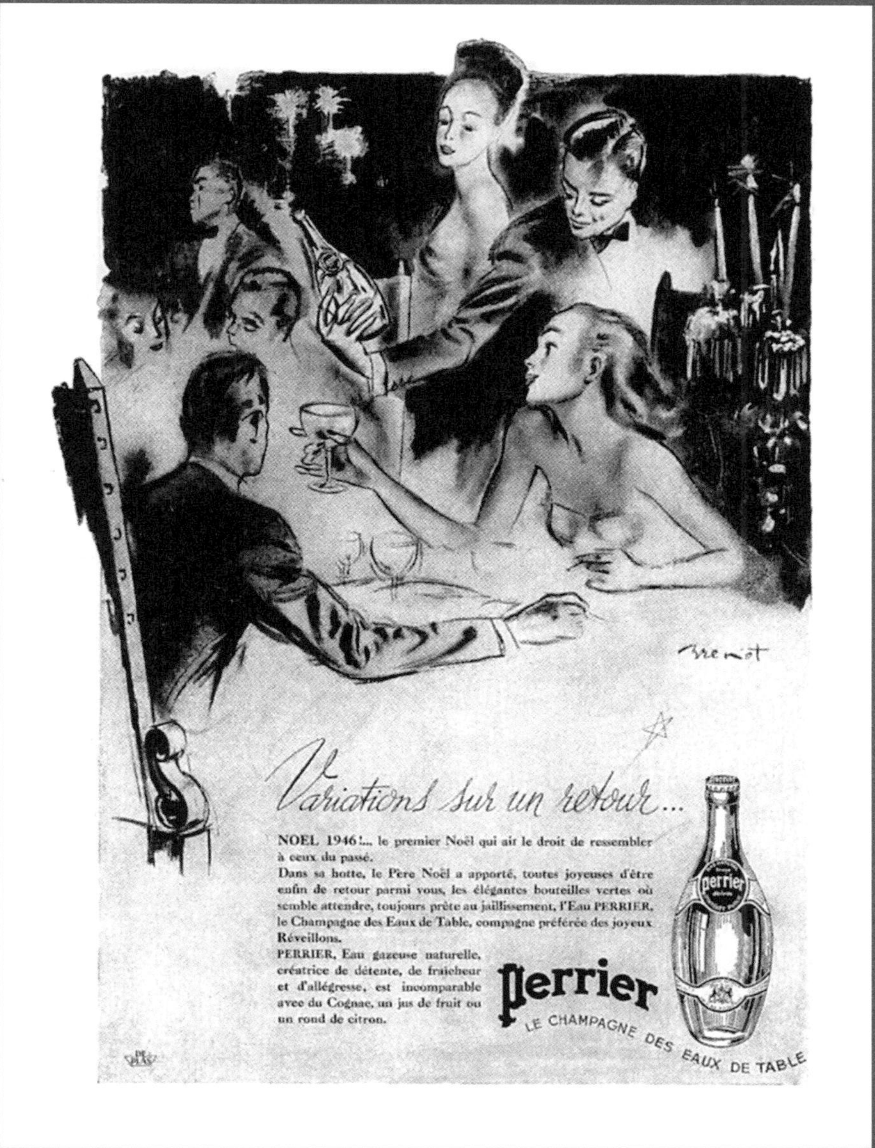

Brenot

This campaign marked the start of the career of poster designer Brenot, who was born in Paris in 1913 and had previously produced fashion plates for the top designers and sketched major artists and society ladies for magazines. He immortalized the Le Lido cabaret and its stunning dancers and established the credentials of the French post-war pin-up.

l'eau qui fait pschitt

This happy slogan invented by Jean Davray, imitating the fizz of a bottle of Perrier being opened, captured the spirit of the 1950s and early 1960s. Its good-humored message really hit the spot in France during the 30-year post-war boom. "Pschitt" reappeared in the strapline of a variety of campaigns, but was illustrated and used by top poster designers and illustrators from 1949. Elite poster designers Carlu, Morvan and Savignac all produced their "Monsieur Pschitt", giving free rein to their imaginations and huge creative talents. Magazines could not get enough of illustrators Peynet and Kiraz, who were also invited to add their very own twist to the "Pschitt" theme. "Pschitt" also picked up on the latest dance crazes and, in 1962, Perrier became the water that could do the Twist.

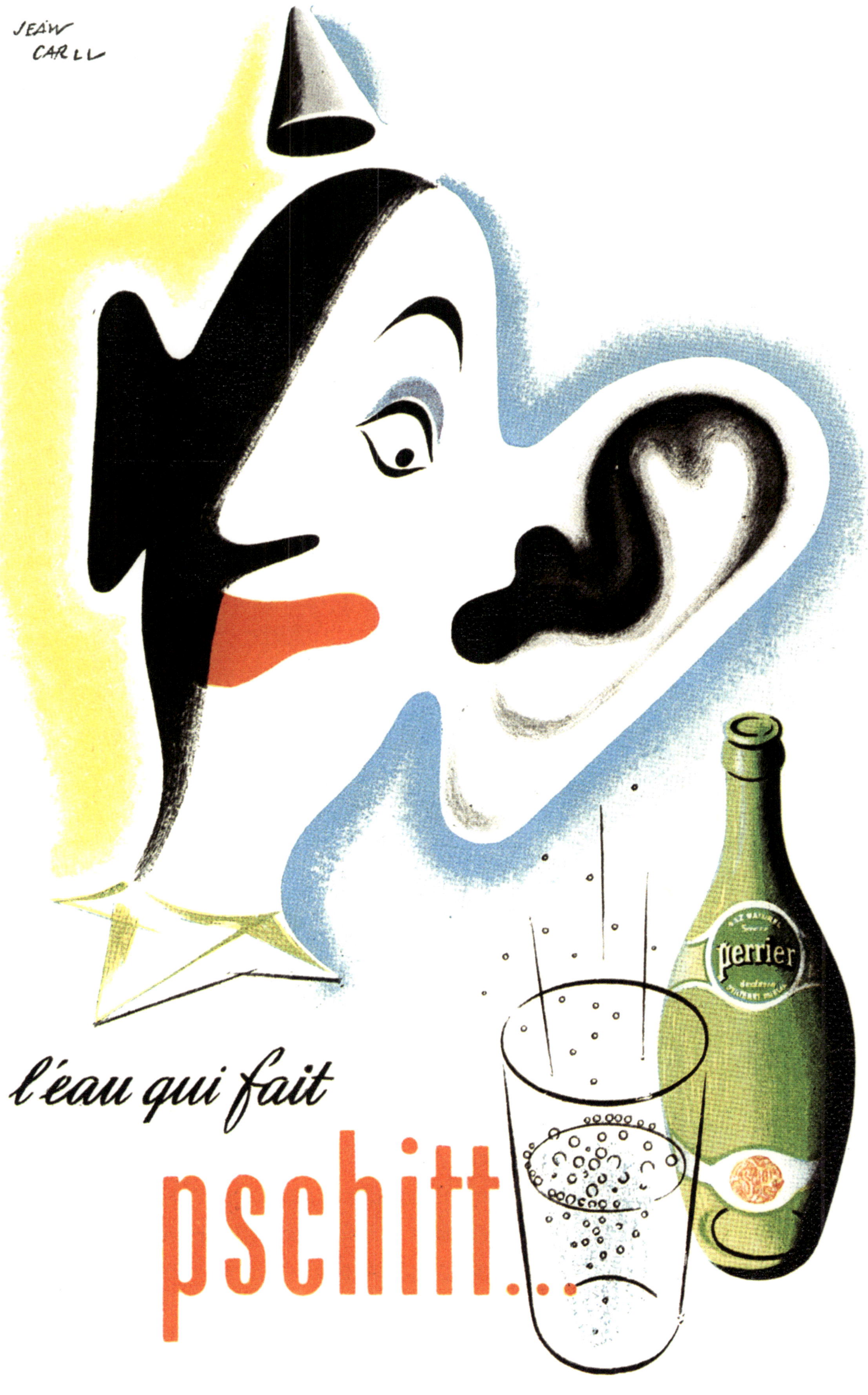
JEAN CARLU
Perrier
l'eau qui fait
pschitt...

Jean Carlu

Jean Carlu, was born in 1909 in Paris, and earned a reputation in the mid-1920s as one of the top advertising illustrators. He was initially drawn to Cubism and, under the influence of Juan Gris, he brought a surreal touch to his work. During World War II in the United States, the artist drew a number of posters to bolster the US war effort.

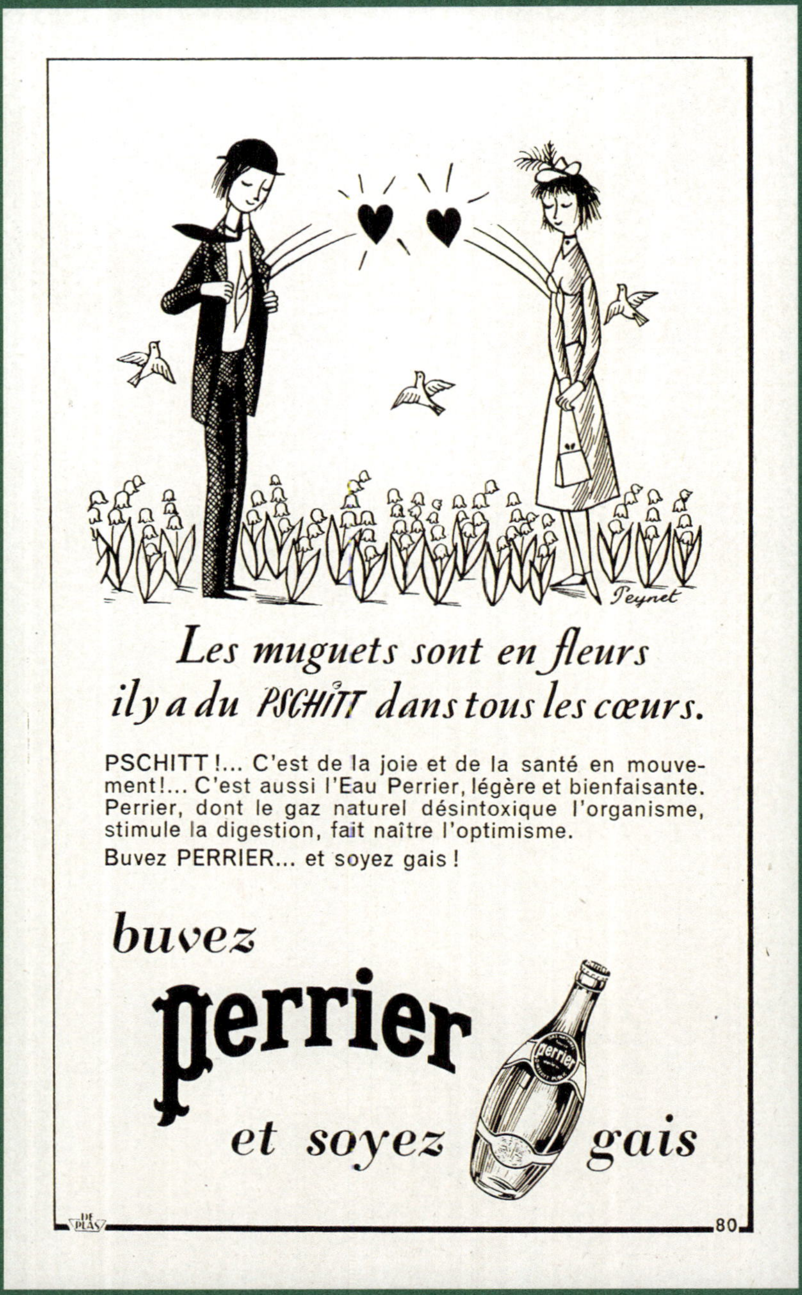

Raymond Peynet

Raymond Peynet, who was born in Paris in 1908, was the king of hearts. As a newspaper illustrator, he created a couple sitting on a bench representing the poet and his muse in 1942. Peynet's Lovers were known worldwide, becoming indelibly associated with Valentine's Day.

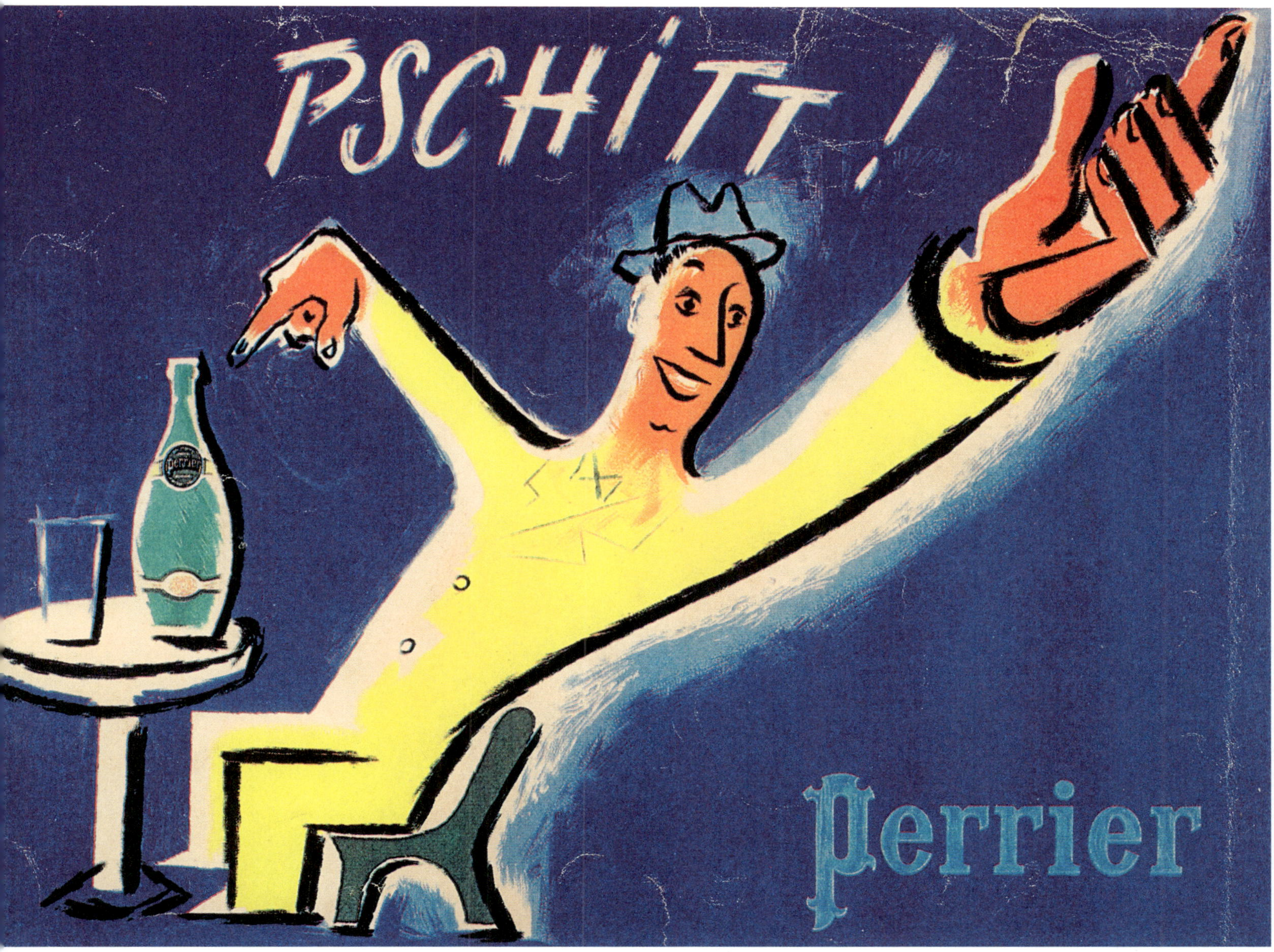

Hervé Morvan

Hervé Morvan, who was born in Brittany in 1917, loved happy, smiling characters. He started his career decorating movie theater facades then designed movie posters. He invented the Gitane cigarette brand flamenco dancer, modernized advertising for the Banania chocolate drink and l'Alsacienne biscuits and brought his zany brand of humor to the poster world over several decades.

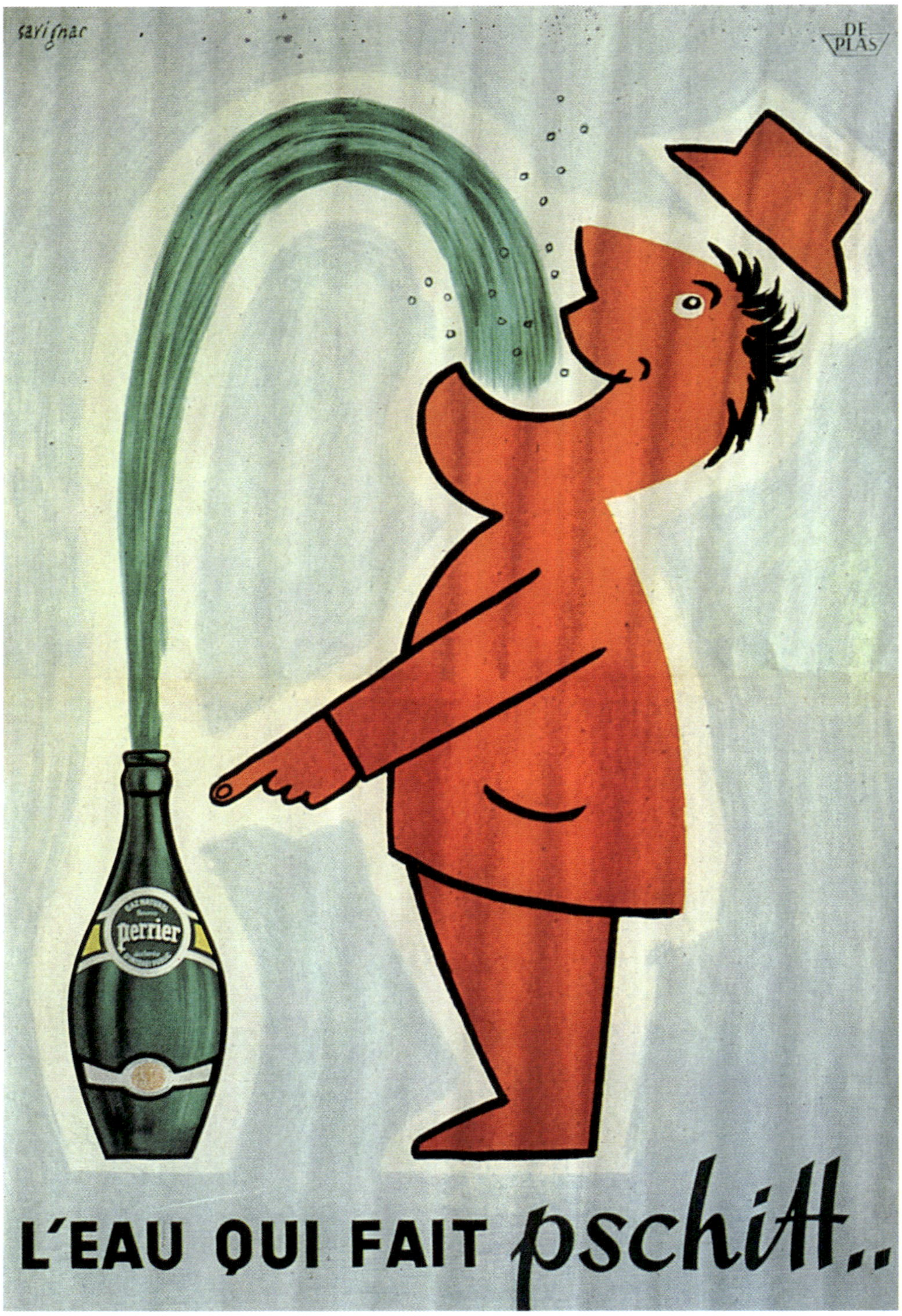

Raymond Savignac

Raymond Savignac was born in Paris in 1907 and brought cheer to the lives of the French in the post-war era for nearly half a century. This man, who designed some 600 posters, had two loves - Charlie Chaplin and the town of Trouville - and conveyed humor and simplicity in an effective yet poetic style.

Kiraz

Kiraz was born Edmond Kirazian in Cairo in 1923 and settled in Paris in 1946. He created his Parisian women for the magazine *Jours de France* in 1959. Kiraz's long-legged *parisiennes* came to epitomize those stylish icons of the 1960s and 70s, who never aged or put on weight.

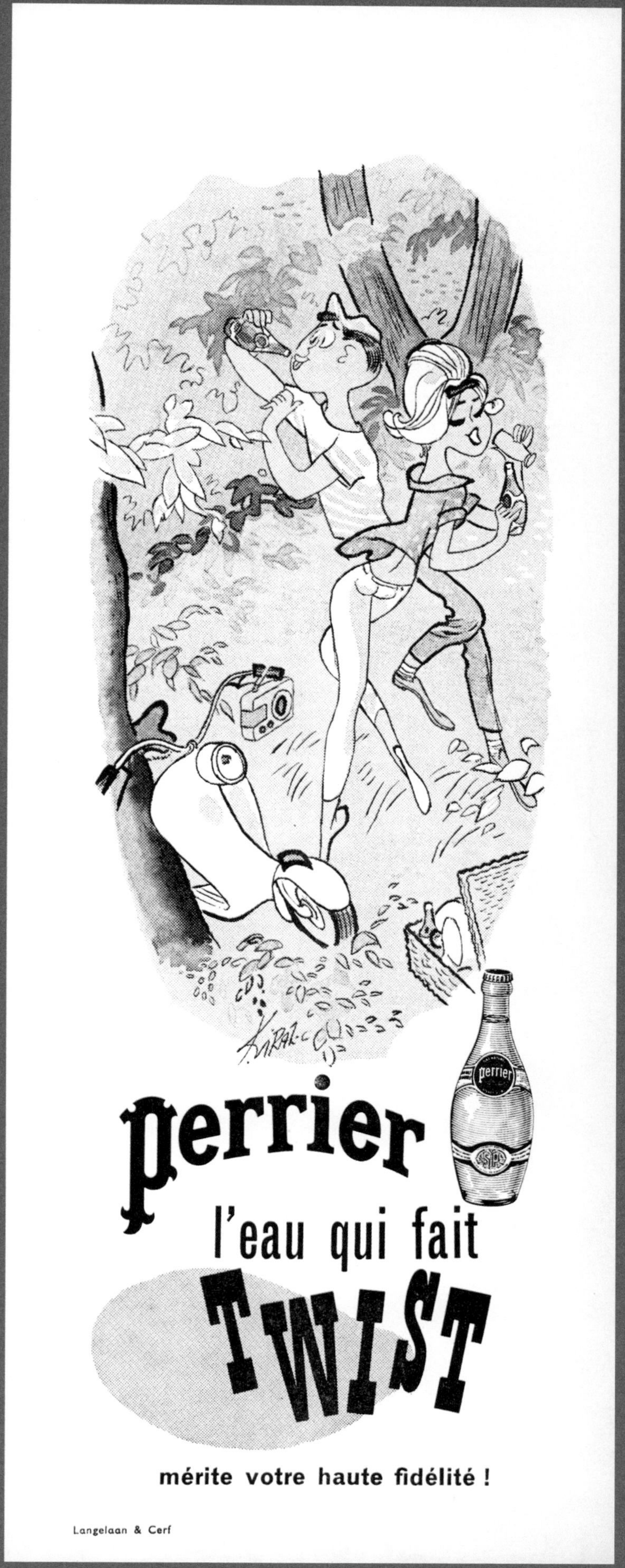

the bestiary

Perrier moved into comedy with a bestiary of animals ranging from cows and camels to parrots from the pen of André François in a series of press advertisements which opted for humor and pushed it to a whole new level. The campaign took people by surprise, made them laugh or raised a smile with a menagerie of original animals, making Perrier a firm fixture on the comedy scene of the day.

pour

activer

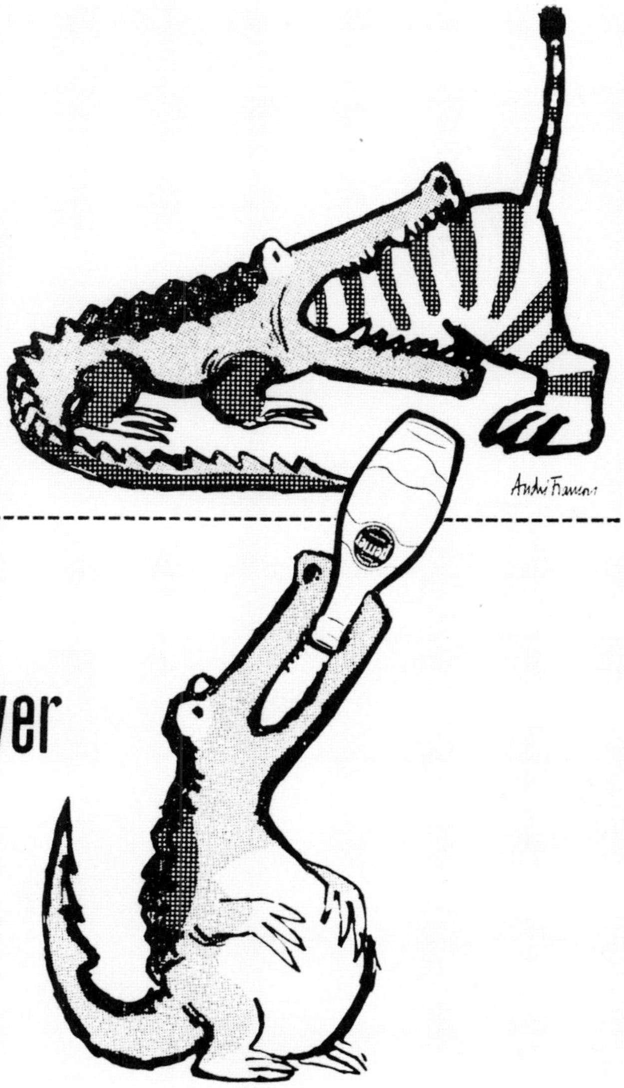

la digestion !

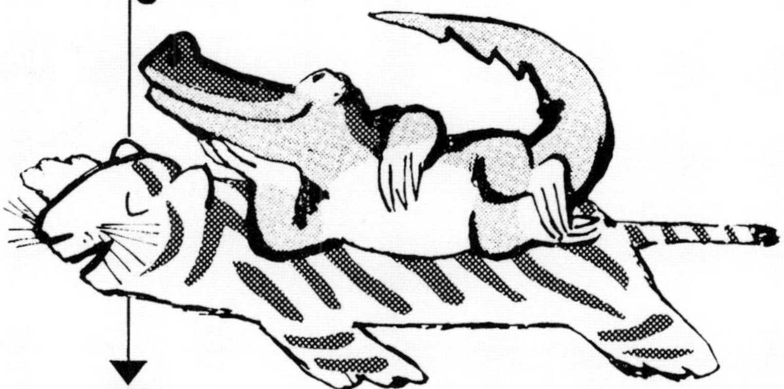

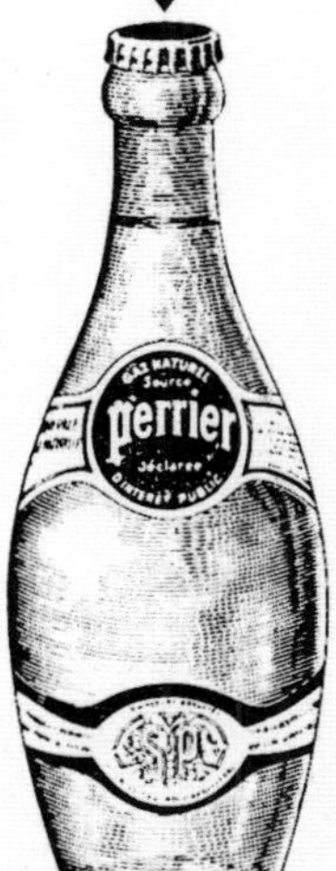

Langelaan & Cerf

Vous êtes en train de trop manger et, déjà, vous savez que vous allez payer votre gourmandise du prix d'une digestion laborieuse. C'est alors qu'il faut faire intervenir le coup du milieu : un grand verre d'eau Perrier coupant la suite des plats. L'eau Perrier, minérale, gazeuse naturelle, pure ou coupée de vin blanc, est l'eau des digestions heureuses !

MINÉRALE GAZEUSE NATURELLE

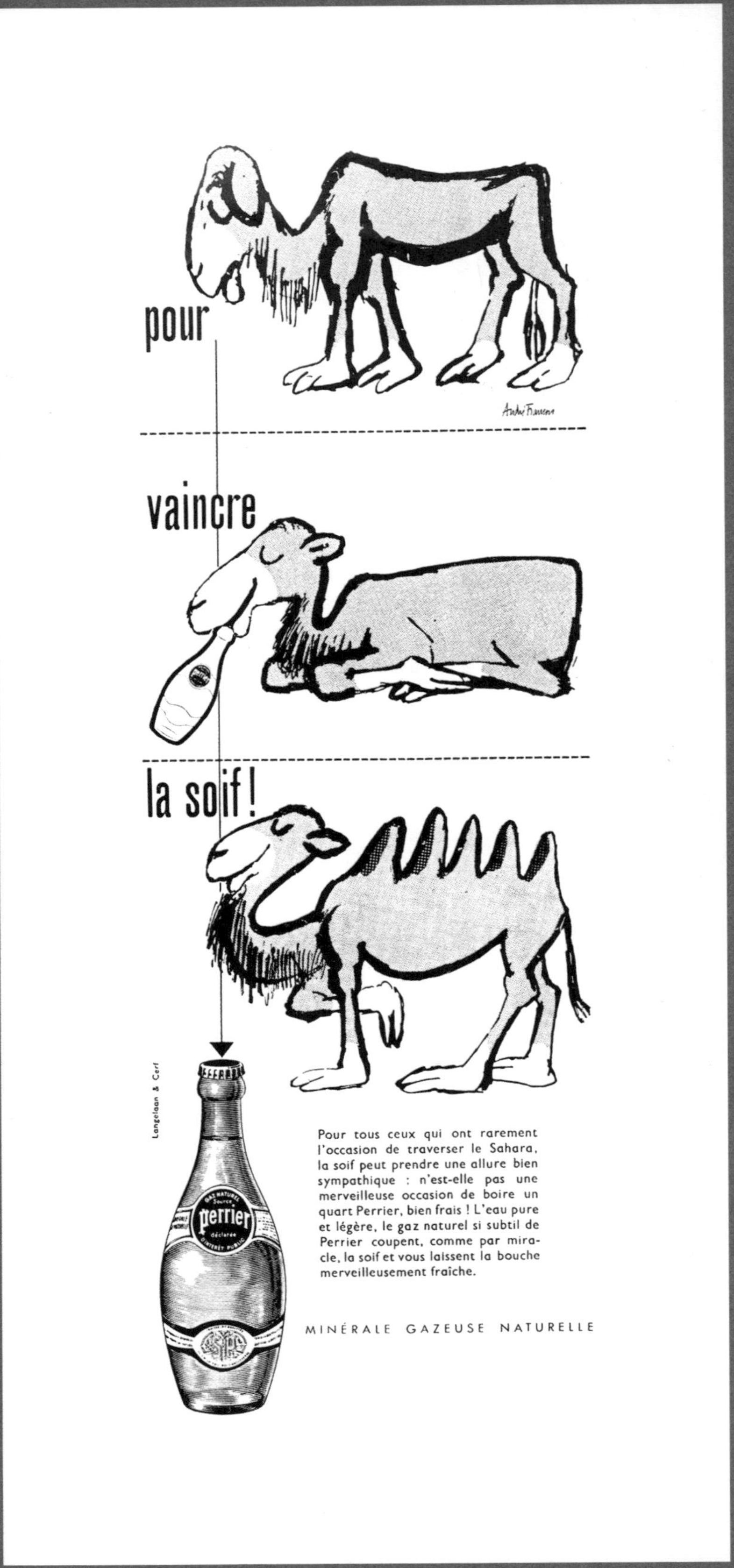
pour
vaincre
la soif !
Langelaan & Cerf
Perrier
Pour tous ceux qui ont rarement l'occasion de traverser le Sahara, la soif peut prendre une allure bien sympathique : n'est-elle pas une merveilleuse occasion de boire un quart Perrier, bien frais ! L'eau pure et légère, le gaz naturel si subtil de Perrier coupent, comme par miracle, la soif et vous laissent la bouche merveilleusement fraîche.
MINÉRALE GAZEUSE NATURELLE

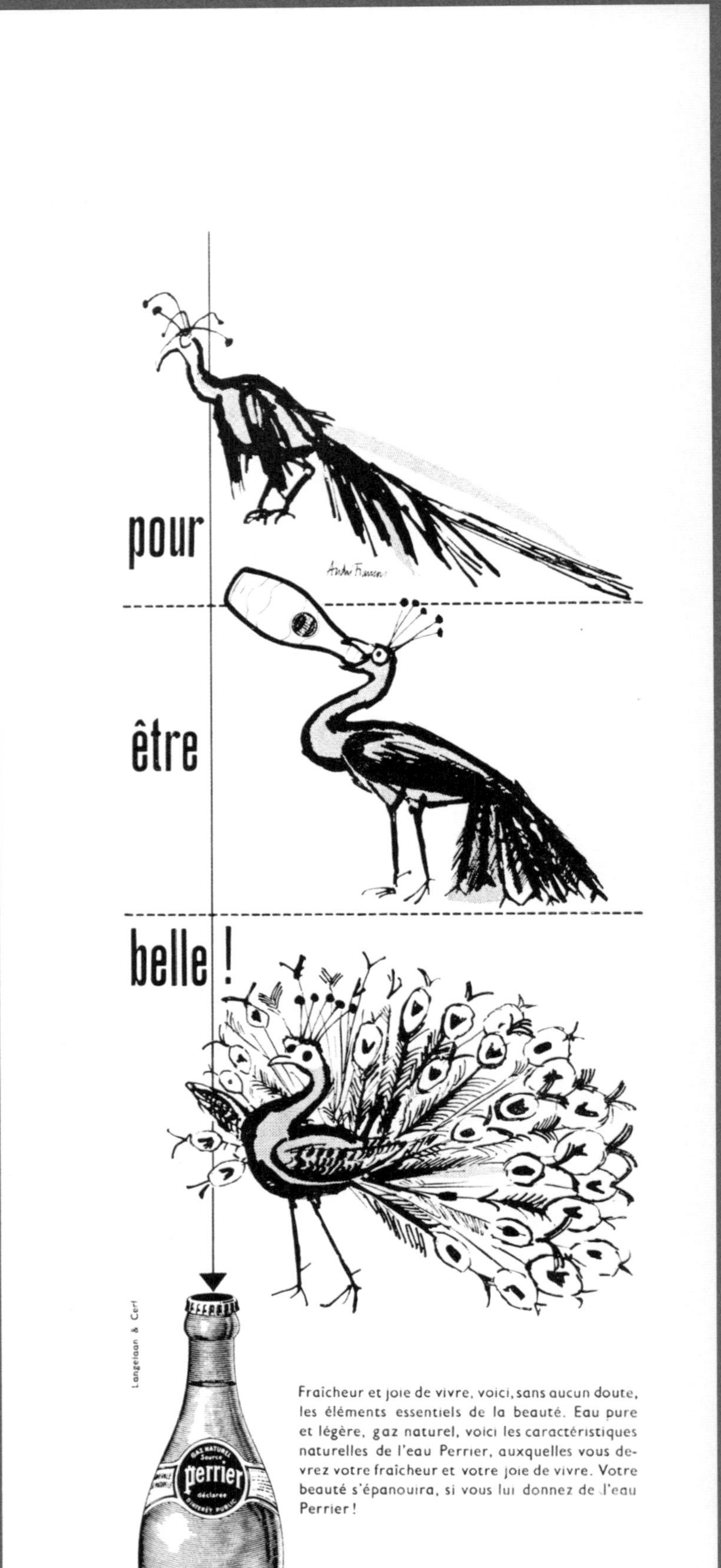
pour
être
belle !
Langelaan & Cerf
Perrier
Fraîcheur et joie de vivre, voici, sans aucun doute, les éléments essentiels de la beauté. Eau pure et légère, gaz naturel, voici les caractéristiques naturelles de l'eau Perrier, auxquelles vous devrez votre fraîcheur et votre joie de vivre. Votre beauté s'épanouira, si vous lui donnez de l'eau Perrier !
MINÉRALE GAZEUSE NATURELLE

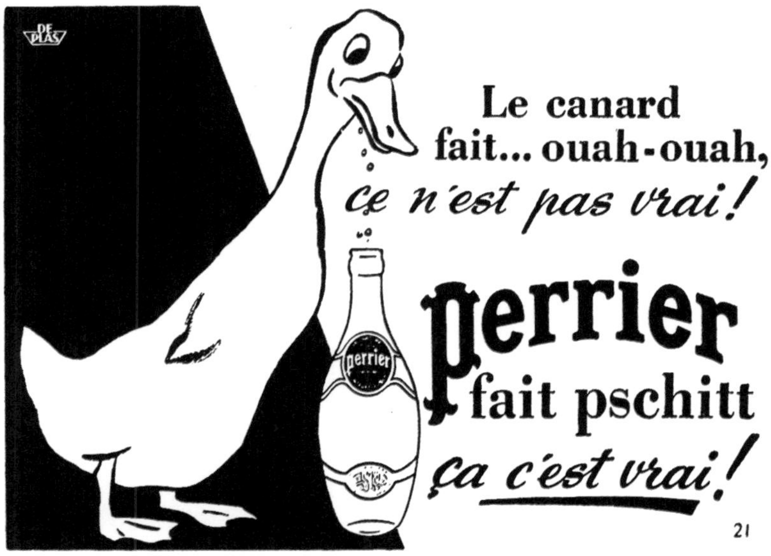

21

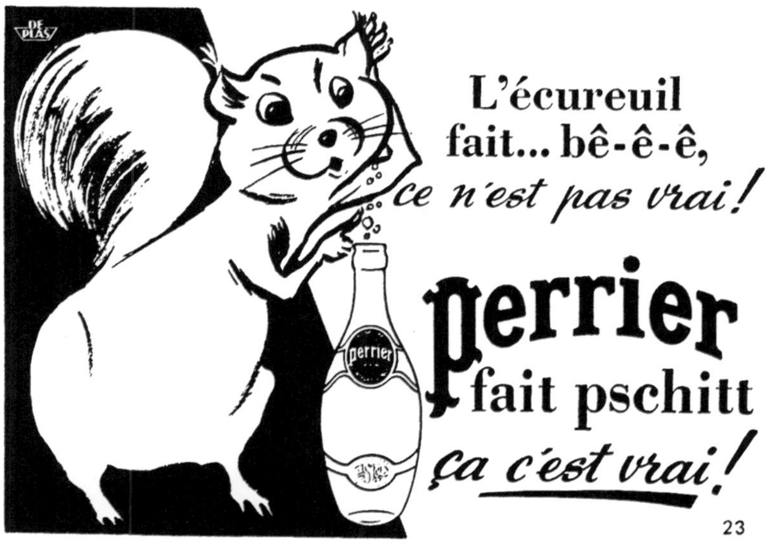

23

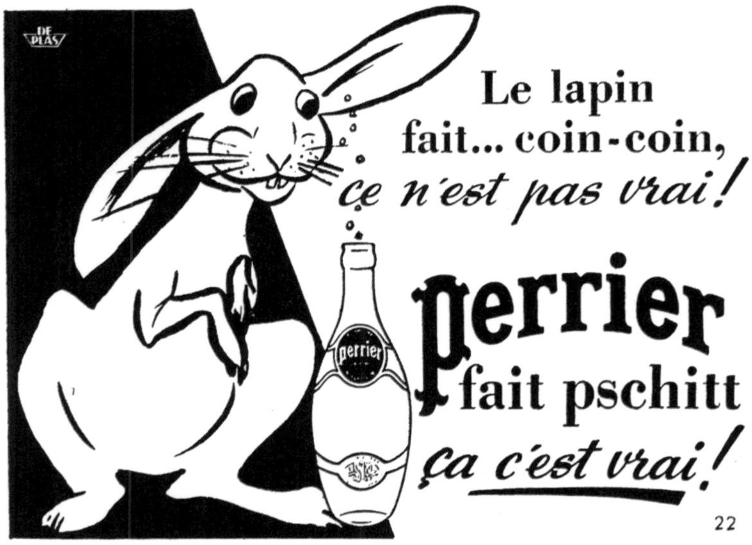

22

André François

André François designed the animal campaign. Born André Farkas in 1915, in a Hungarian town which would become Timisoara in Romania, he settled in France in 1934. As an illustrator, painter and sculptor, he created unusual and poetic worlds full of hybrid characters and animals both real and imaginary.

the quarter pschitt

The bottle, a true jewel in the Perrier crown, became an advertising star in its own right and still tops the bill. Campaigns in the 1950s pulled out all the stops to make the little Perrier bottle a fully-fledged character singing “Chantons Pschitt”. The bottle appeared in all sorts of guises going back through time, including a matriarch, soldier and aristocrat. Each quarter liter bottle corresponded to a popular song from the traditional repertoire, with a new twist. In the 1960s, the quarter liter bottle had a facelift and bounced back in stylized form from the pen of Deransart. Perret’s work featured a whole cast of characters, for whom it was always Perrier time, irrespective of the time of day.

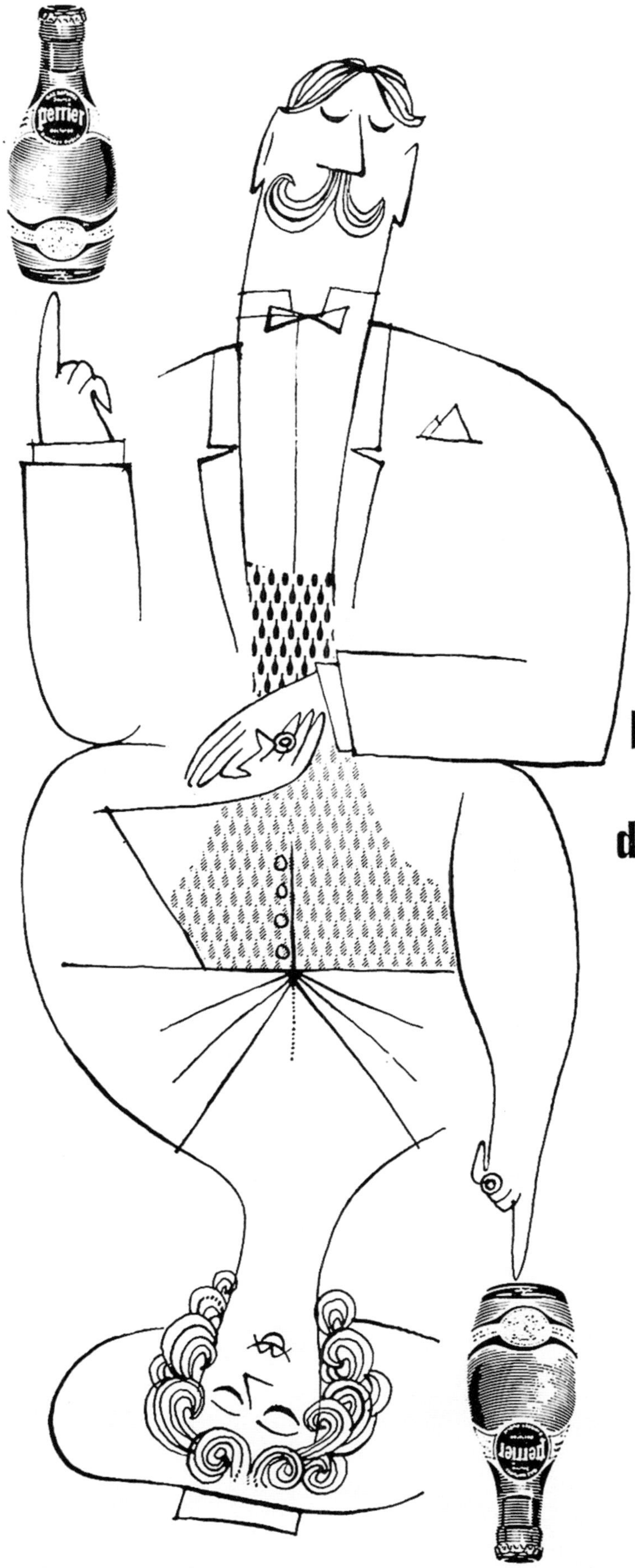

Pour moi et ma moitié...
deux quarts Perrier

Dessin de DERANSART
Langelaan & Cerf

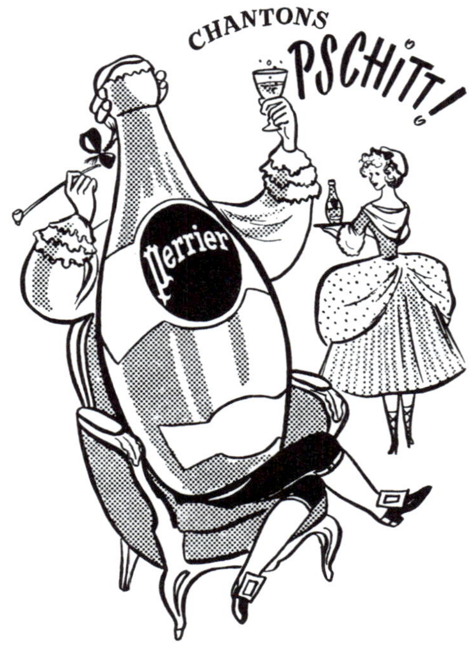

**Au jardin de mon père
l'Eau Perrier est servie**

"Auprès de ma blonde" chantaient nos aïeux, le cœur tout content. Les blondes sont toujours là, les brunes aussi, mais aujourd'hui l'Eau Perrier vient ajouter à cette vieille gaîté française le dynamisme, la fantaisie de ses mille bulles joyeuses. Gazeuse naturelle, l'Eau Perrier est pure, légère et désaltérante... Elle est Pschitt !

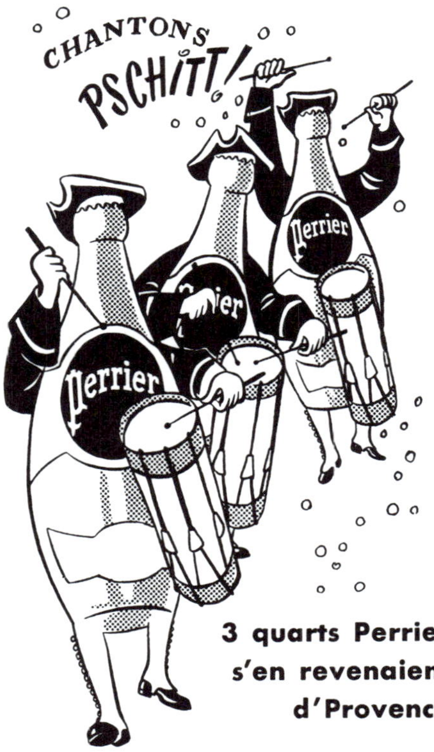

**3 quarts Perrier
s'en revenaient
d'Provence**

Ran tan plan.., Pschitt !... Pschitt !... Pschitt !... Comme les jeunes tambours de jadis, l'Eau Perrier apporte partout l'entrain et la bonne humeur, qui sont depuis toujours l'apanage de la France. Gazeuse naturelle, l'Eau Perrier est pure, légère et désaltérante... Elle est Pschitt !

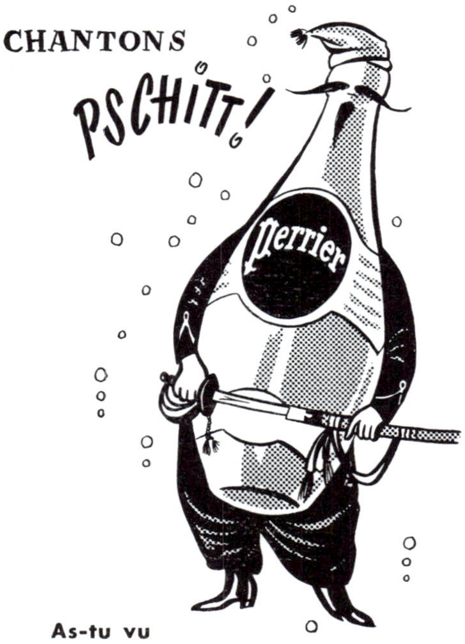

**As-tu vu
la capsule... la capsule,
as-tu vu la capsule,
du quart Perrier !**

Que le Maréchal Bugeaud nous pardonne cette parodie !

Mais l'Eau Perrier, l'Eau qui fait Pschitt, met aussi de la gaîté et du courage au cœur des Français. Gazeuse naturelle, l'Eau Perrier est pure, légère et digestive... Elle est Pschitt !

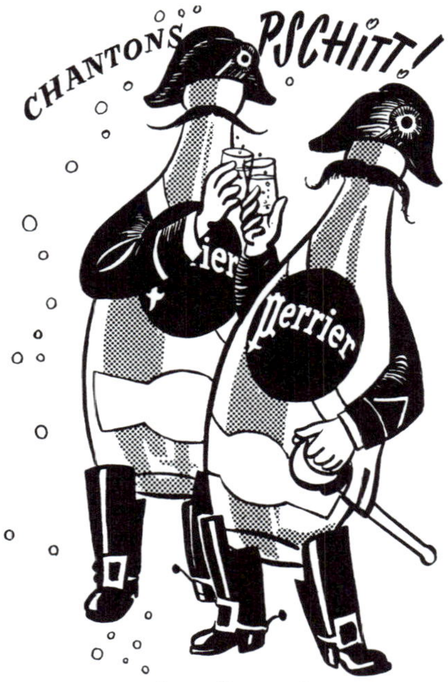

**Quart Perrier, répondit Pandore
Quart Perrier, vous avez raison**

Il n'a jamais été bien contrariant le brave Pandore ! Mais qui ne l'approuverait quand il célèbre les vertus de l'Eau Perrier ? Gazeuse naturelle, l'Eau Perrier est pure, légère et digestive... Elle est Pschitt !...

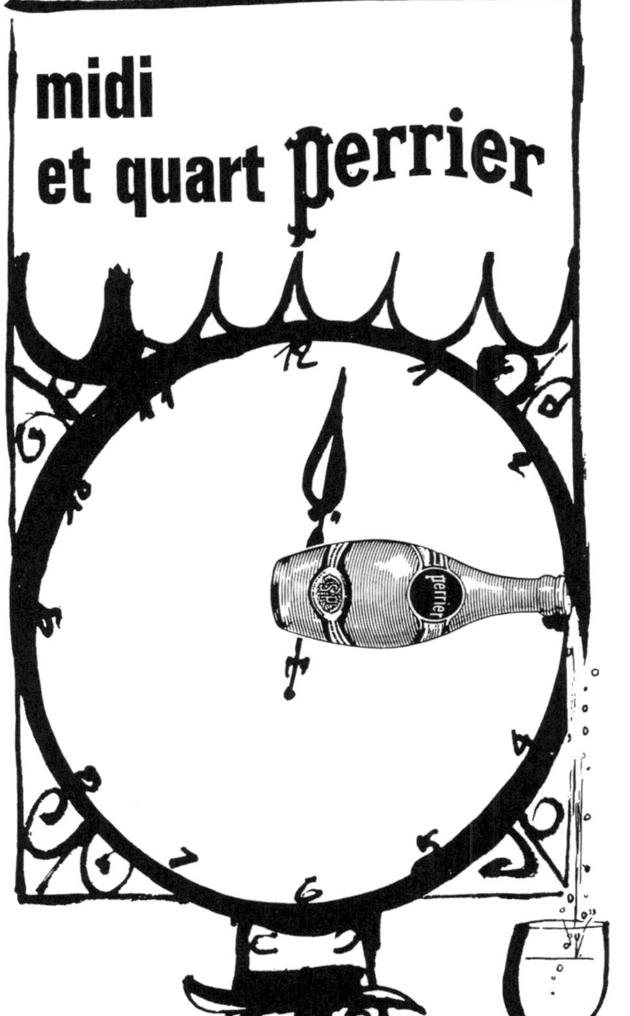

l'heure amicale de l'apéritif

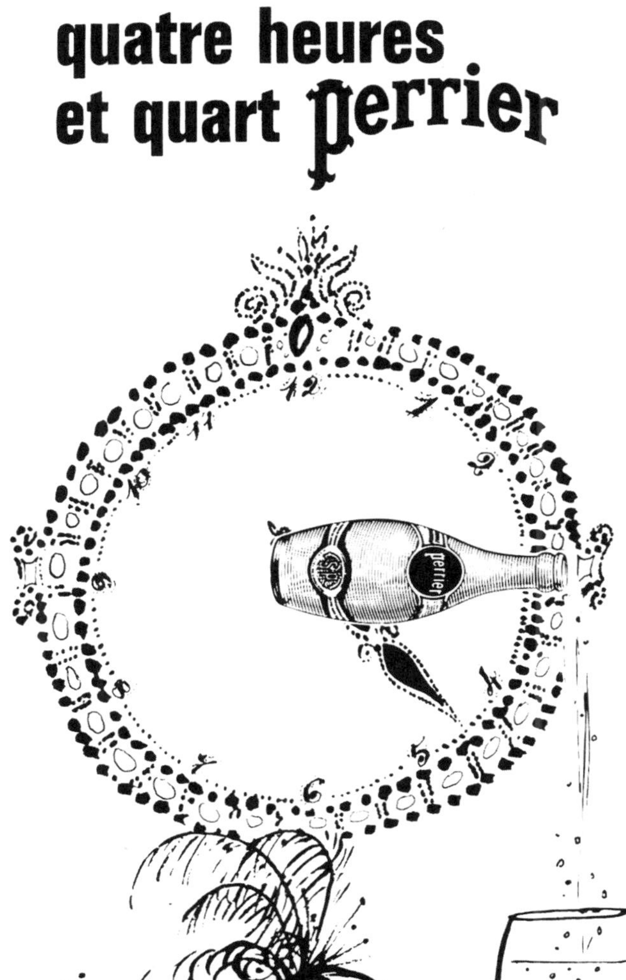

l'heure joyeuse du goûter

crazy bubbles

Perrier went wild with the comic books of Jean-Claude Forest in 1967. The crazy bubbles accompanied his wonderful leopard skin-clad or mermaid-tailed creations.
Jean-Claude Forest's women, with their ultra-modern graphic identity, heralded the psychedelic age and the first flush of the sexual revolution. Perrier campaigns became provocative and daring and made a pioneering foray into the world of the comic strip, which was yet to establish its artistic credentials.

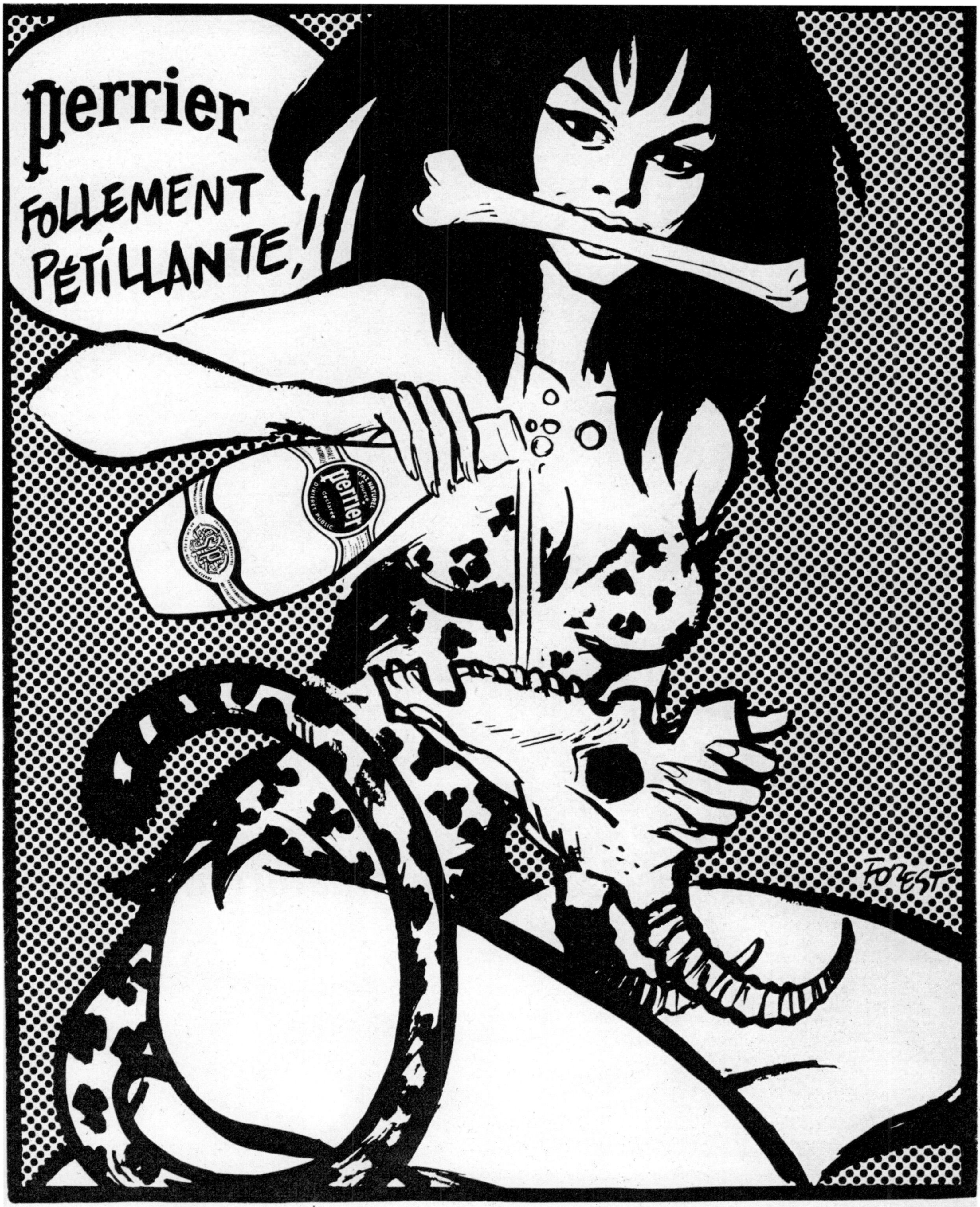

C'EST **FOU** COMME ELLE FAIT BIEN DIGÉRER!

Langelaan & Cerf

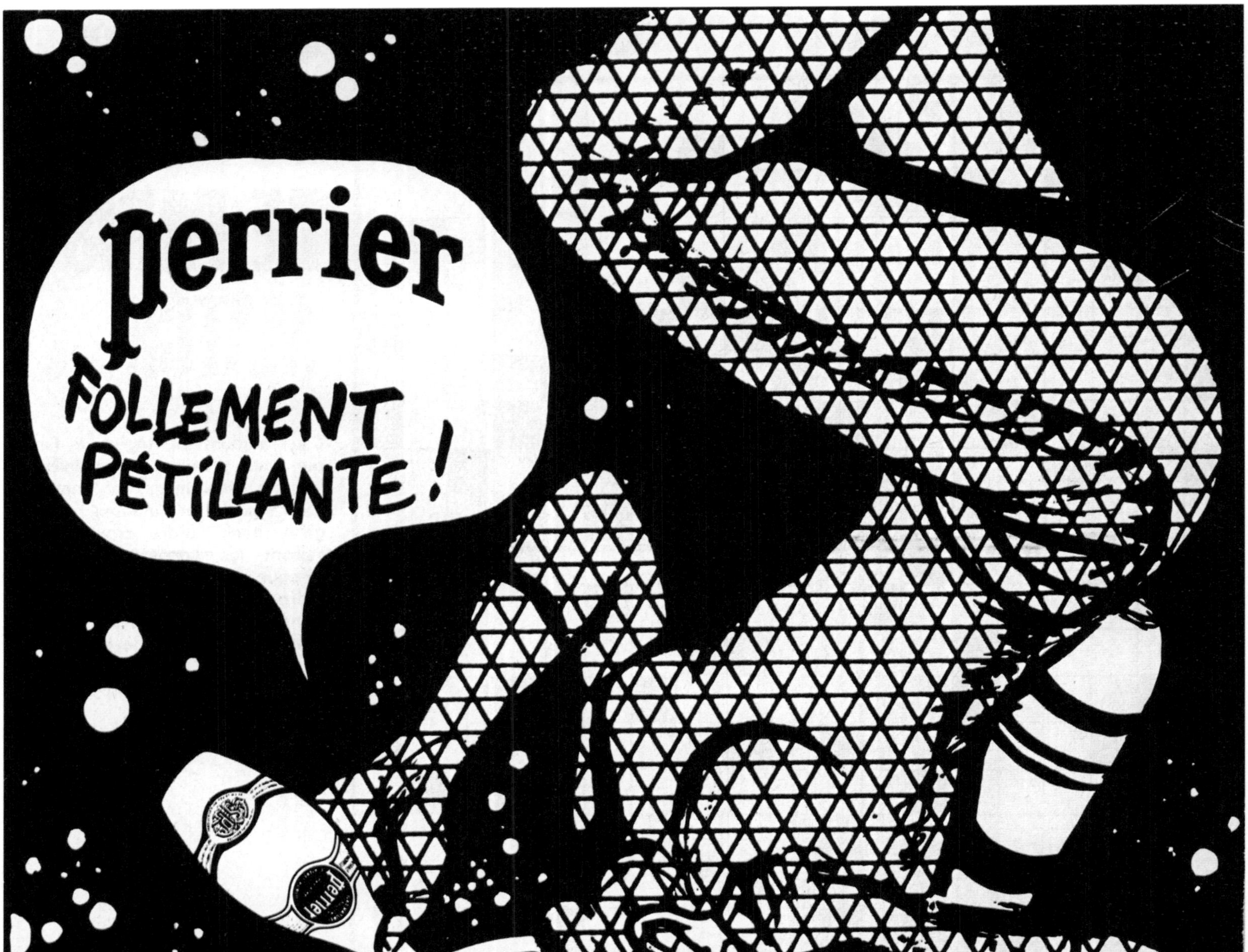
Perrier
FOLLEMENT PÉTILLANTE !
perrier
FOREST

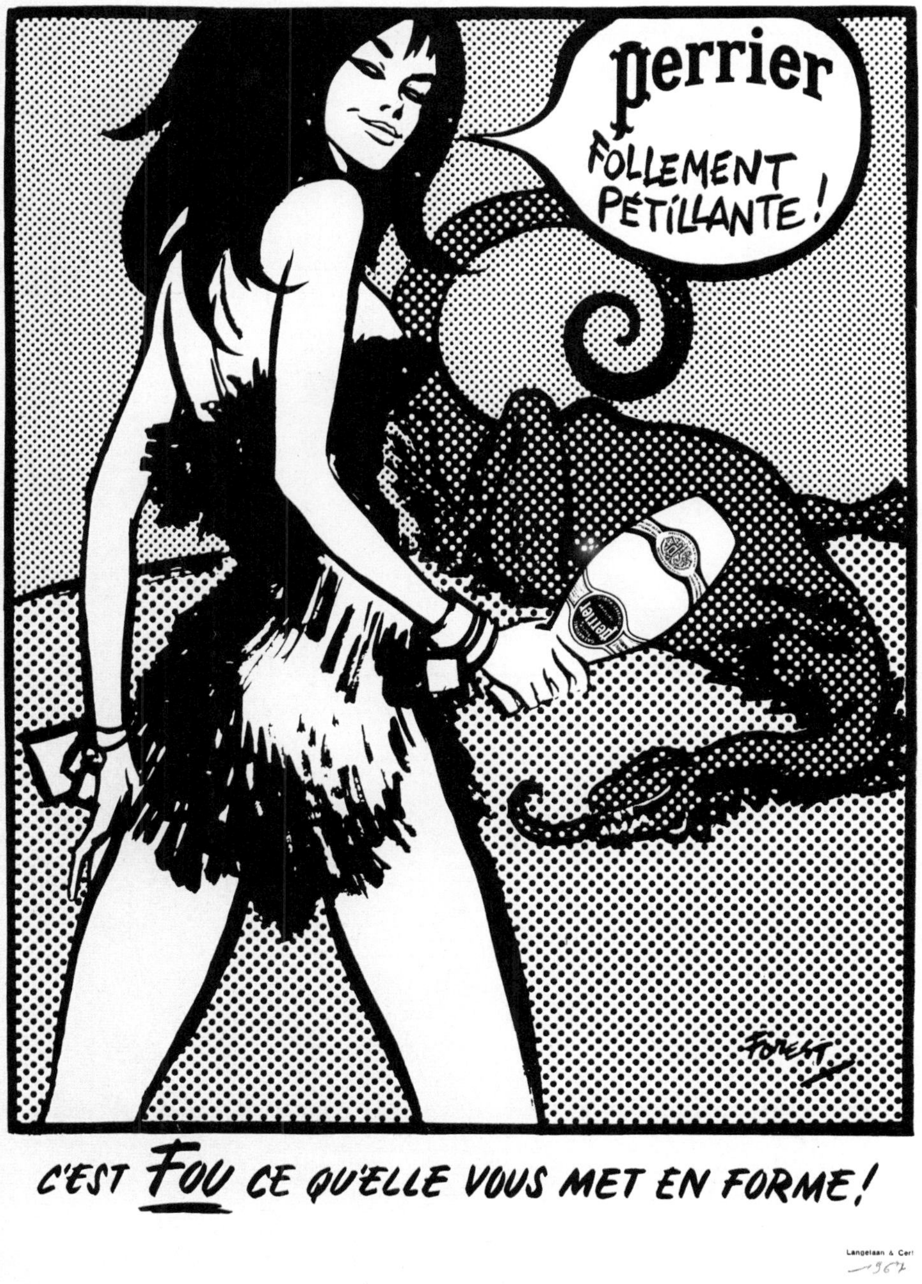

Jean-Claude Forest

Jean-Claude Forest, who was born in Paris in 1930, worked on a number of children's books before creating the sexy heroines who revolutionized the French comic strip scene.
In the early 1960s, he created the character Barbarella, brought to life by Jane Fonda in the movie version.

une fraîcheur de rêve

The year 1968 was marked by revolution and by the explosion of photography, which stole a march on illustration. Perrier struck poses in an ambience of sea, sex and sun and invented the slogan "Une fraîcheur de rêve" (a miracle of freshness). Young people from California to Paris were dreaming of a new, free, natural world. Bright colors and soft focus were the keynote of the campaign by photographer Jean-Claude Dewolf, who ramped up the party atmosphere, ambient vibe and summer fun as couples hooked up and broke up.

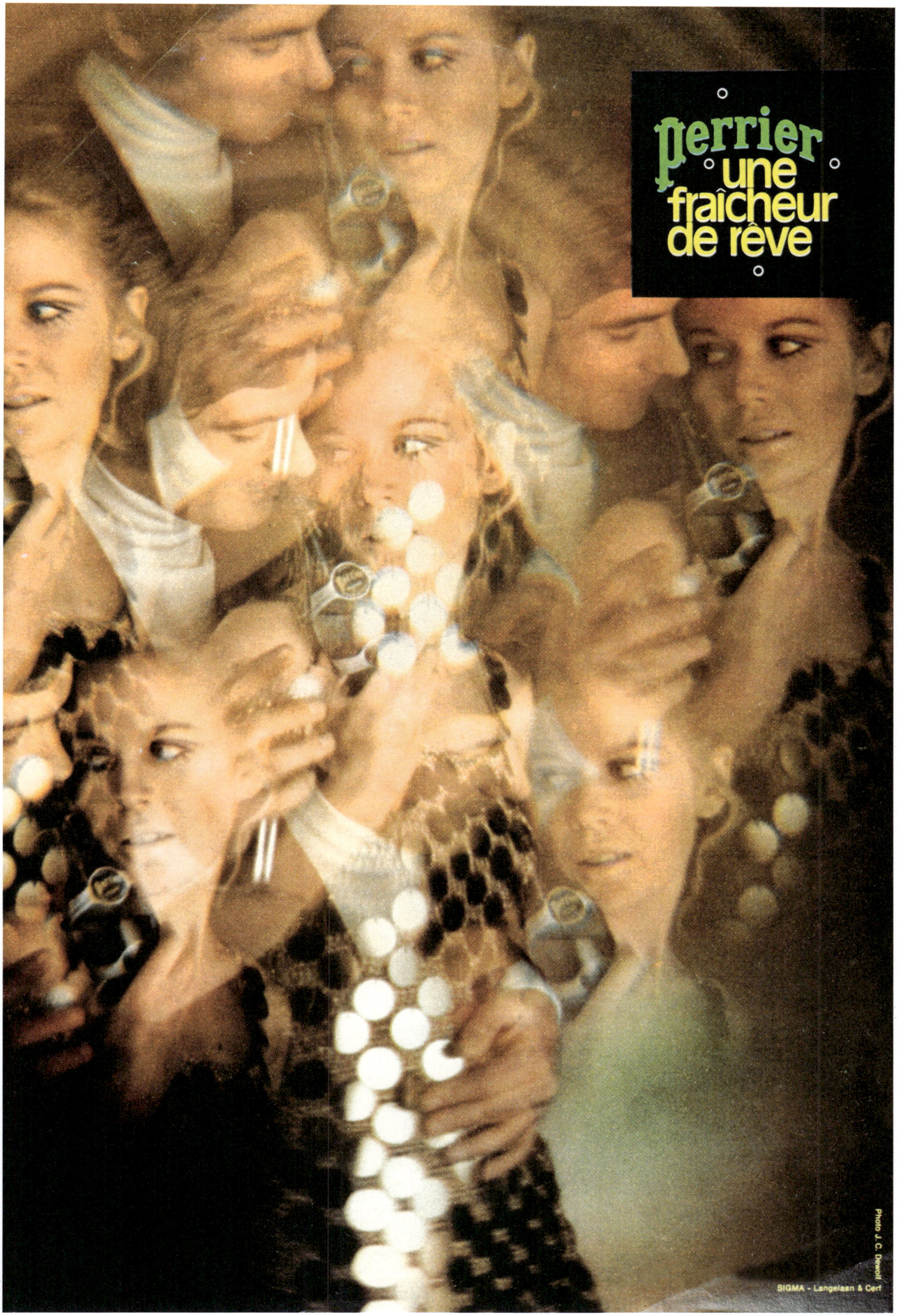
Perrier
une fraîcheur de rêve
Photo J. C. Dewolf
SIGMA - Langelaan & Cerf

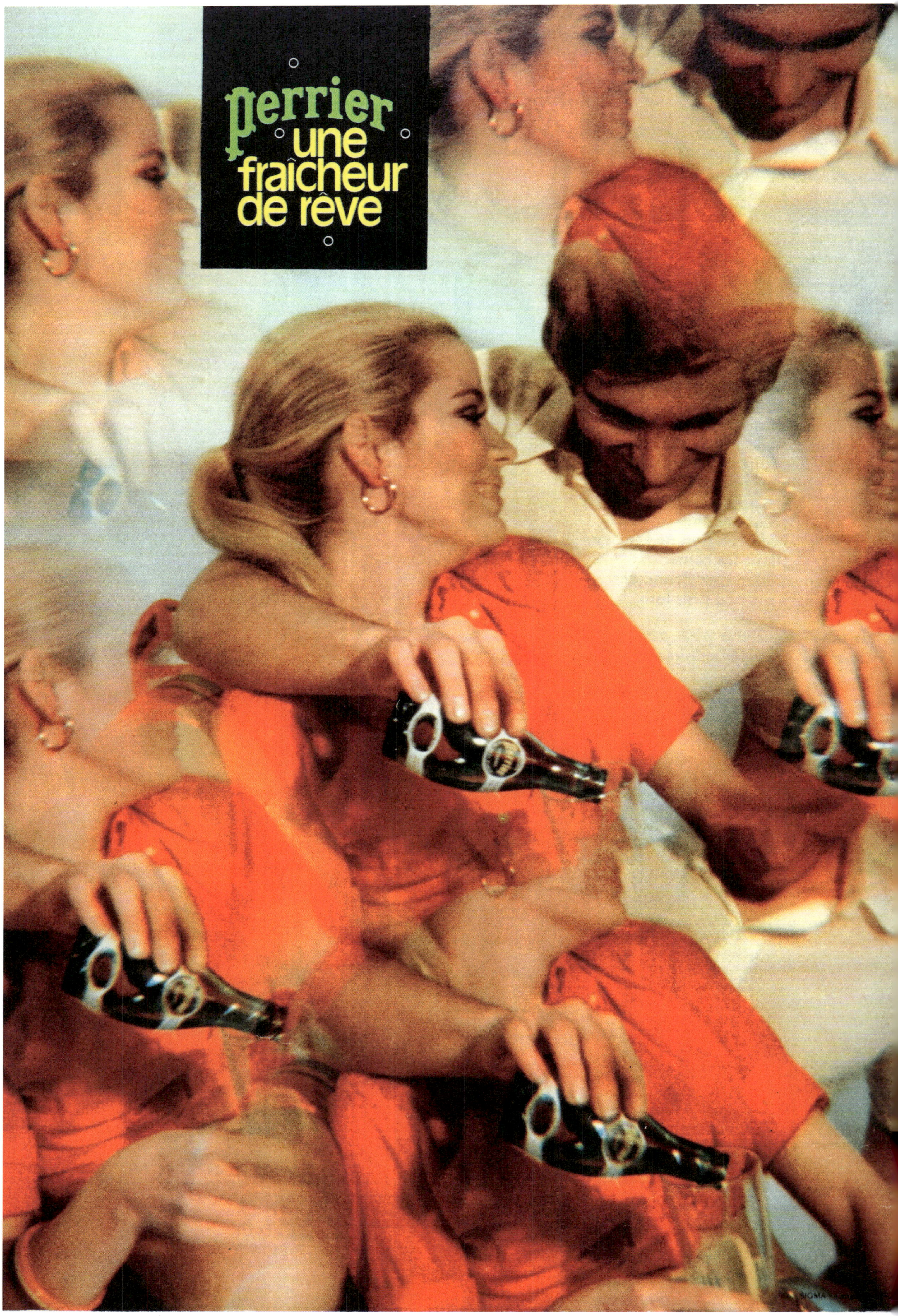
perrier
une
fraîcheur
de rêve

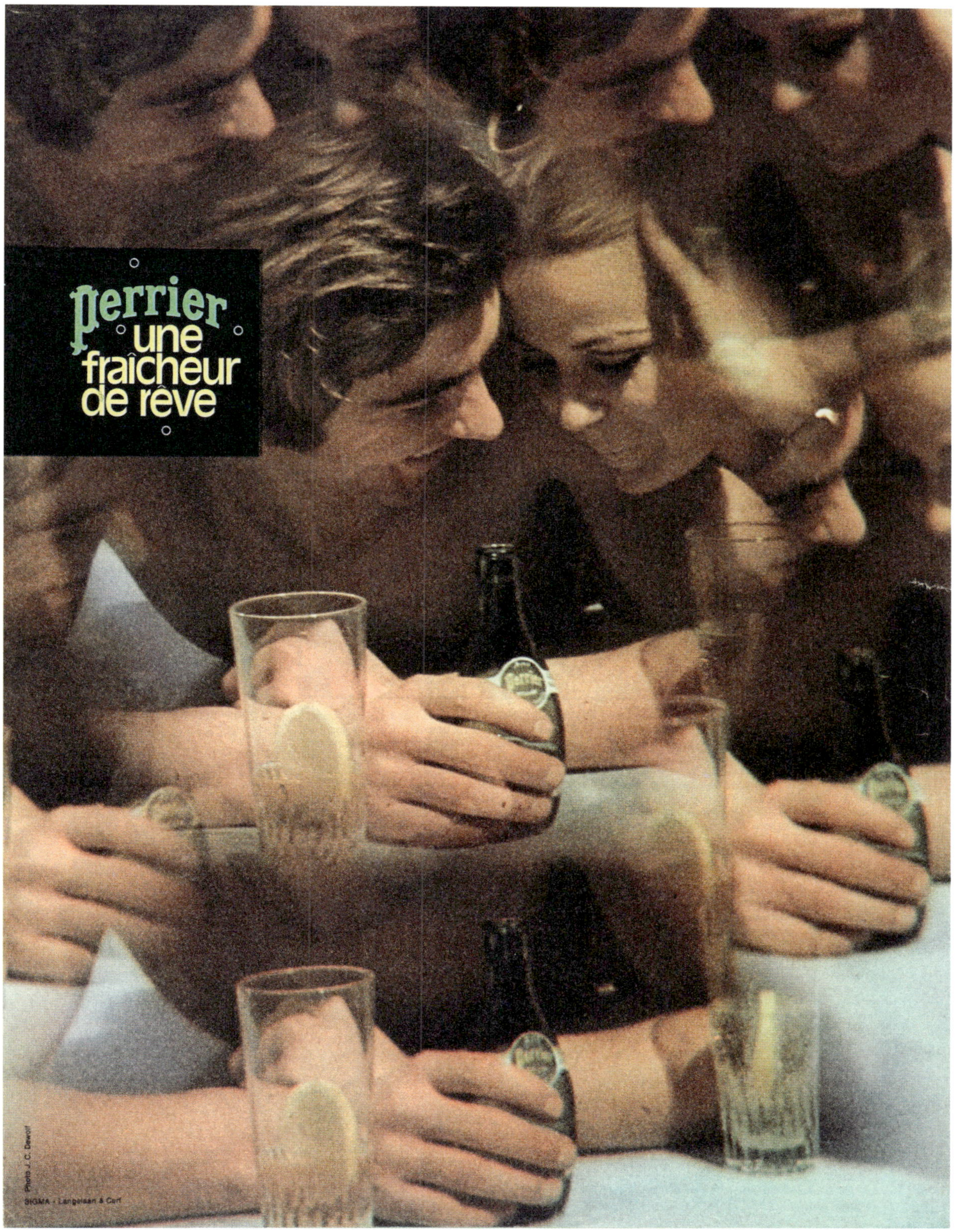
Perrier
une
fraîcheur
de rêve
Photo J. C. Dewolf
SIGMA - Langelaan & Cerf

no Perrier, no pleasure

Mockery was the order of the day in the early 1970s and Perrier established its credentials. Jean-Claude Dewolf's photos took it to the next level by featuring caricatured bourgeois followed by their faithful butler. Three years later, the bourgeois had been jettisoned, but the manservant was back on duty with a modern cast of thrill-seekers indulging in parachute jumps and diving. The white-gloved manservant with his little bottle of water on a tray also conveyed the message that you could not enjoy life to the full and take part in your favorite pastimes without Perrier – "No Perrier, no pleasure."

Pas de vrai plaisir
sans Perrier

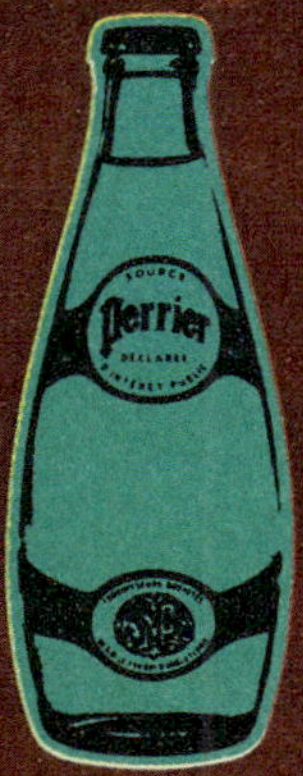

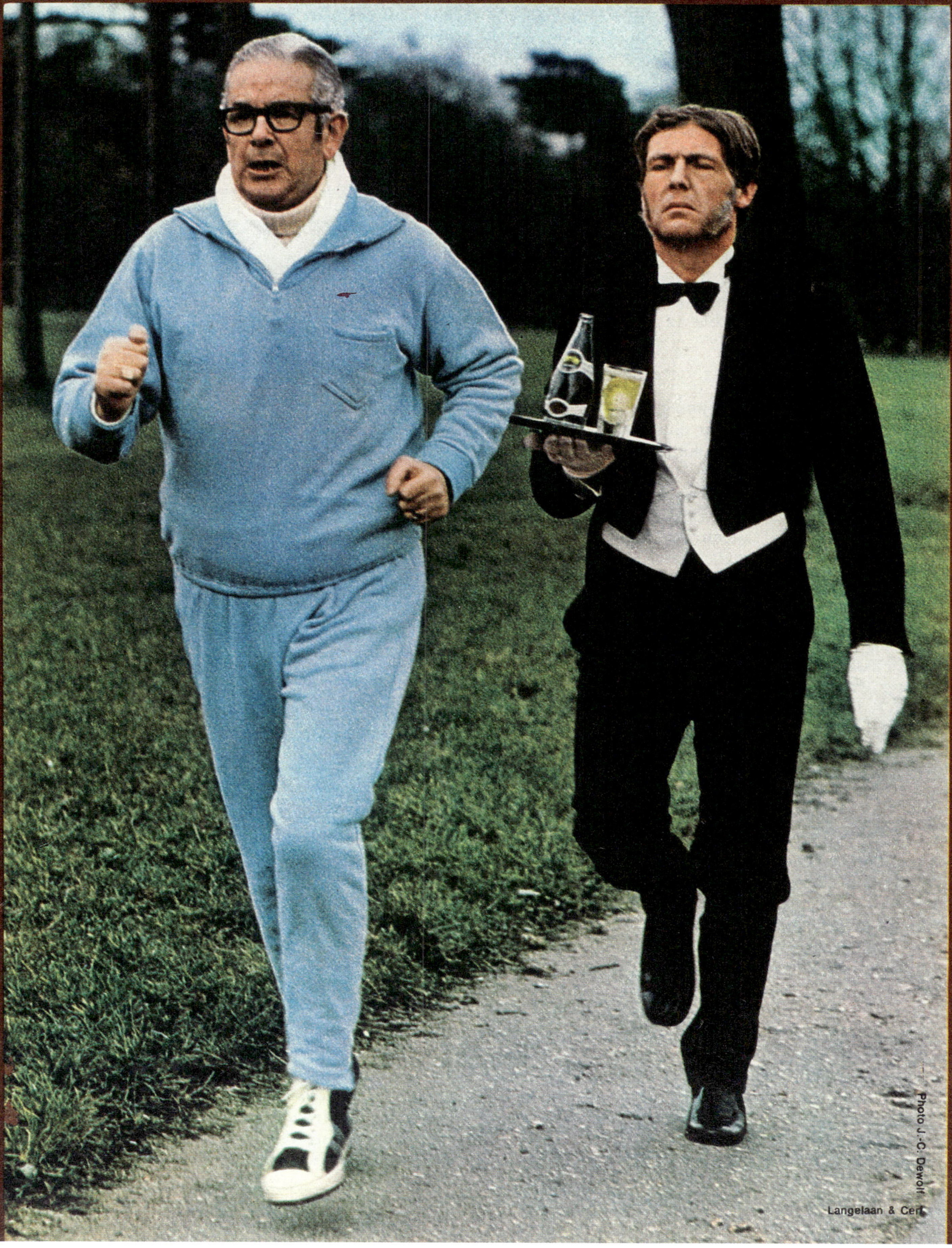

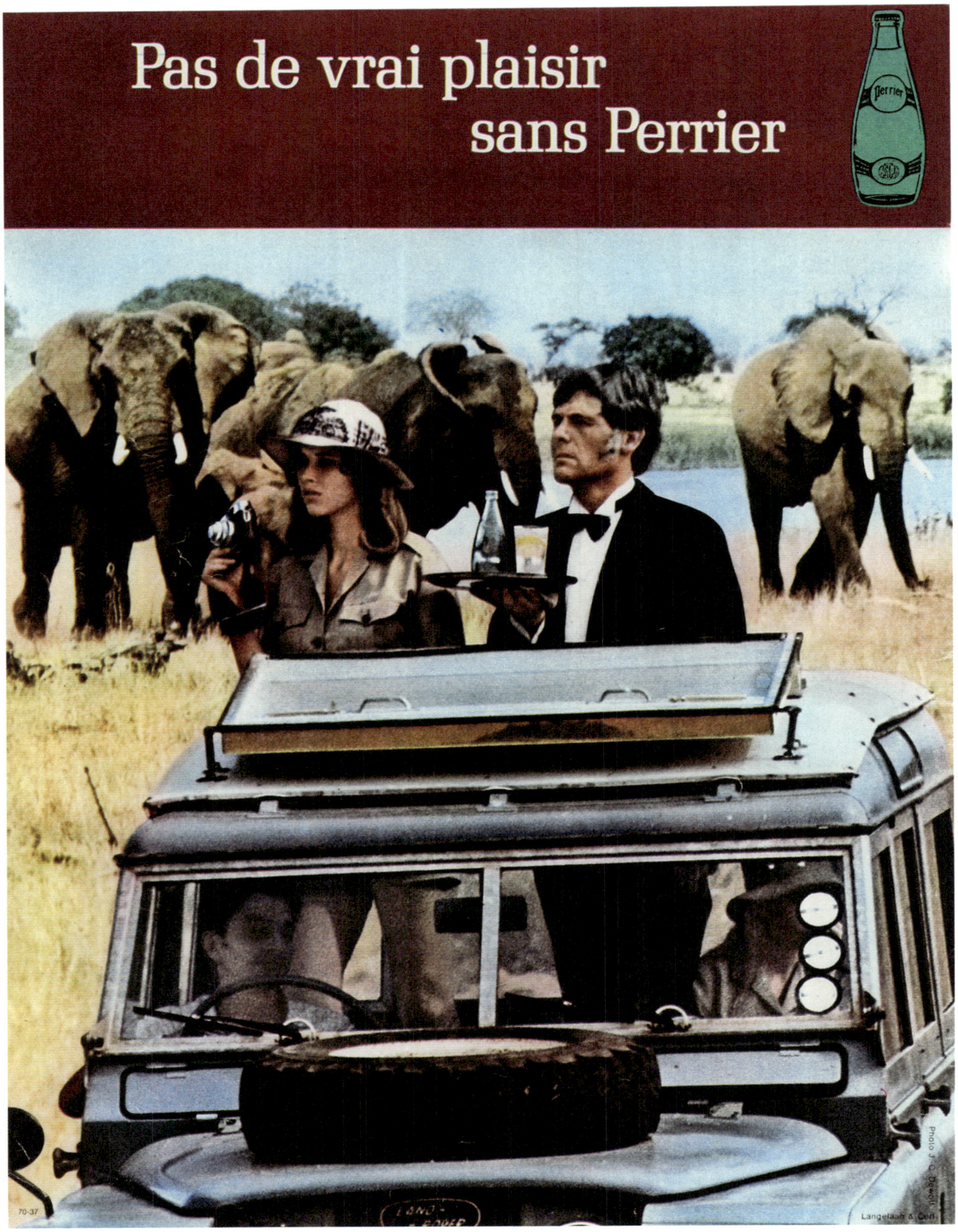
Pas de vrai plaisir
sans Perrier
Perrier
70-37
Langelaan & Cen.

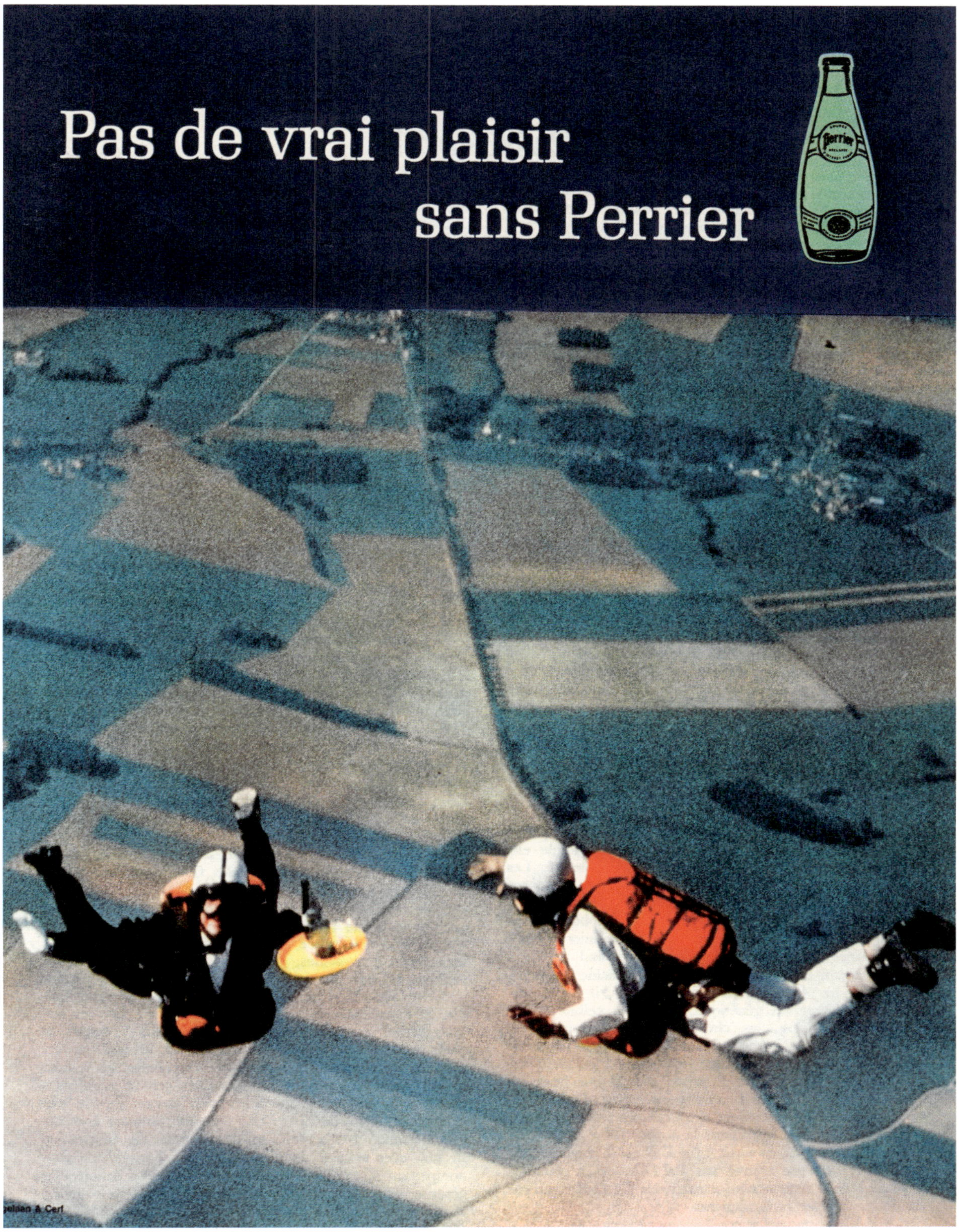
Pas de vrai plaisir
sans Perrier

Perrier c'est fou

"Perrier c'est fou" (Perrier is zany) was the third major iconic slogan for Perrier after the "Champagne of table waters" and "l'eau qui fait Pschitt" and became an advertising staple, illustrated first of all by that master of the poster, Bernard Villemot, then picked up by Patrick Arlet in his own inimitable style, before being subverted by Daniel Vignat. Whereas previous campaigns had focused on photography, Perrier now returned to its roots in drawing. Bernard Villemot's creations made a big impact, as he was the first to illustrate the crazy side of Perrier with his black woman wearing bottles around her neck as a tribute to Josephine Baker and her banana skirt. Ranging from embracing couples to bottles in the shape of sails plowing through the waves, Villemot's colorful designs were in keeping with the spirit of "Perrier, c'est fou". He was joined by Arlet, who created a timeless, upbeat world where Harlequin became a waiter. Vignat then decided to turn the slogan "Perrier, c'est fou" on its head to read "Ferrier, c'est Pou".

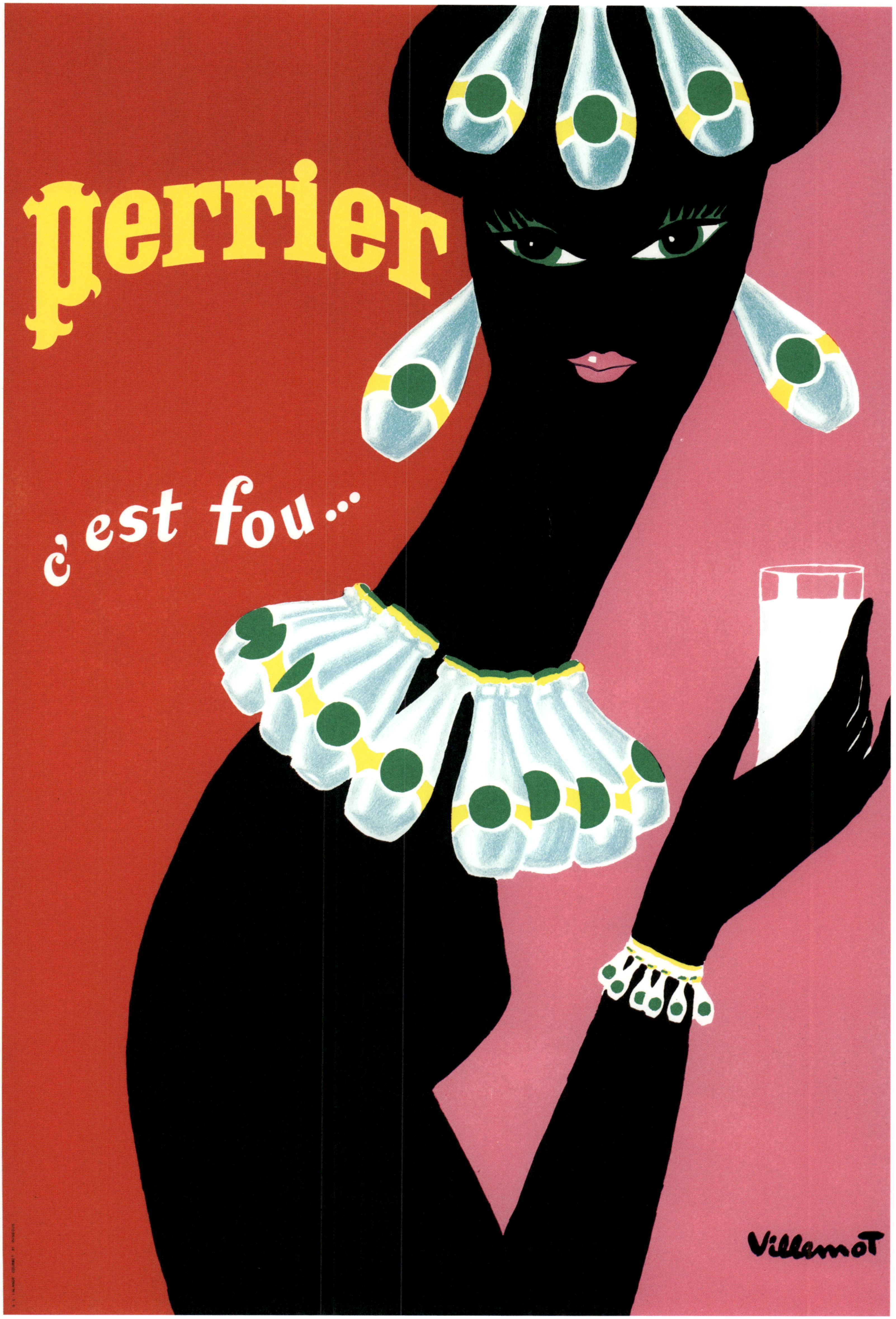
Perrier
c'est fou...
Villemot

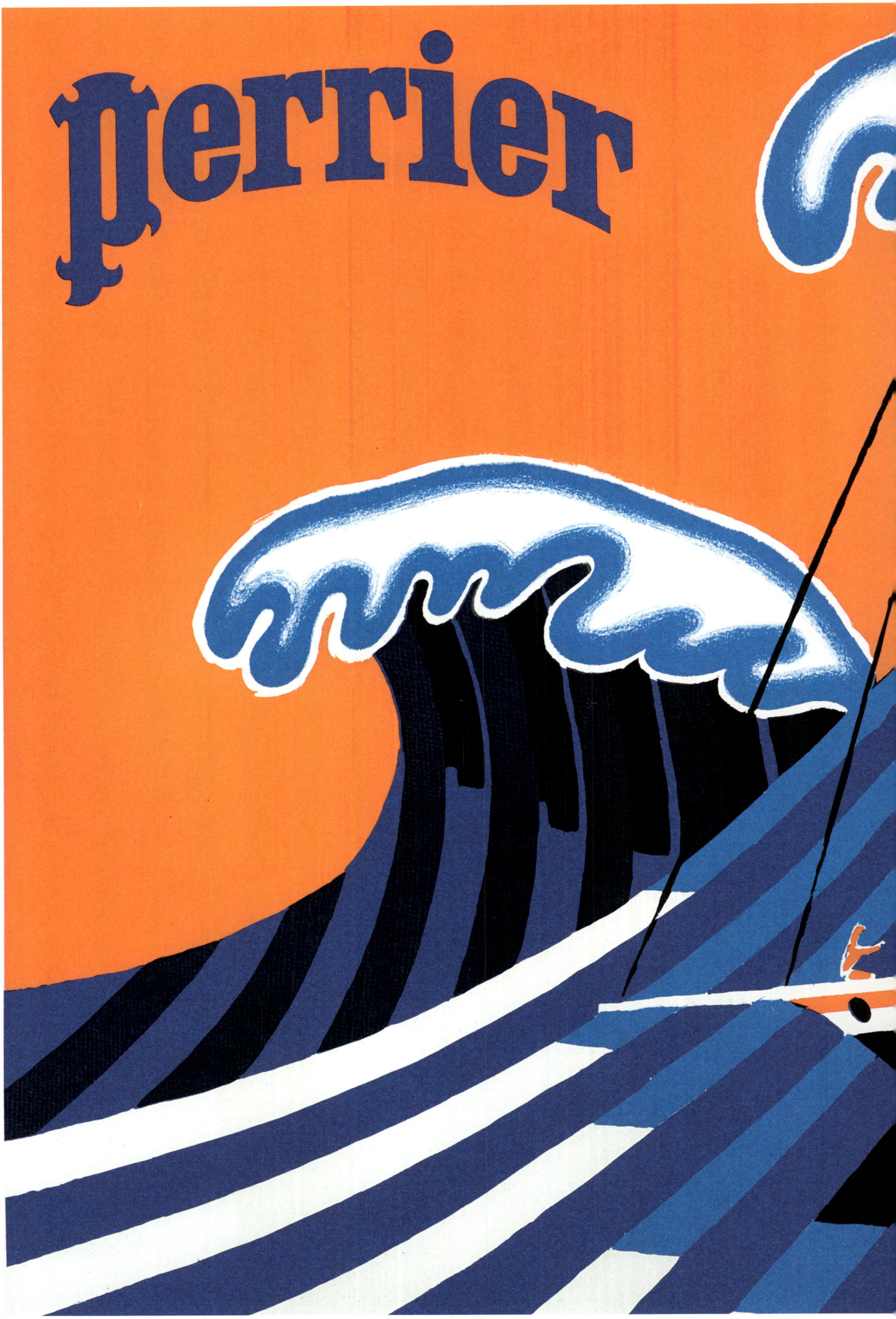
Perrier

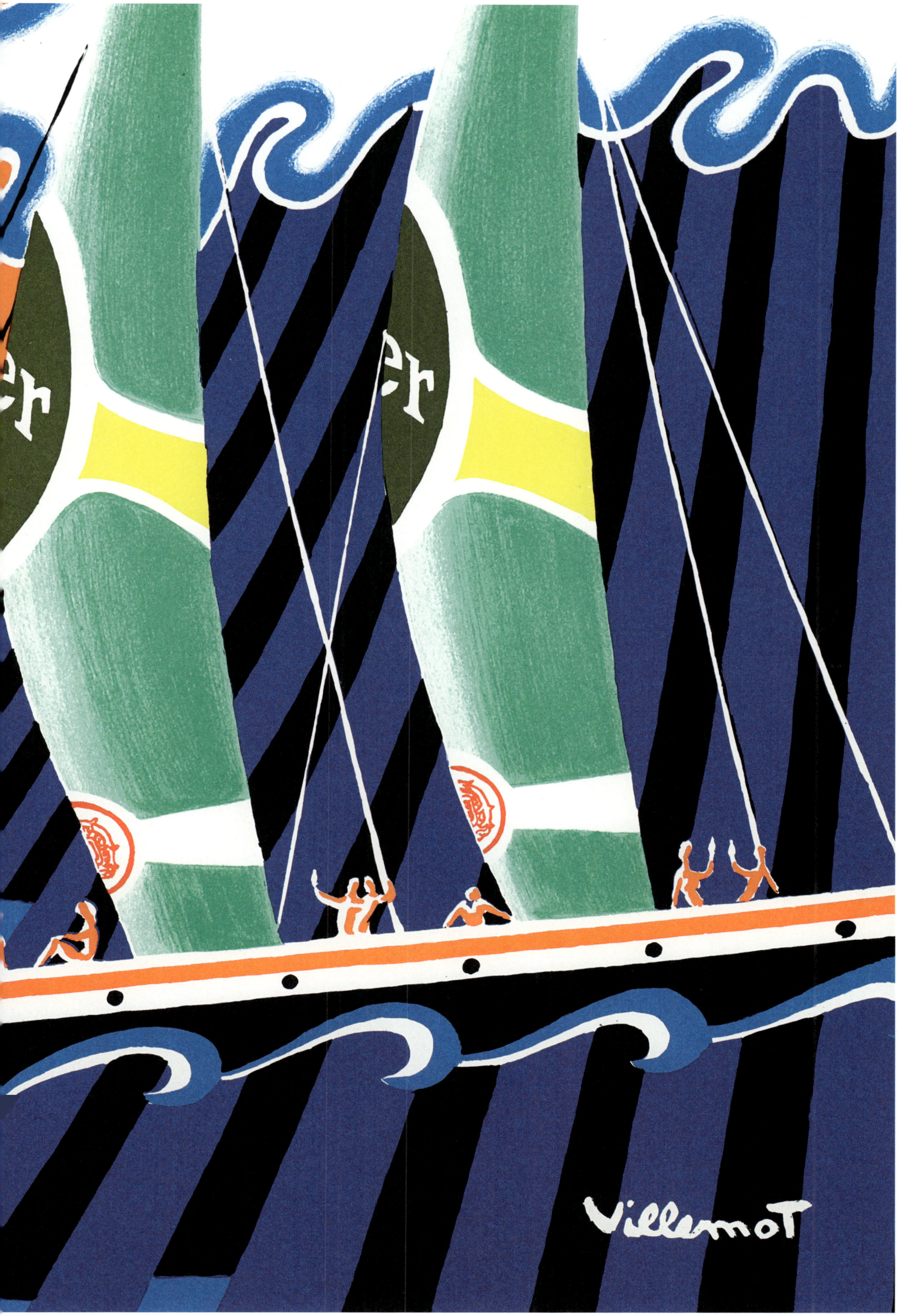
Villemot

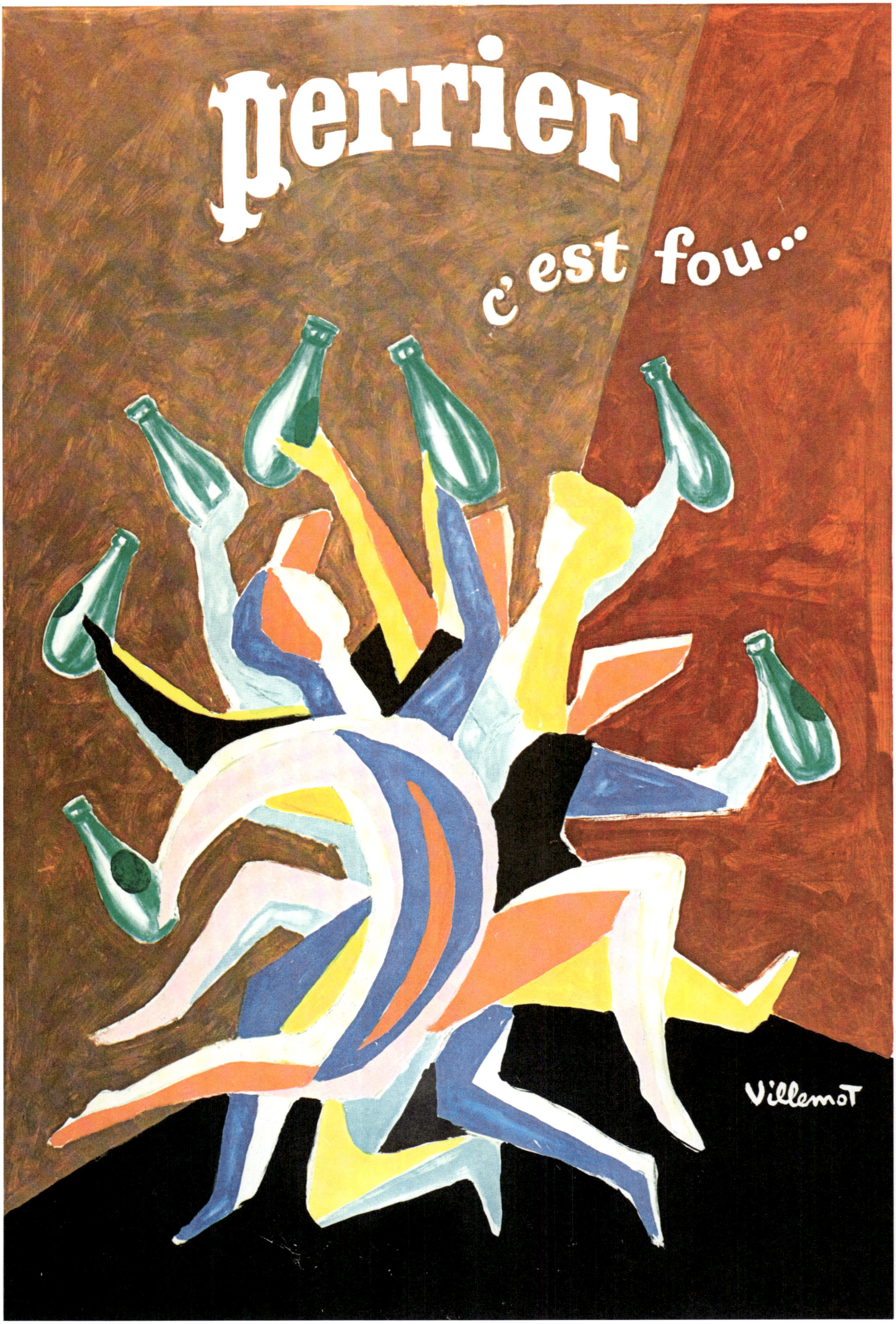
Perrier
c'est fou...
Villemot

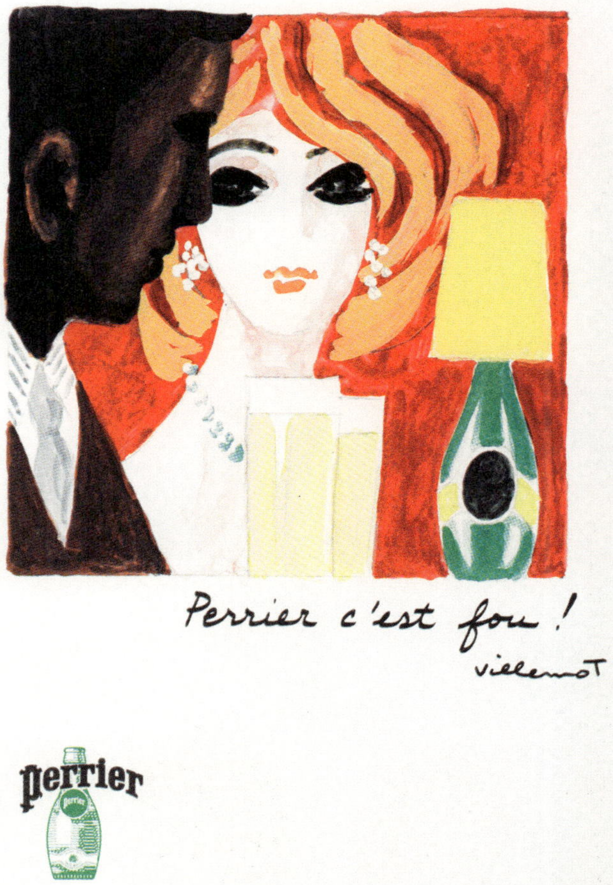

Bernard Villemot

Bernard Villemot, was born in 1911 in Normandy, the son of a cartoonist. He began his career as a poster designer for the movies in the 1930s, influenced by Cassandre, Paul Colin and Cappiello. He was responsible for a number of major national campaigns, both during and after the war. He was known as the 'poster painter' and worked loyally for Perrier for nearly twenty years, demonstrating his trademark love of color..

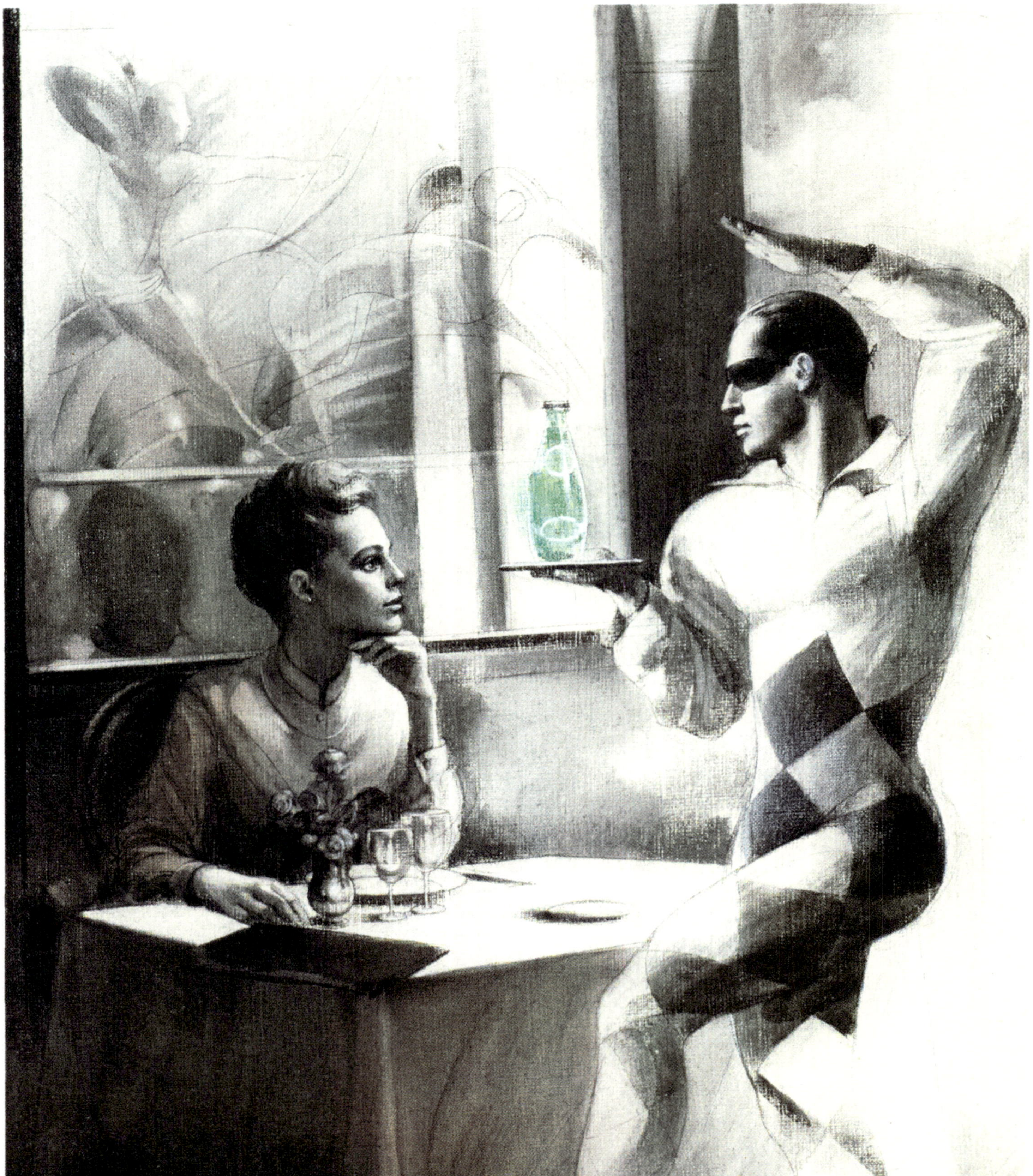
Perrier
c'est fou

Daniel Vignat

Daniel Vignat was born in 1940 near Paris and began his career at the Nina Ricci fashion house as a creative and advertising consultant. After several years as Creative Director at Publicis, he worked for Perrier as a freelancer and came up with a new form of craziness: the “Ferrier c’est Pou” poster. Daniel Vignat then worked with prestigious couturiers and perfumers before making a complete career change and becoming a therapist.

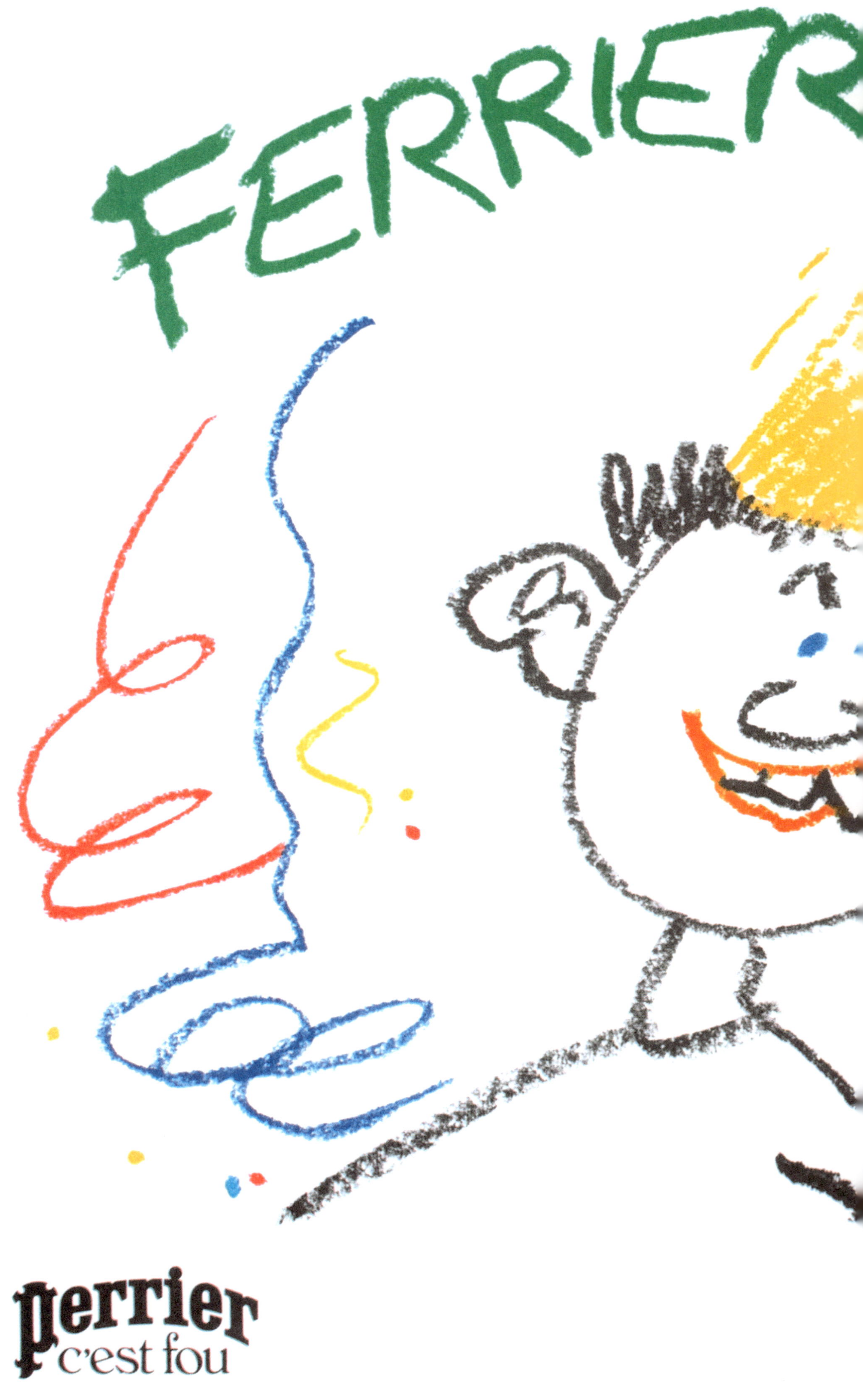
FERRIER
perrier
c'est fou

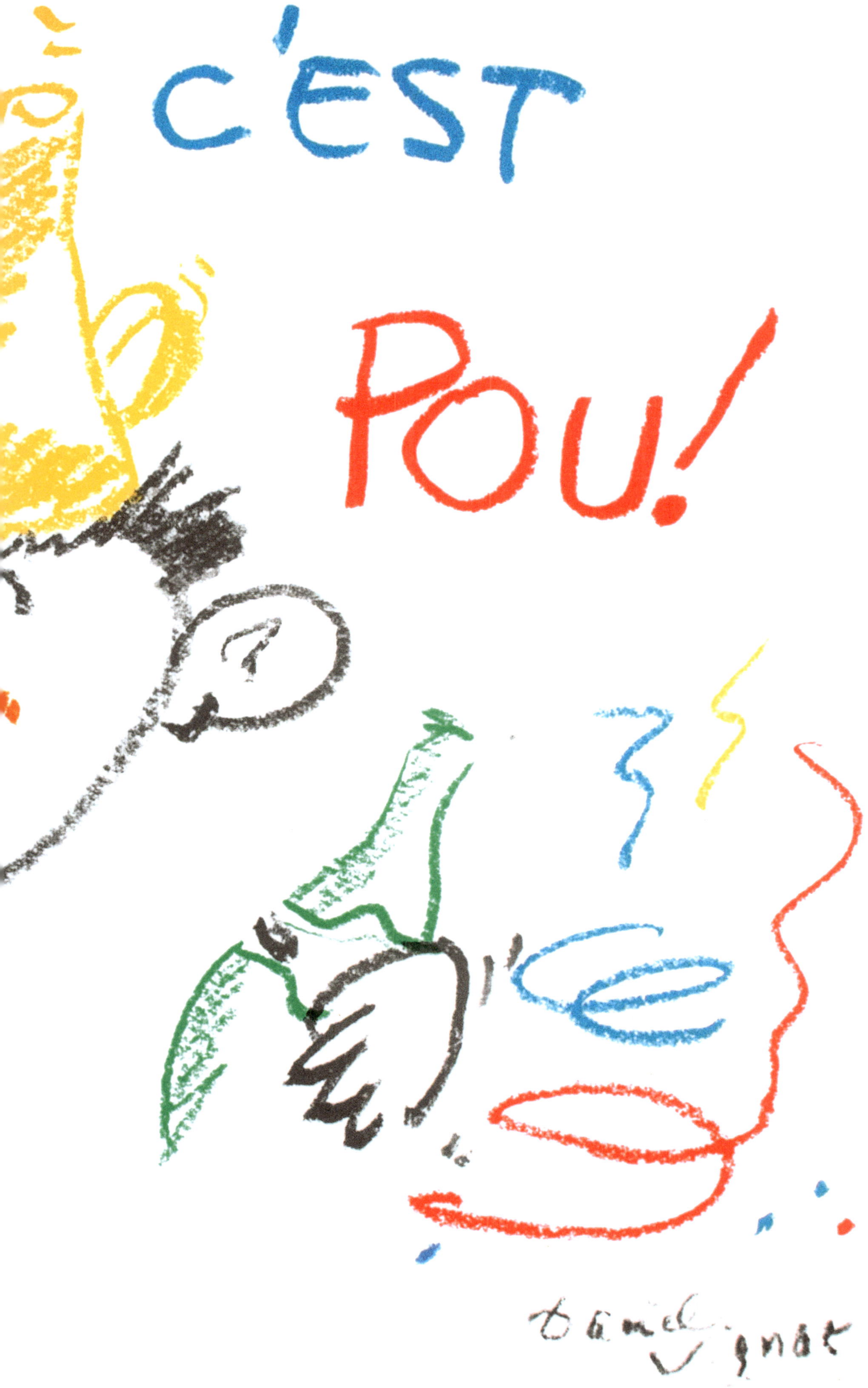
C'EST
POU!

so near and yet so far

When Perrier crosses borders, its campaigns blend its French origins with local color. When Perrier hit the East Coast in 1976, the Statue of Liberty declared, "Perrier. It's only natural", holding aloft a bottle of sparkling mineral water instead of a torch. This was followed by the explosive slogan "Earth's First Soft Drink". Perrier surveyed Americans from the pinnacle of its 120 million year legacy and described its history of purity and naturalness dating back to prehistoric times. This concept was illustrated by major artists. Robert O. Blechman created an inventive gem of an animated film and the great Milton Glaser was inspired to draw two legendary posters.

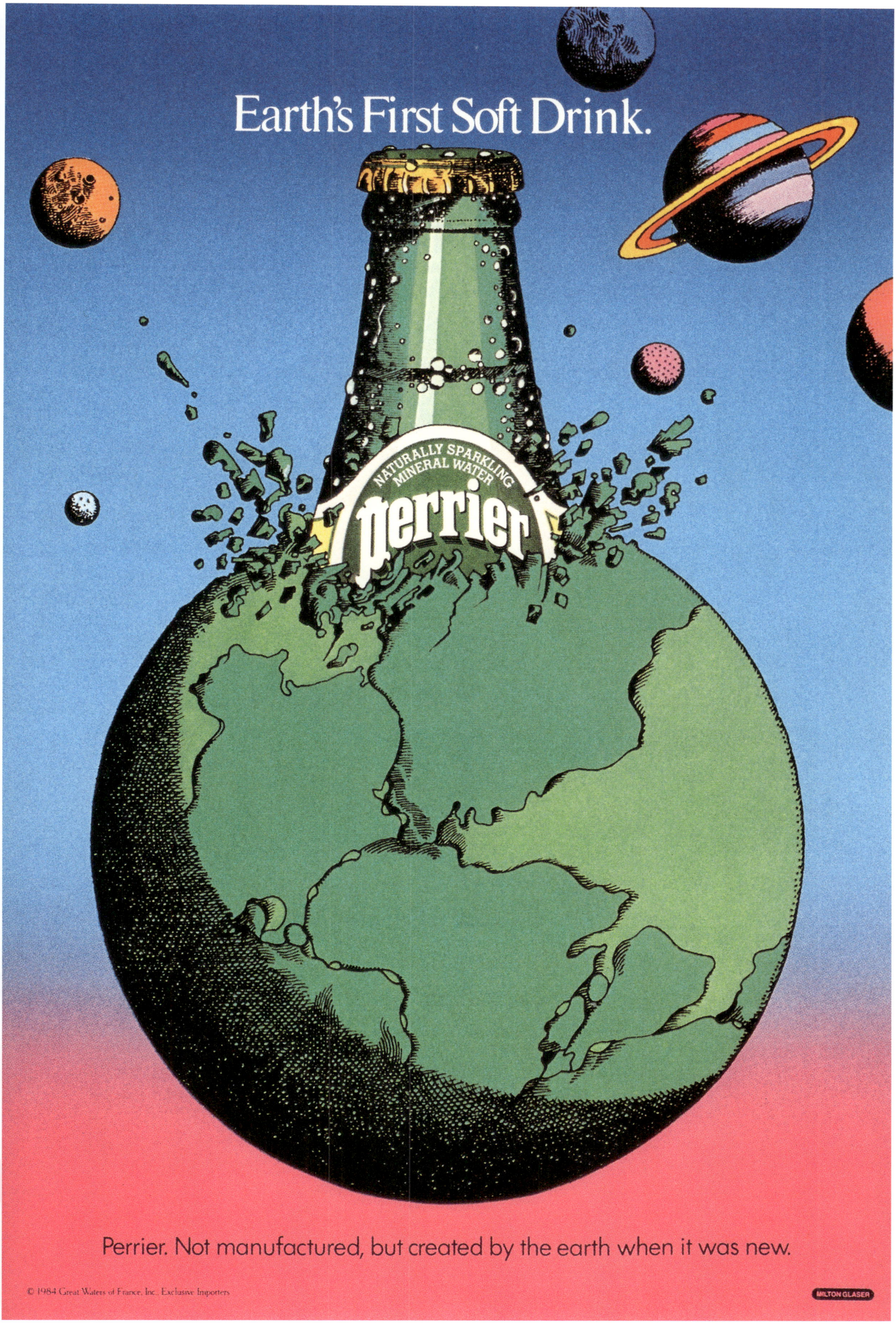
Earth's First Soft Drink.
NATURALLY SPARKLING
MINERAL WATER
Perrier
Perrier. Not manufactured, but created by the earth when it was new.
© 1984 Great Waters of France, Inc., Exclusive Importers
MILTON GLASER

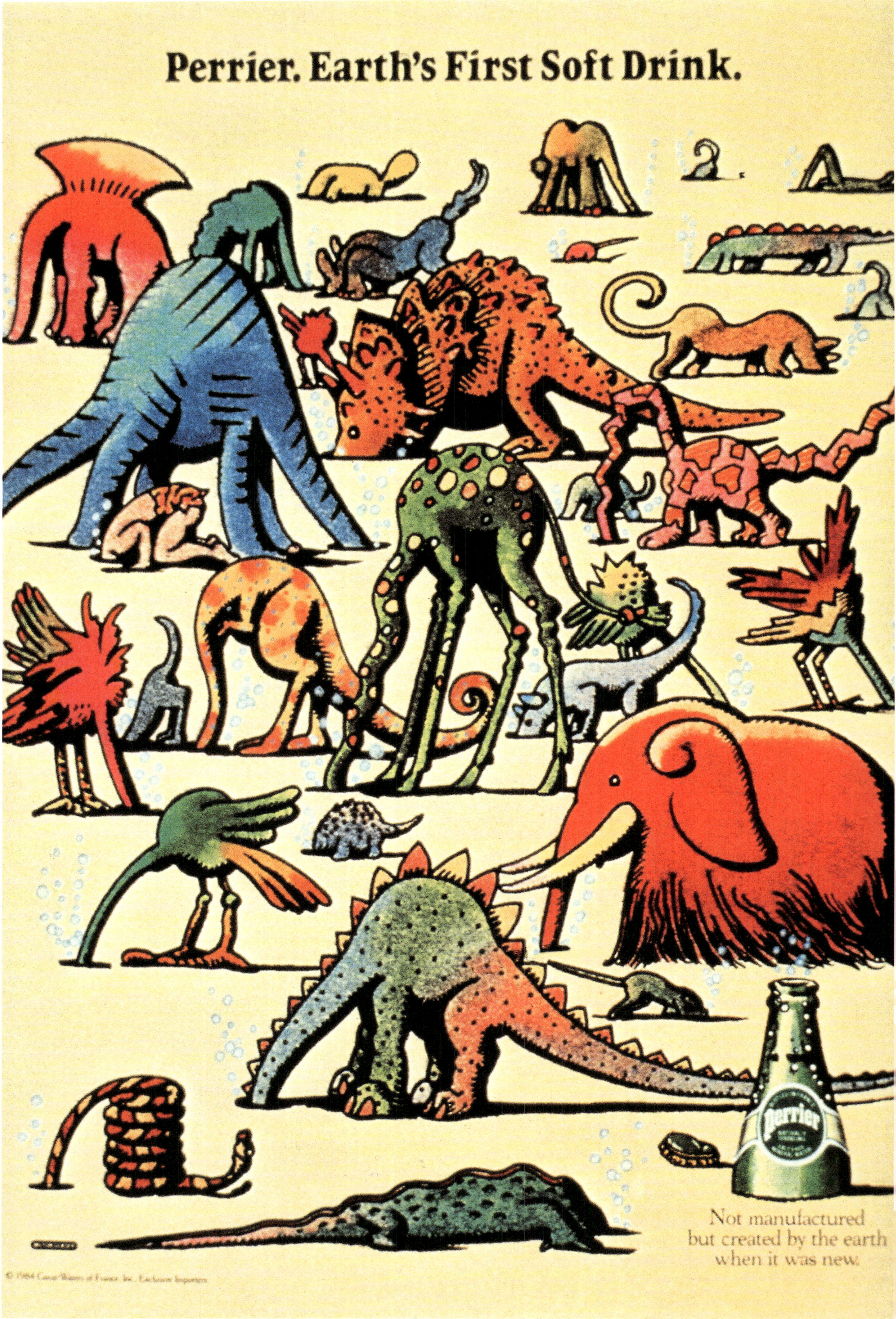
Perrier. Earth's First Soft Drink.
Perrier
Not manufactured
but created by the earth
when it was new.

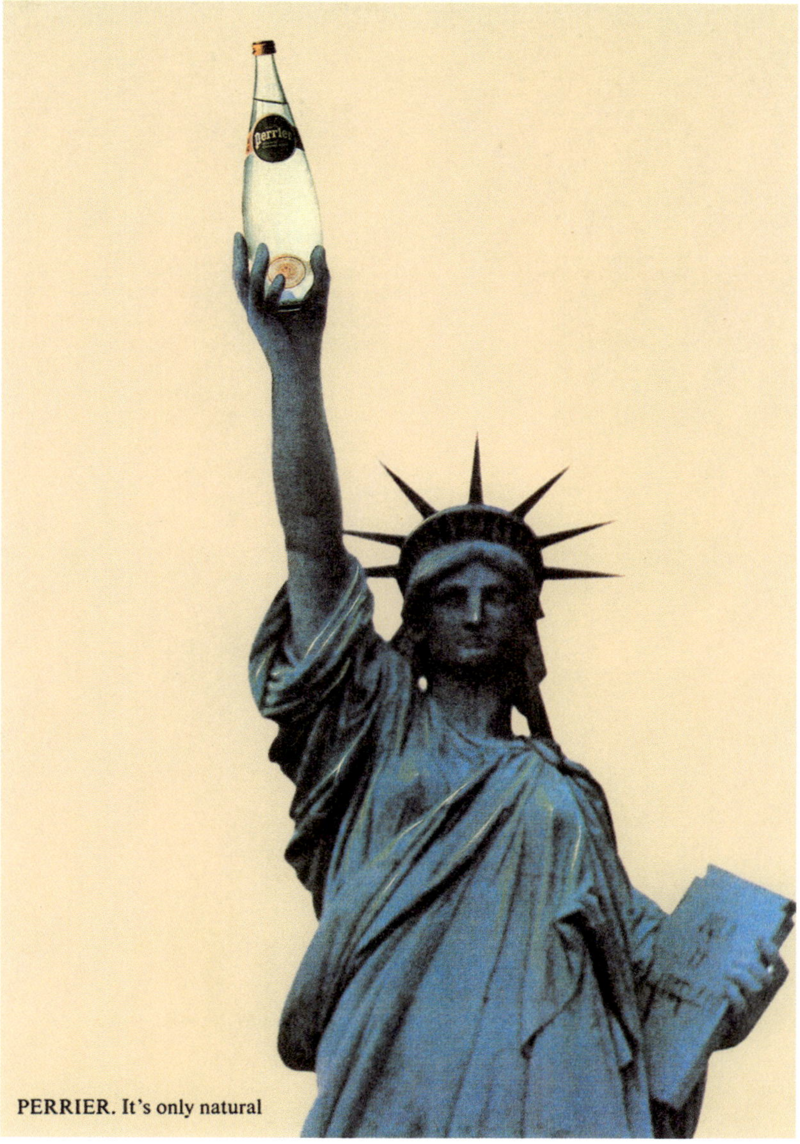

Milton Glaser

Milton Glaser dreamed up the slogan "I love New York", with the heart replacing the verb. He was born in 1929 in New York, and earned a reputation as one of the greatest graphic designers of the twentieth century. The creator of a number of covers and illustrations for prestigious magazines and record sleeves, including Bob Dylan's 1967 album, he launched *New York Magazine* in 1968. The work of this godfather of American graphic art featured in exhibition at the Pompidou Center in Paris in 1977.

Home sweet home: to return to its roots in the land of its early adopters, Perrier went straight to the heart of the British temperament. In the birthplace of humor, a variety of campaigns played on water-based puns in everyday expressions. Perrier and water became inseparable from "H2 Eau" and "Eau revoir", not forgetting "Incogniteau", "Eau-la-la", "Bistreau" and the inspired "Picasseau", complete with a Cubist bottle.

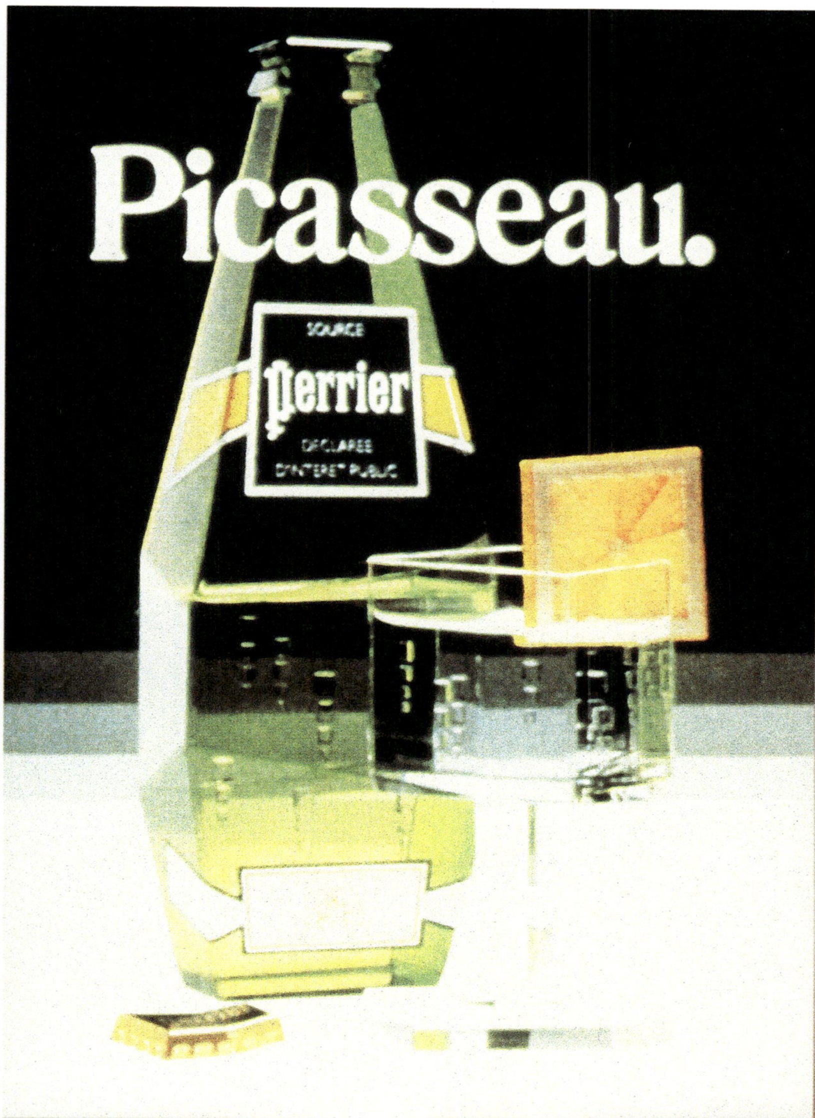
Picasseau.
SOURCE
Perrier
DECLAREE
D'INTERET PUBLIC

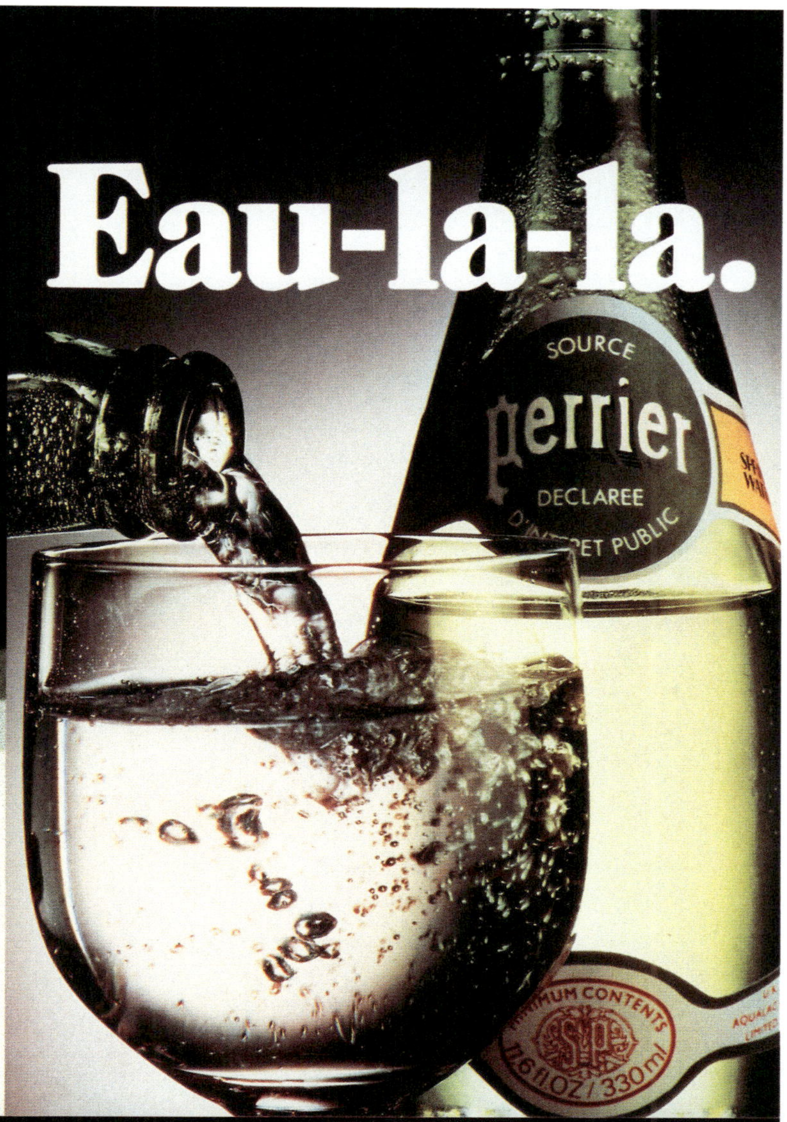
Eau-la-la.
SOURCE
Perrier
DECLAREE
D'INTERET PUBLIC
MINIMUM CONTENTS
11.6 fl OZ / 330 ml

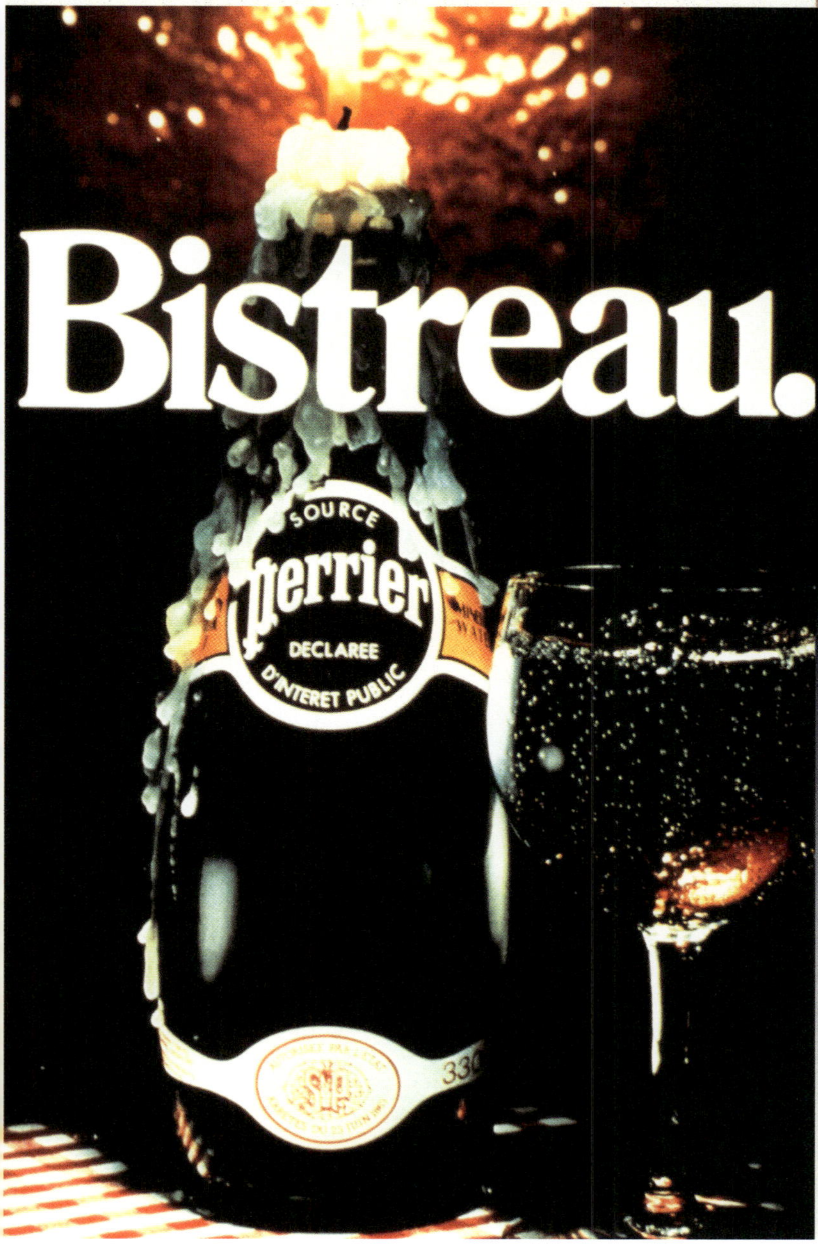
Bistreau.
SOURCE
Perrier
DECLAREE
D'INTERET PUBLIC

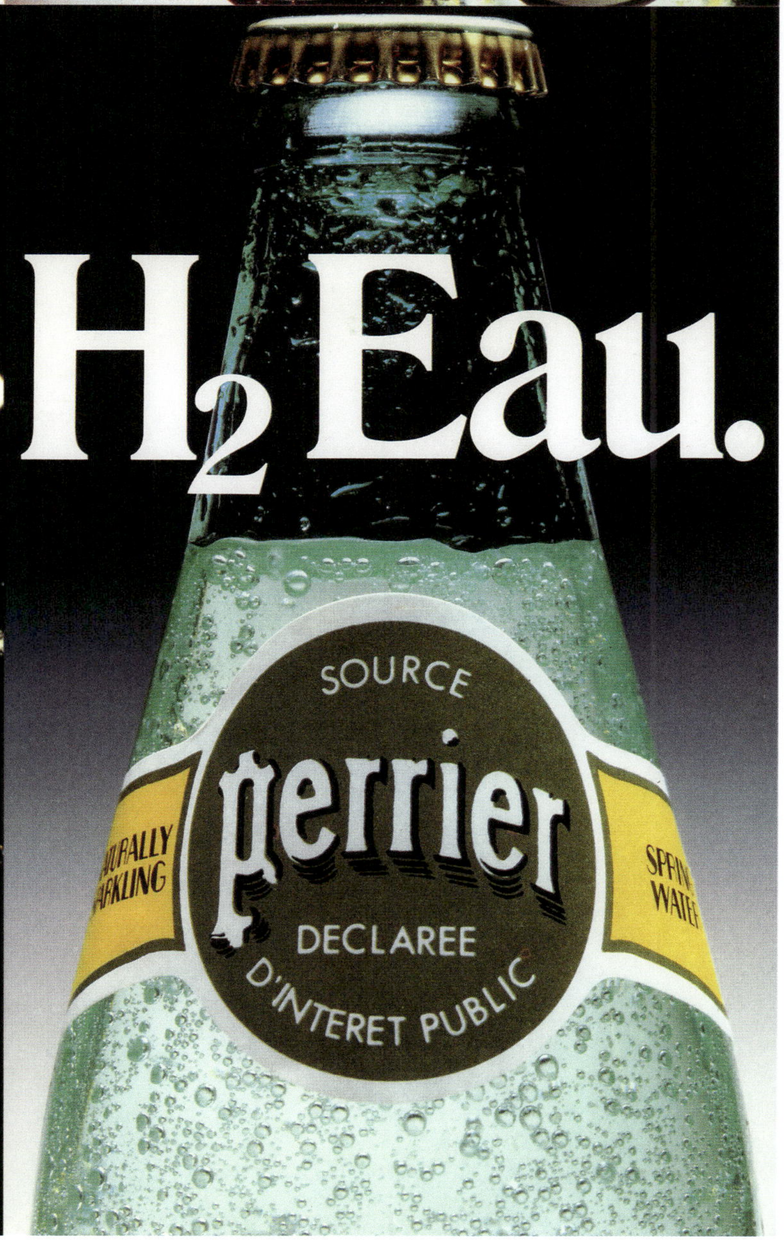
H_2Eau.
SOURCE
Perrier
DECLAREE
D'INTERET PUBLIC

In Japan, graphics ruled the roost and advertising deployed them with relish, playing with ideograms and setting the bubbles in a traditional landscape without compromising their origins in any way - "Perrier is Perrier" when all is said and done. In a different vein, Perrier stood out from the crowd in Belgium with its humorous posters. Generation Perrier made sperm twist and shout and fertilize the future in a manner reminiscent of Woody Allen's 1972 film "Everything you always wanted to know about sex... (but were afraid to ask)", which featured a sperm "launcher".

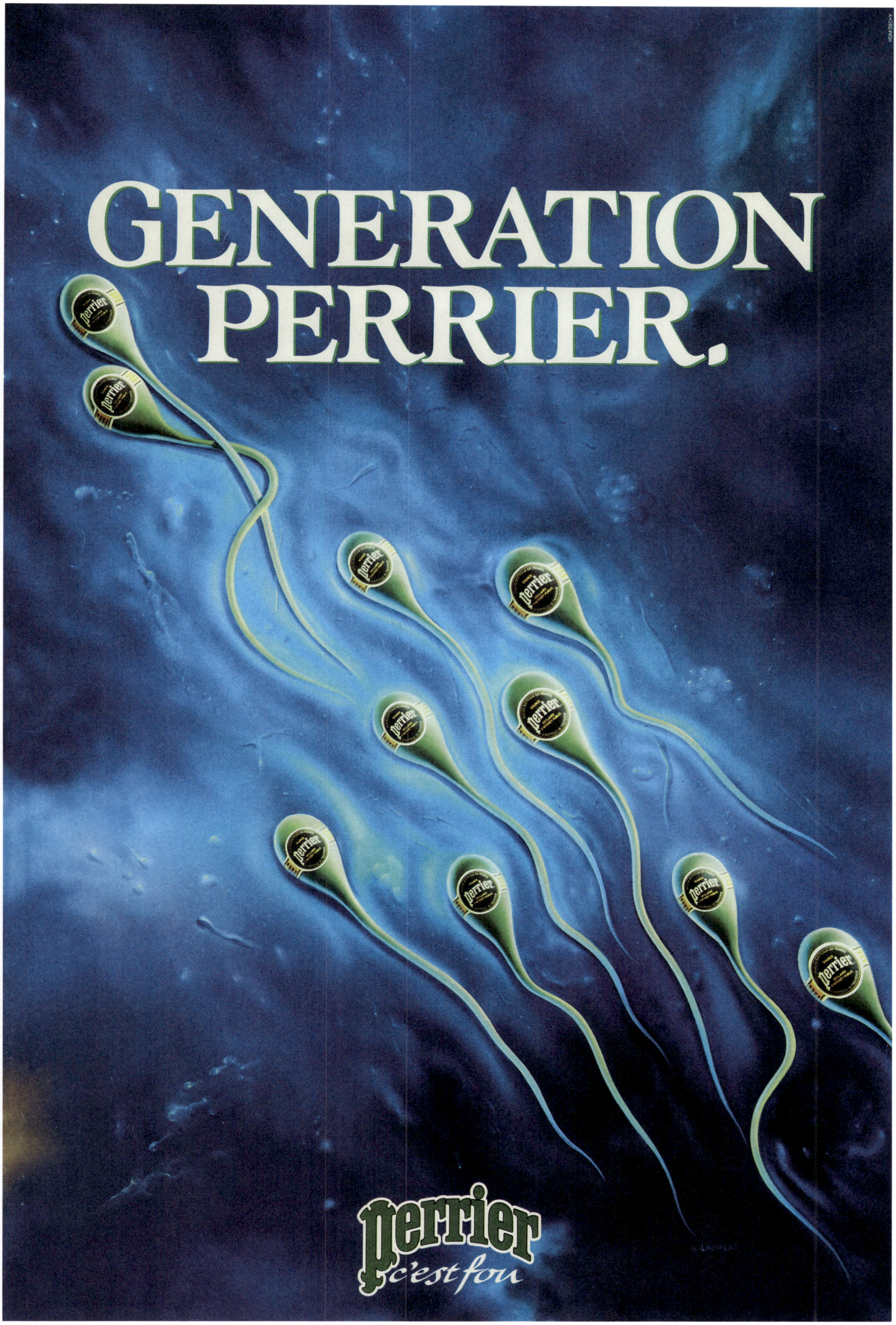
GENERATION
PERRIER.
perrier
c'est fou

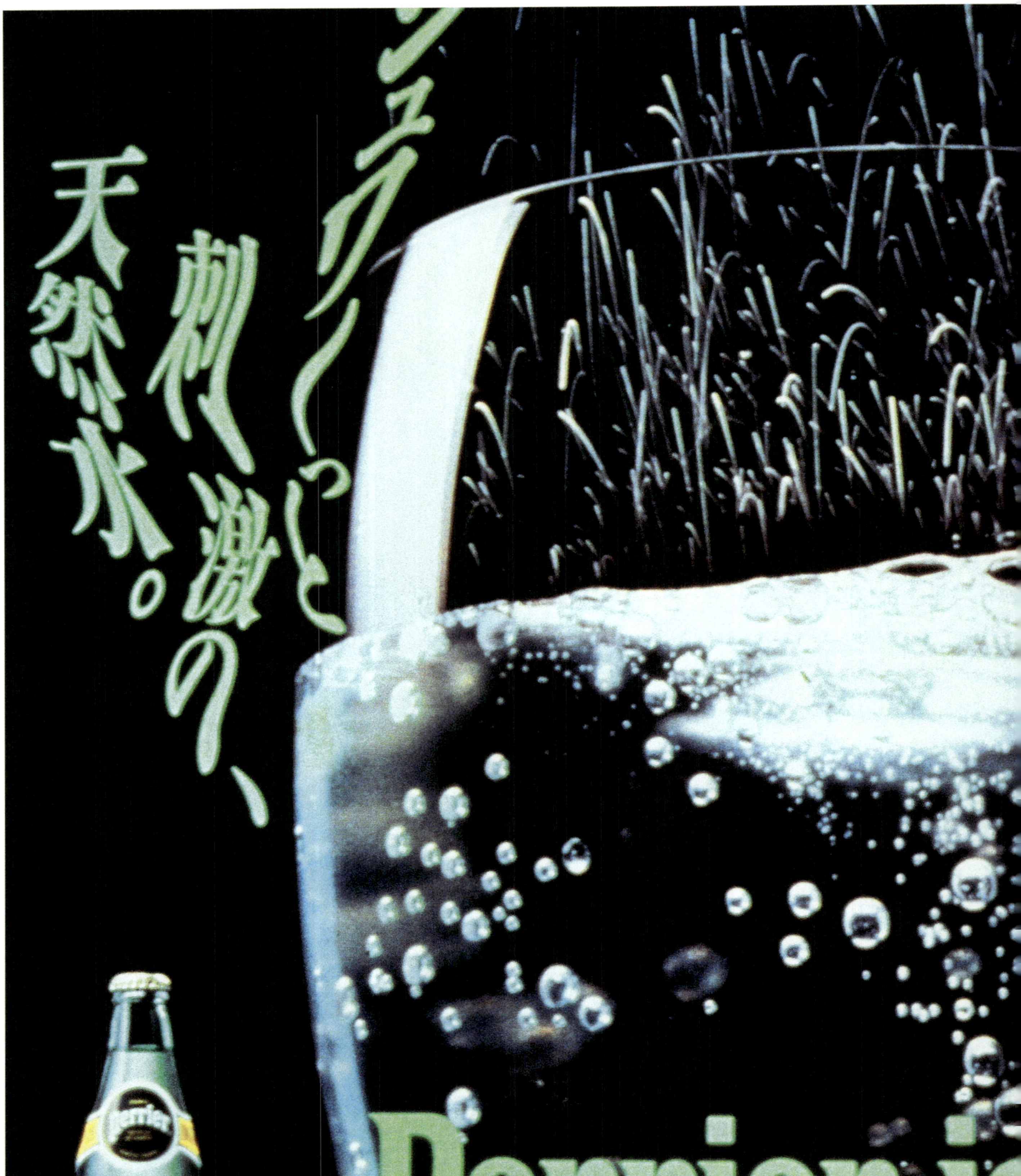
ュワリっと
刺激の、
天然水。
Perrier is

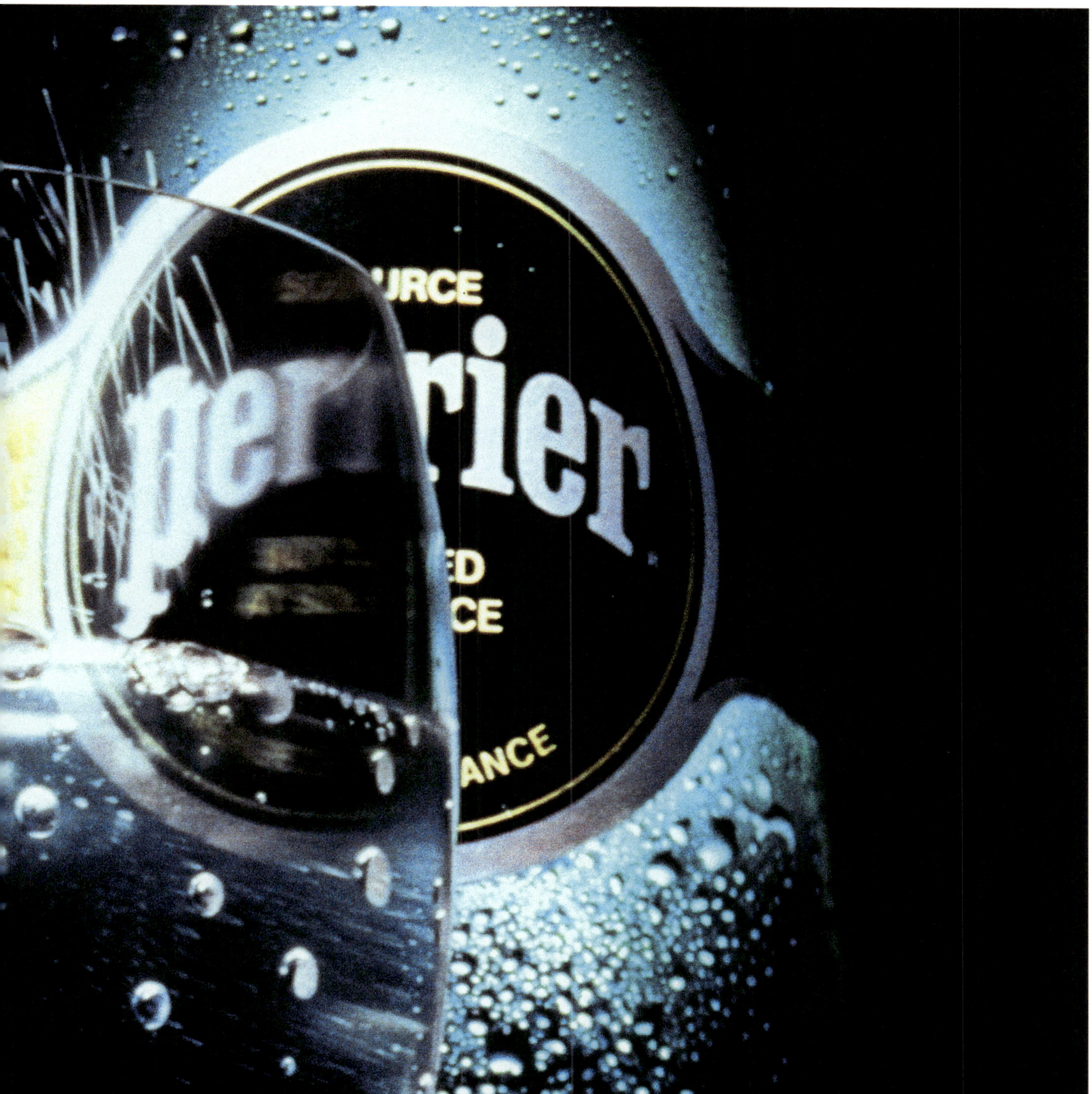
Perrier

t-shirt

This is not a t-shirt, as Magritte might have said, but a poster where t-shirts and Perrier become all-American stars. The campaign was launched in 1997 with four posters by the photographer Vincent Dixon, including one featuring Einstein sticking his tongue out towards a glass of Perrier. This daring idea won him the French poster award in 1998. Riding the wave of this success, new characters appeared on t-shirts. The actor Marty Feldman, star of Mel Brooks' Frankenstein Junior, rubbed shoulders with his distant movie cousin Nosferatu the Vampire, then came a creature straight out of Jaws and even the famous Captain Haddock, winning Dixon a second consecutive French poster award in 1999.

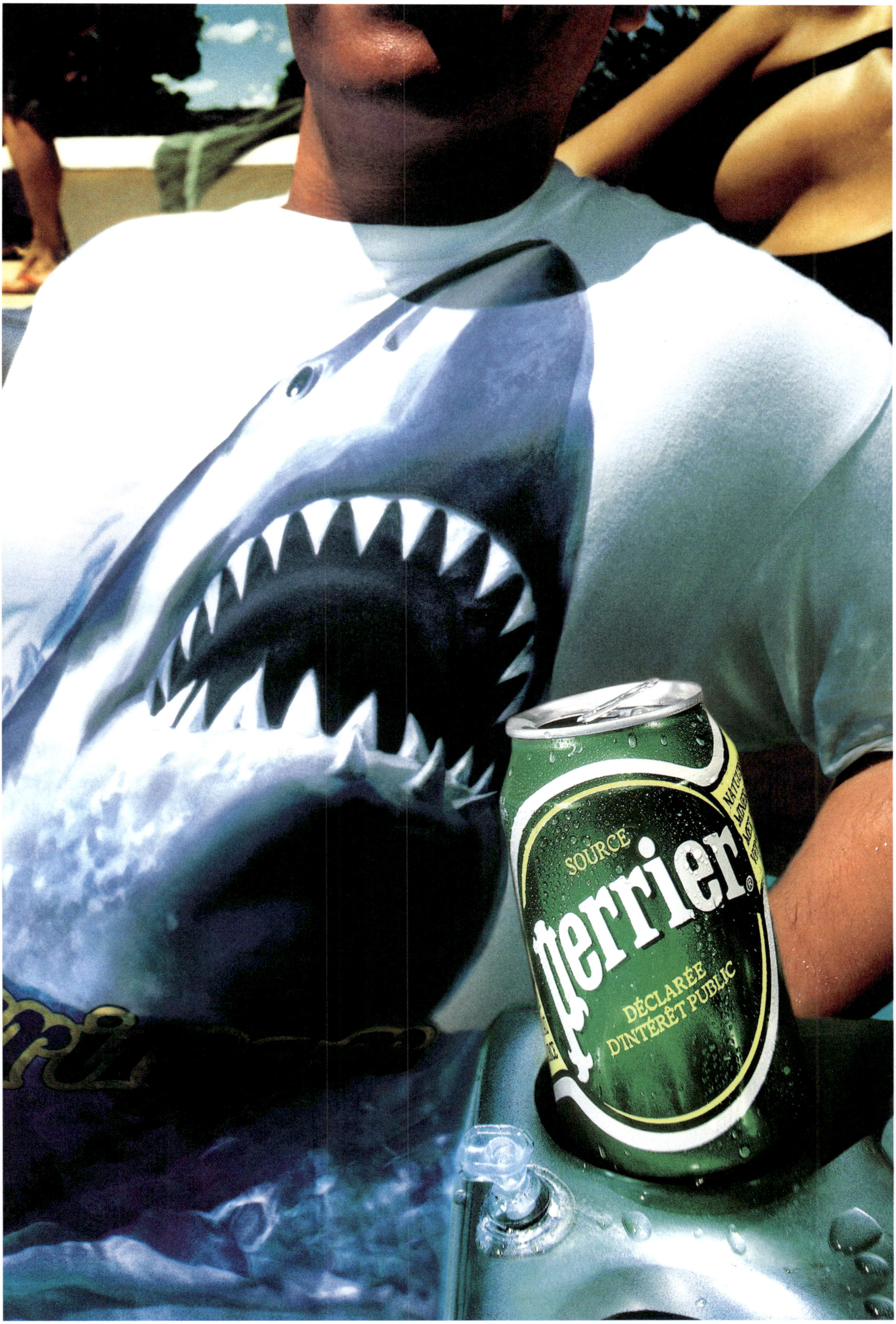
SOURCE
Perrier®
DÉCLARÉE
D'INTÉRÊT PUBLIC

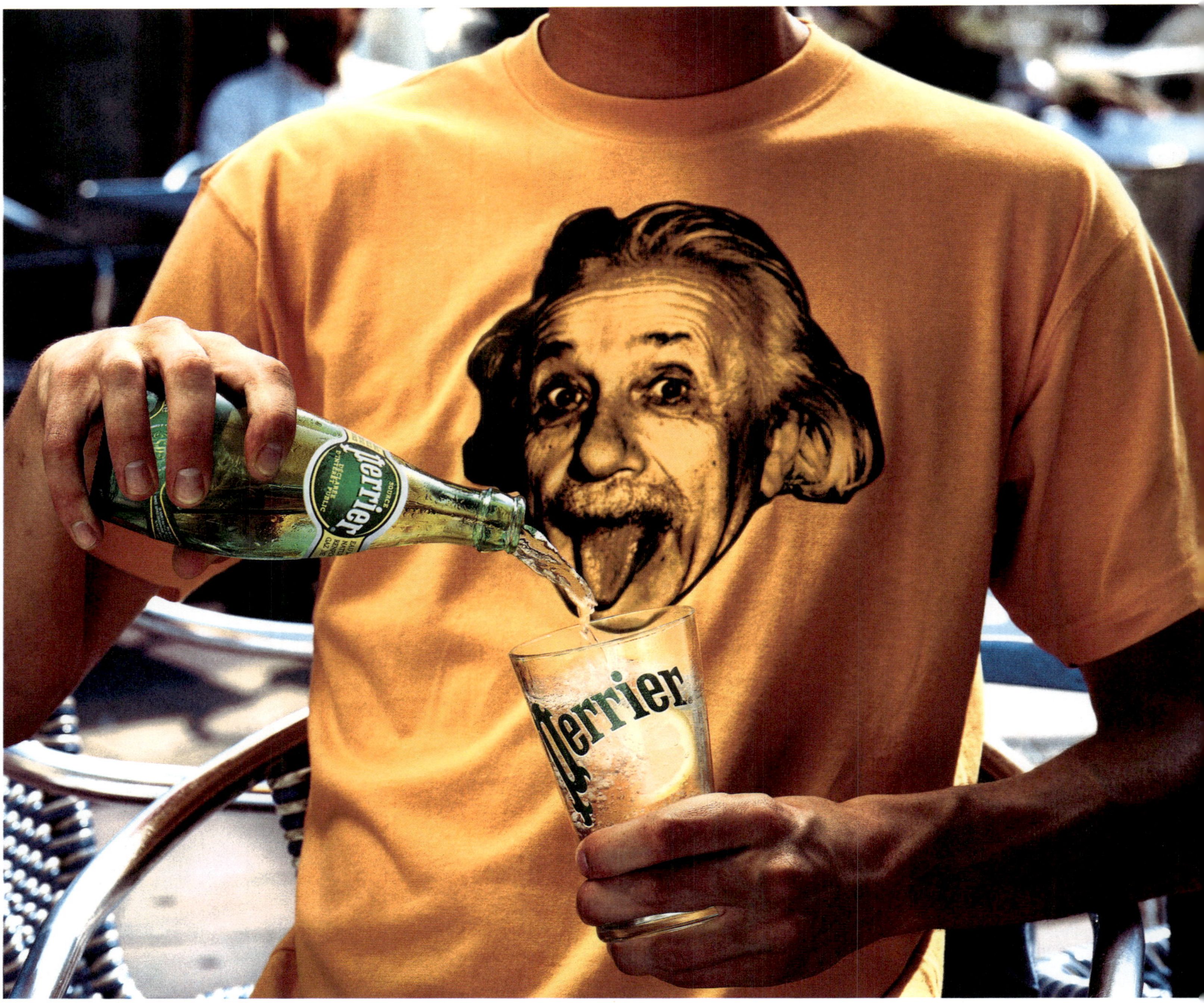
Perrier
Perrier

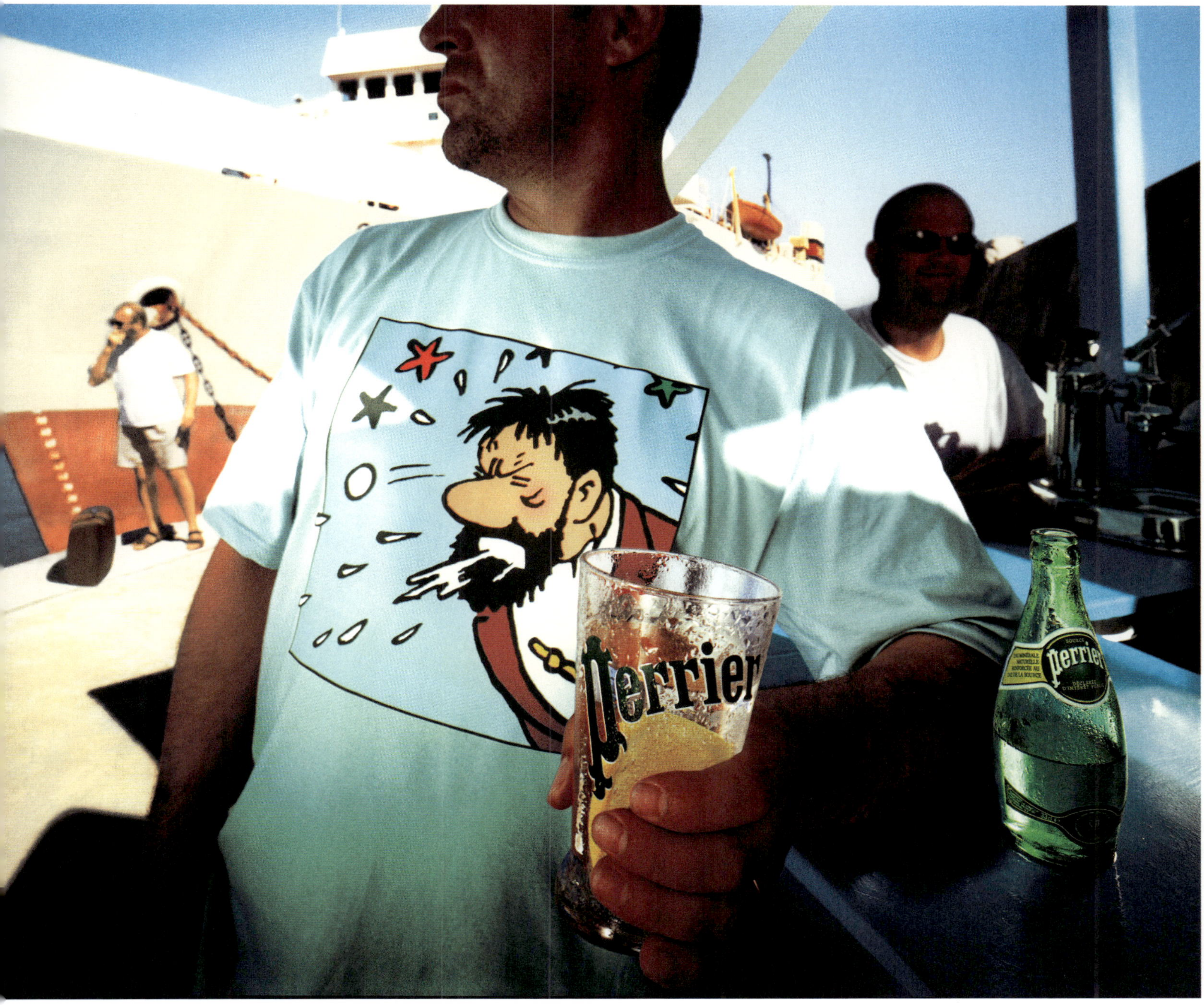
Perrier
Perrier

water, air, life

How do you follow "Perrier, c'est fou"? What looked at first sight like an impossible challenge was taken up with flair in the new simple strapline: "Water, air, life". Times were changing, but Perrier was still drawing on the very best talents and its campaigns swept the board at awards ceremonies in an upbeat advertising industry. The launch of "Water, air, life" was marked by three breathtaking films, each little advertising gems. The first, The Lion, in which a thirsty young woman and lion fight over a bottle of Perrier, was directed by Jean-Paul Goude. The following two films were directed by Ridley Scott. The director of Alien made the planets dance to the James Brown hit Sex Machine and then transported tennis champion John McEnroe into The Mirage, where the player grew old all alone in an apocalyptic universe in which his only memories were playing tennis and drinking Perrier. In 1991, The Lion won the Grand prix at the Cannes International Advertising Festival and The Mirage received a Bronze Lion award. In 1994, La Madelon, directed by Ken Ralston and featuring lead soldiers launching an assault on a refrigerator, was awarded the Grand Prix Stratégies and a Silver Lion at Cannes.

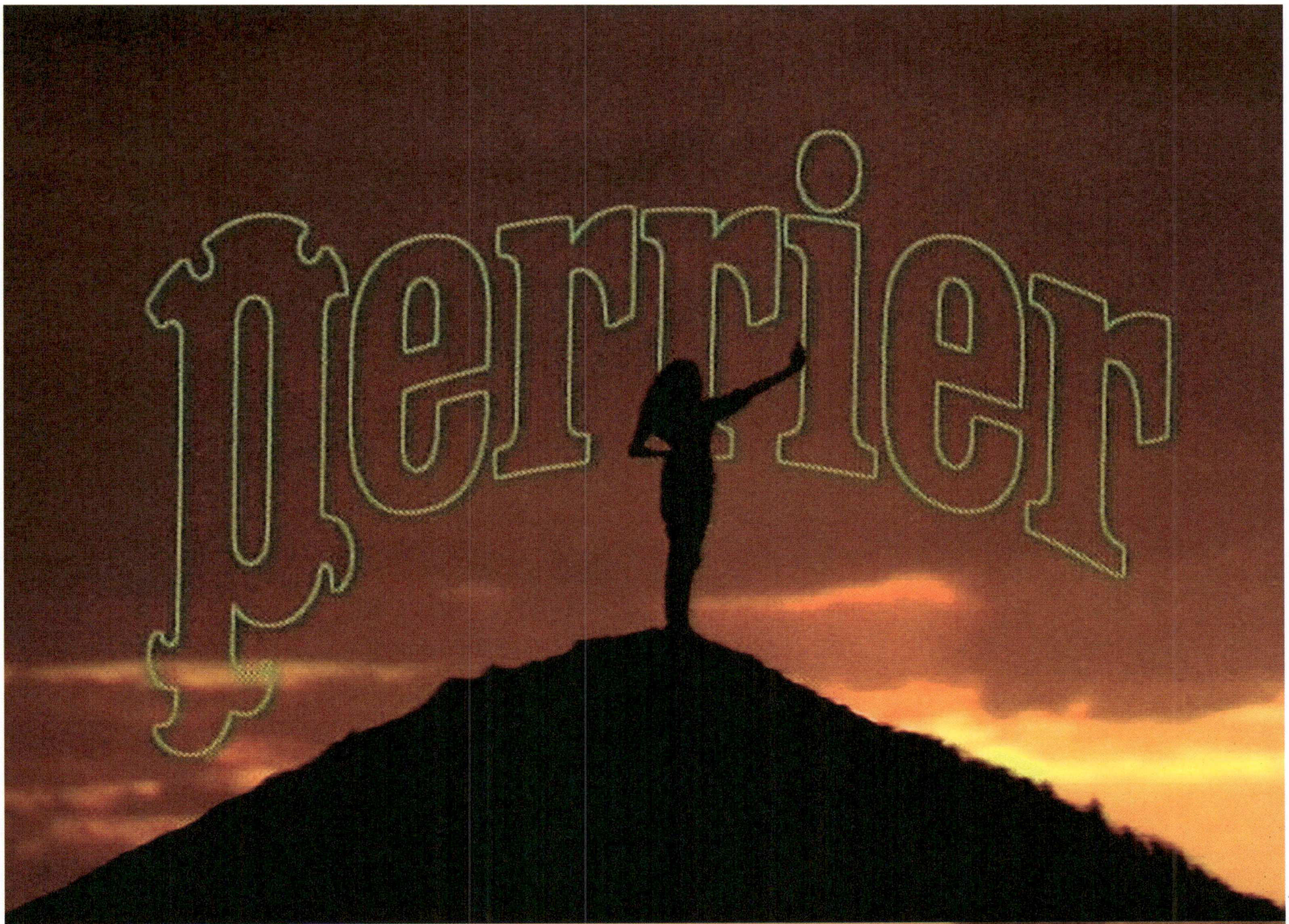
perrier
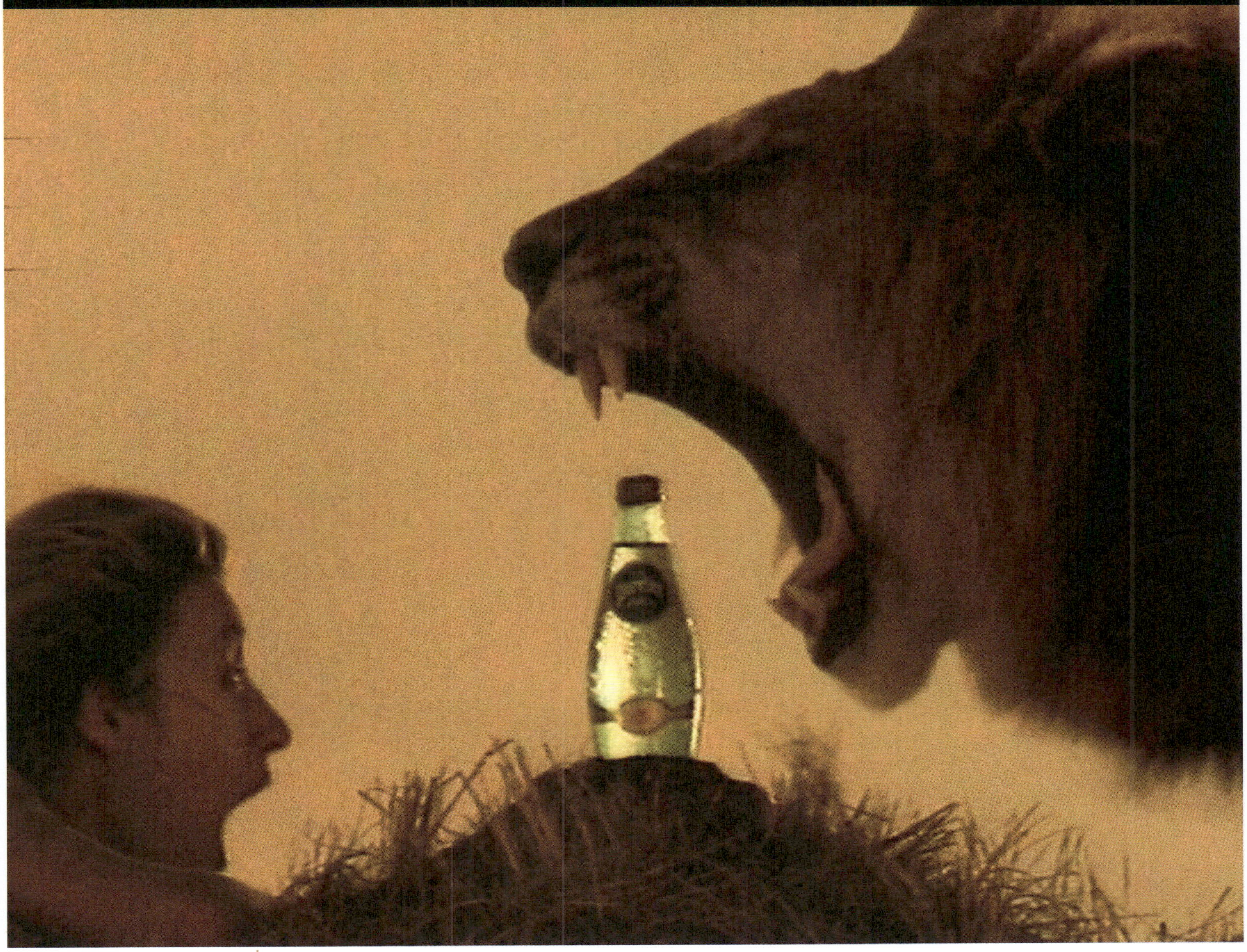

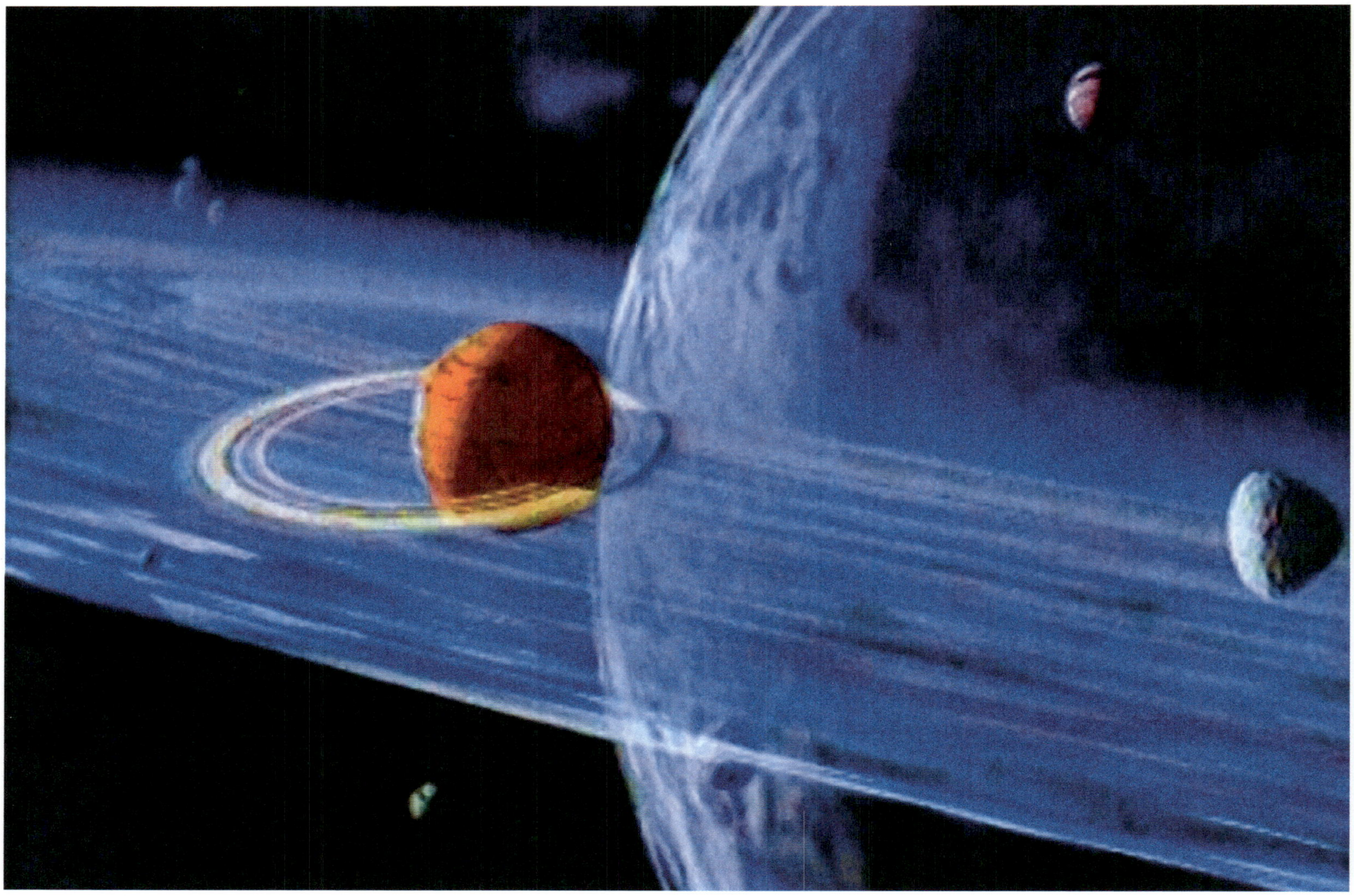

Jean-Paul Goude

Born in 1940, he grew up near Vincennes zoo on the outskirts of Paris. Creative director of *Esquire* magazine in the 1970s, he was a natural risk-taker. He directed the statuesque Grace Jones in a variety of guises and made a number of music videos and commercials which captured the iconic feel of the 1980s. When he returned to French soil, he added his unique stamp to adverts for Kodak or Chanel's Egoïste fragrance. He choreographed the parade for the French Revolution Bicentennial in Paris in 1989.

Ridley Scott

Born in 1937 in England, has directed more than twenty films, several of which have become cult classics. He won one award for *The Duelists* at the 1977 Cannes Film Festival. However, he is best known for his science fiction films, with *Alien* terrifying and fascinating moviegoers in equal measure in 1979. In 1982, he sent Harrison Ford into the unnerving world of the replicants in *Blade Runner*. Ridley Scott came back down to earth in 1991 with the female road movie *Thelma and Louise*, then dived into antiquity with *Gladiator*. He returned to science fiction in 2012 with *Prometheus*.

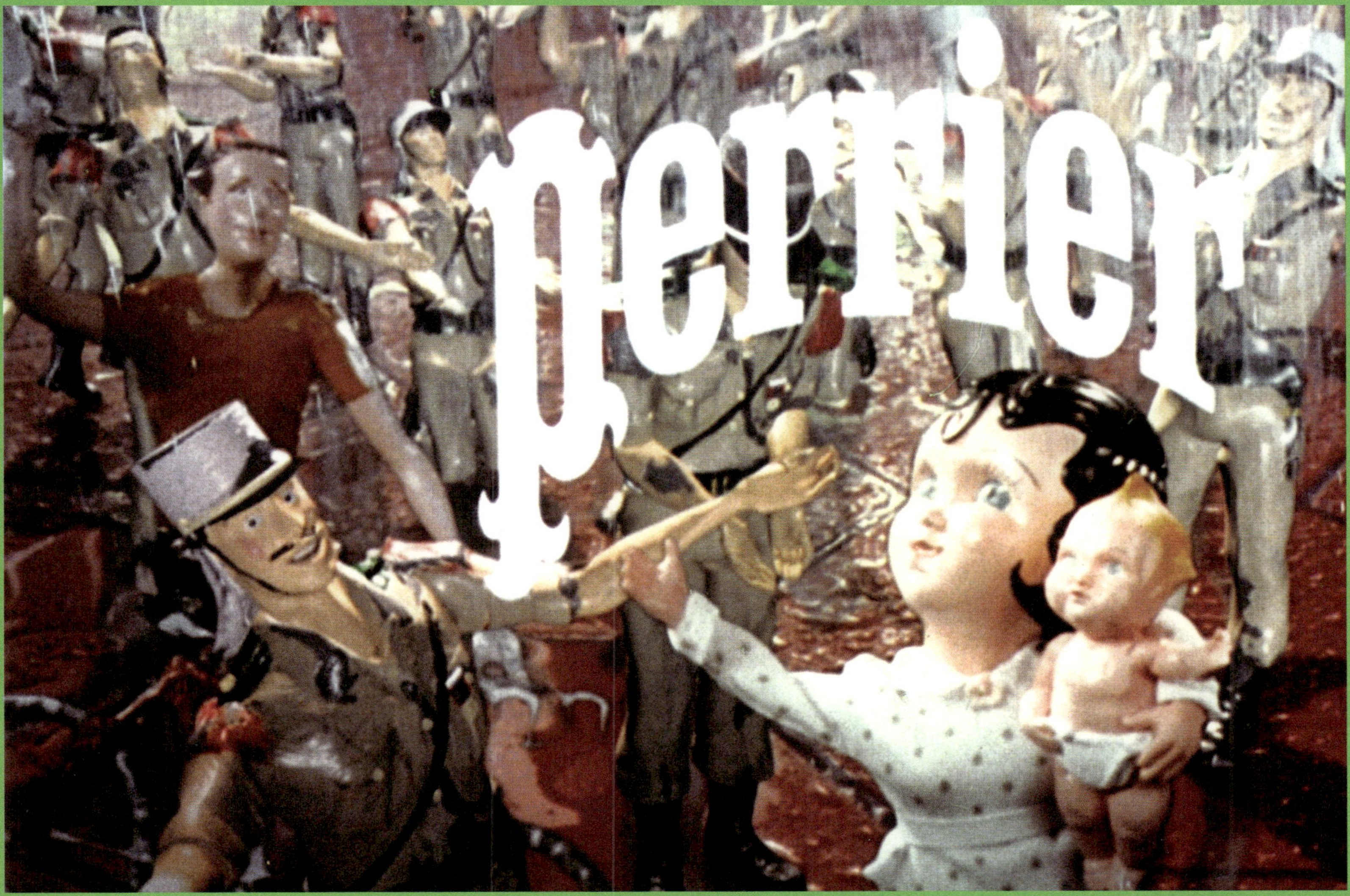

Ken Ralston

Born in 1954 in the United States, the director of the film *La Madelon* is the king of visual effects in Hollywood. He has made his mark on famous feature films ranging from *Star Wars* to *Men in Black 3* and has worked with all the top film-makers. Ken Ralston has won several Academy Awards in the Best Visual Effects category, in particular for *Who Killed Roger Rabbit?*, *Forrest Gump*, *Cocoon* and *Star Wars VI: Return of the Jedi.*

intense refresh-ment

Global warming is the order of the day and Perrier demonstrates its social usefulness once again, refreshing the senses, body and emotions in spectacular settings, from the year 2000 forward. Red hot posters cry out for global cooling with intense Perrier refreshment. As temperatures rise, Perrier the "Thirst quencher" enters the fray in a series of eight sizzling films by Patrice Lecomte. In Melting, a feat of poetic and technical genius, the planet and the entire setting is literally in melt-down. Perrier, the object of every desire and the last recourse before the earth's core goes into fusion, is the only thing to avoid liquefaction in a film by Frédéric Planchon. Destination the sun, as the temperature soars even further in The Drop, which subverts the rules of the science fiction genre and sends a female heroine into space. She saves the world from a heat wave with a drop of Perrier, a new libation to the sun, providing intense refreshment.

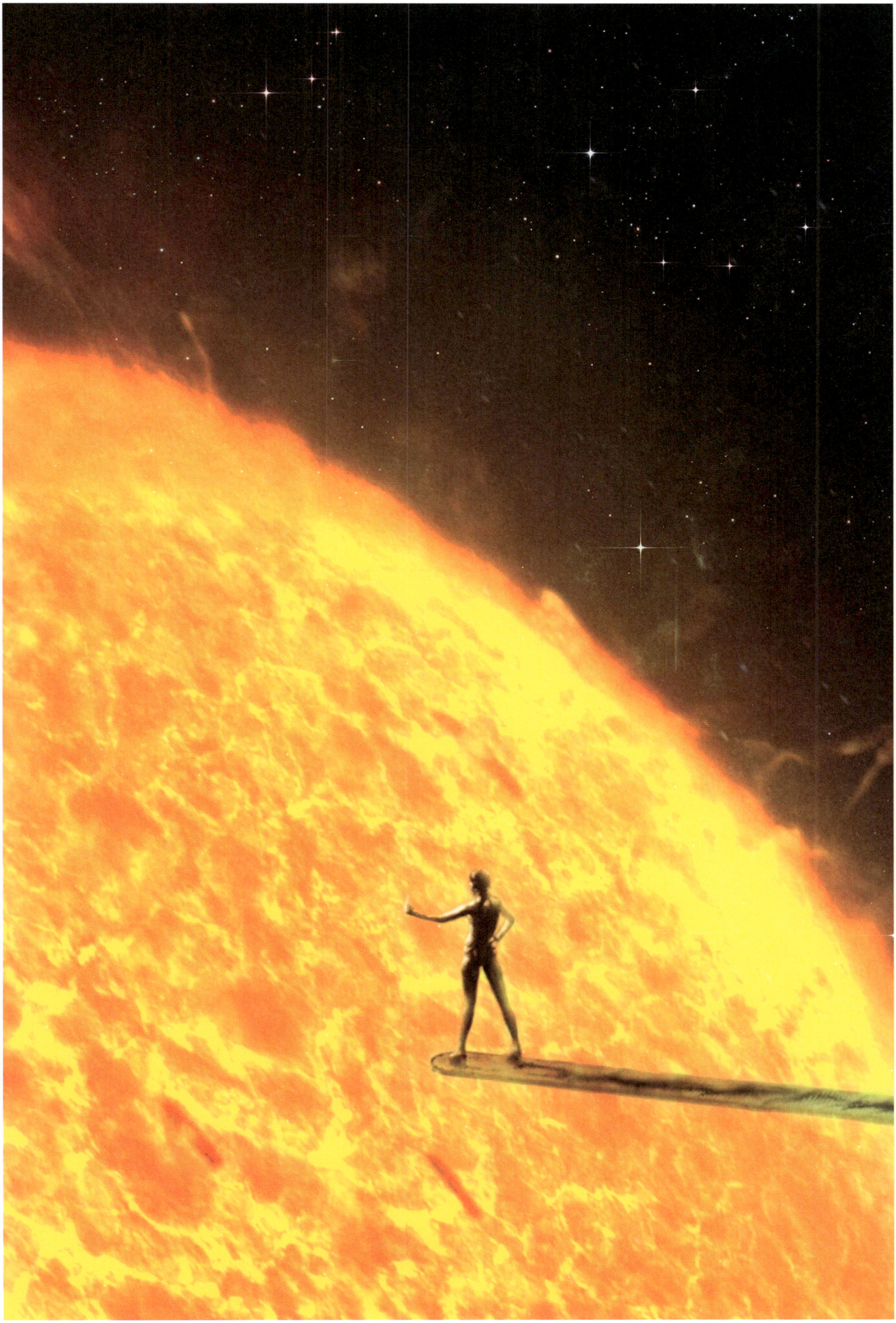

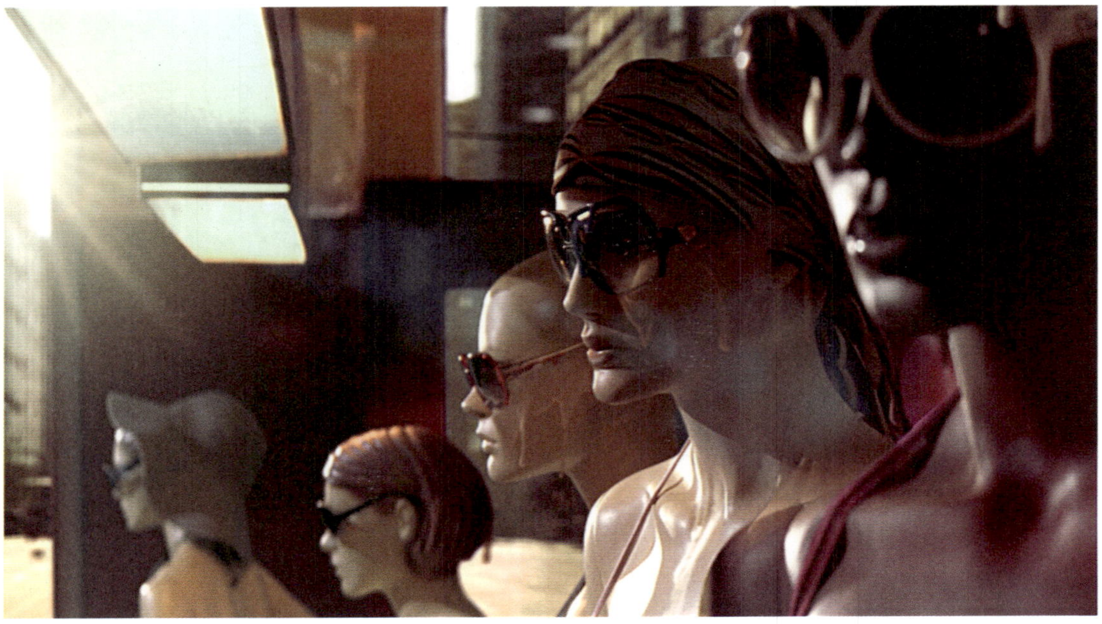

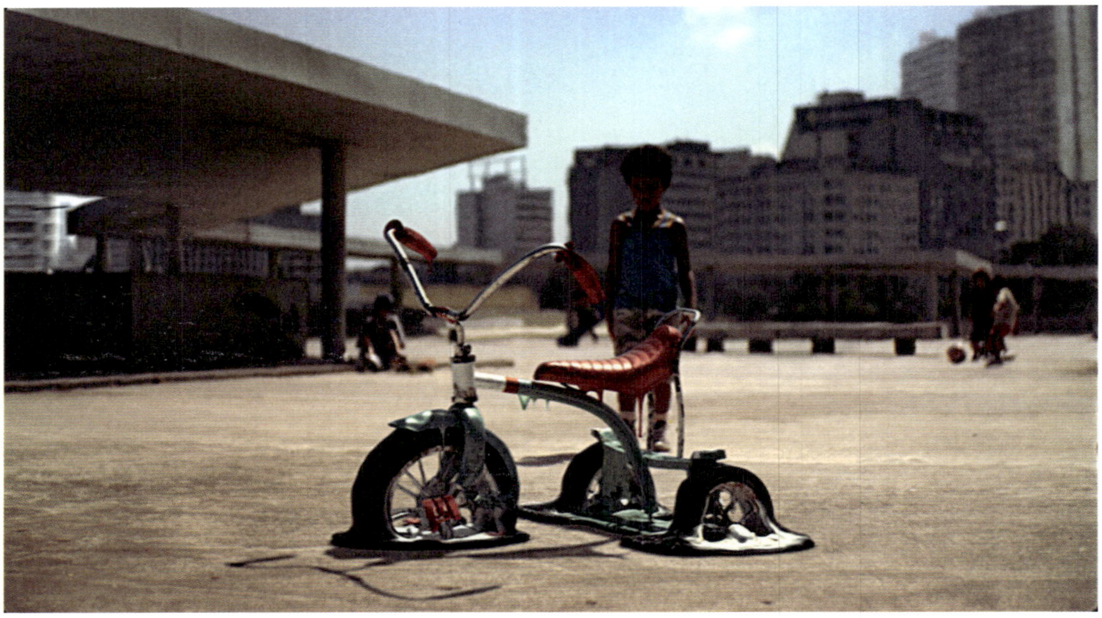

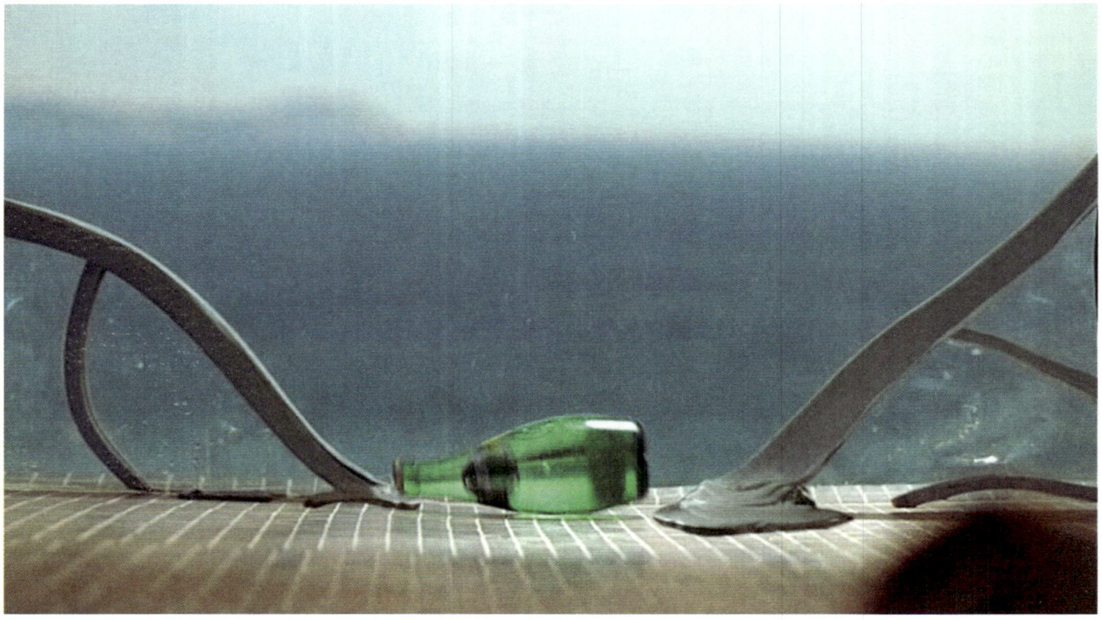

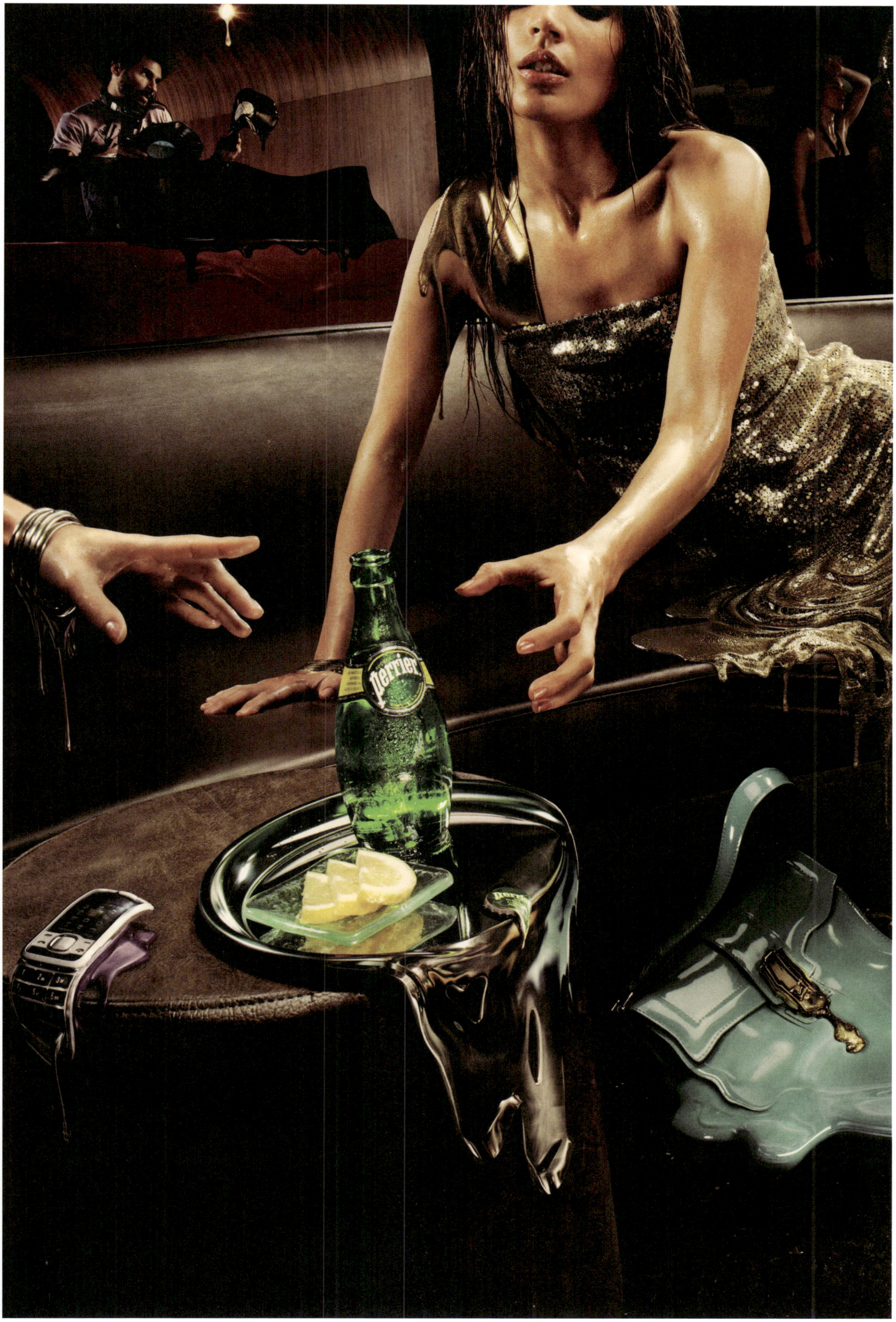
perrier

2.0

Perrier made its mark very early in the digital arena, and with panache. Dita Von Teese, the Perrier muse, embodied this new means of communication for the Facebook and Twitter generation by opening the doors of the "Perrier Mansion", a uniquely sensual world. Internet users who fall for Dita's potent charms can invite themselves to an ultra-private show by the famous burlesque artiste. The interactive adventure moves up a gear with "Le Club", designed exclusively for the internet and social networks. The more visitors there are online, the hotter the content gets. In 2013, "Perrier Secret Place" enters the new realm of interactive gaming, in which unexpected guests appear. Perrier joins the 2.0 age.

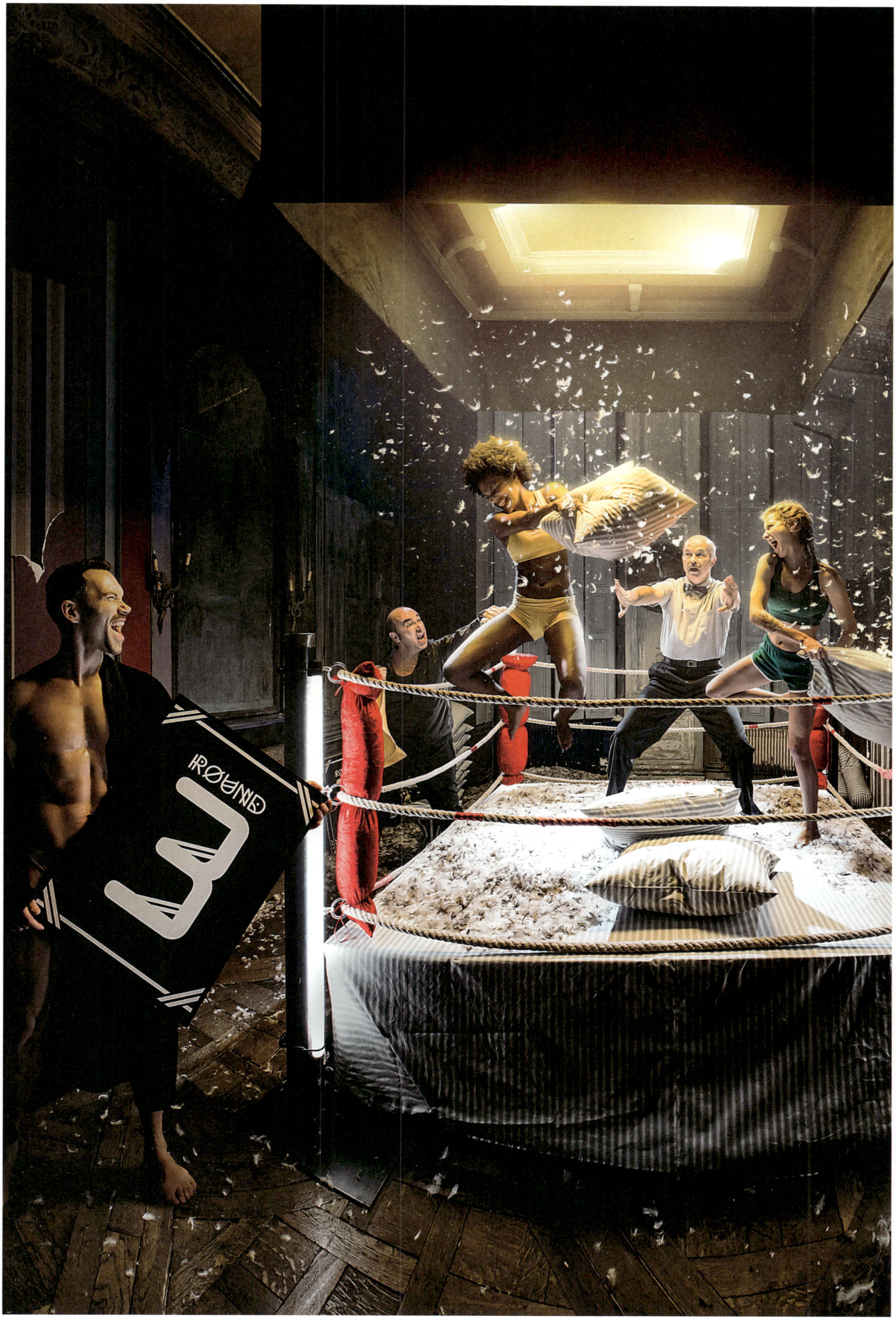
ROUND
3

Perrier Secret Place

Perrier invites internet users to take part in an exclusive secret party packed with unusual features and surprises. Each participant can adopt a persona from a cast of some sixty characters and experience the evening from their perspective.

Perrier Mansion

Modern pin-up girl Dita von Teese is the new Perrier muse. She joins in the Perrier Mansion game, a totally original form of interactive communication which forges a new relationship with consumers and underlines Perrier's pioneering role in the digital arena. The burlesque star also features on the entire Perrier collection.

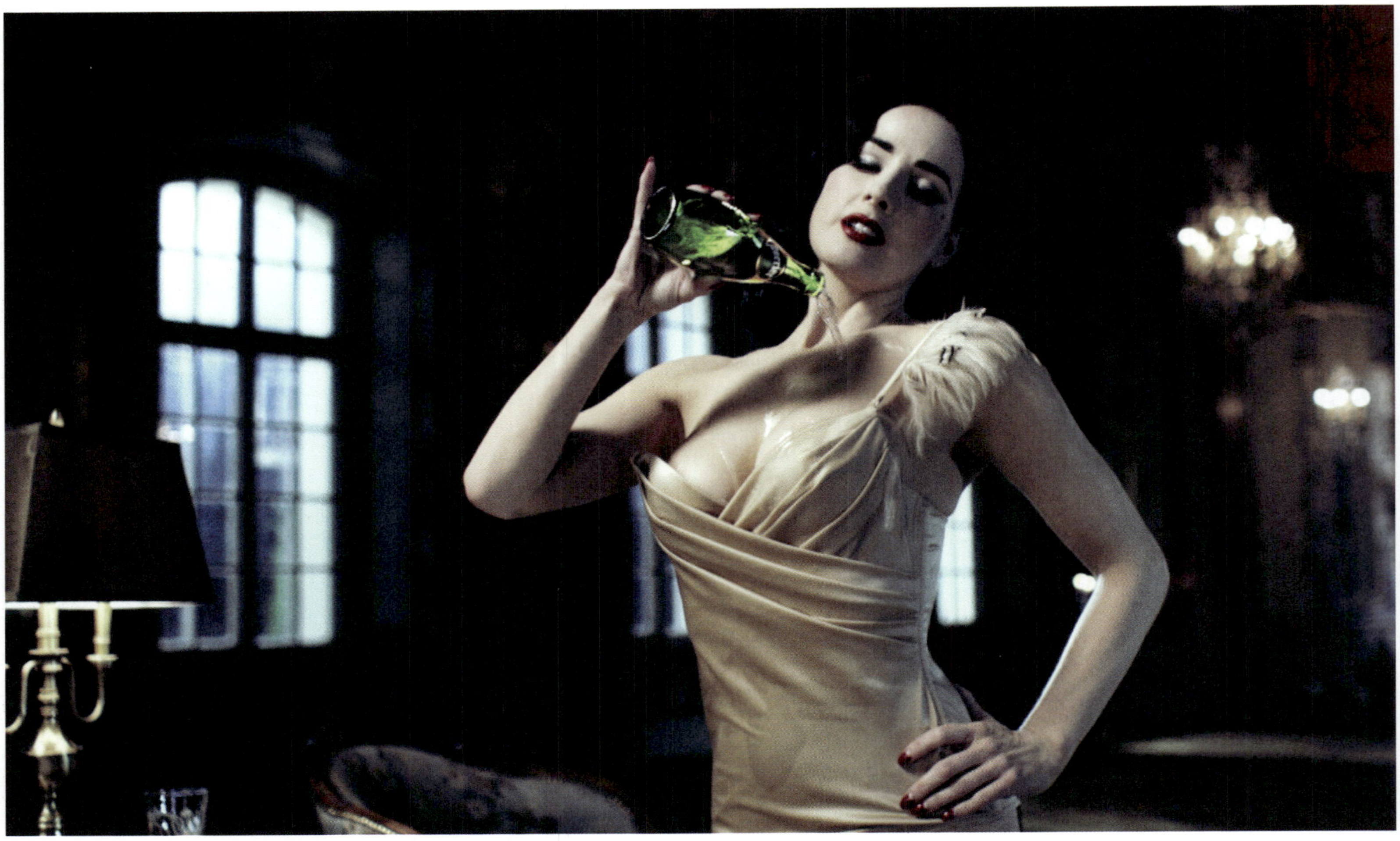

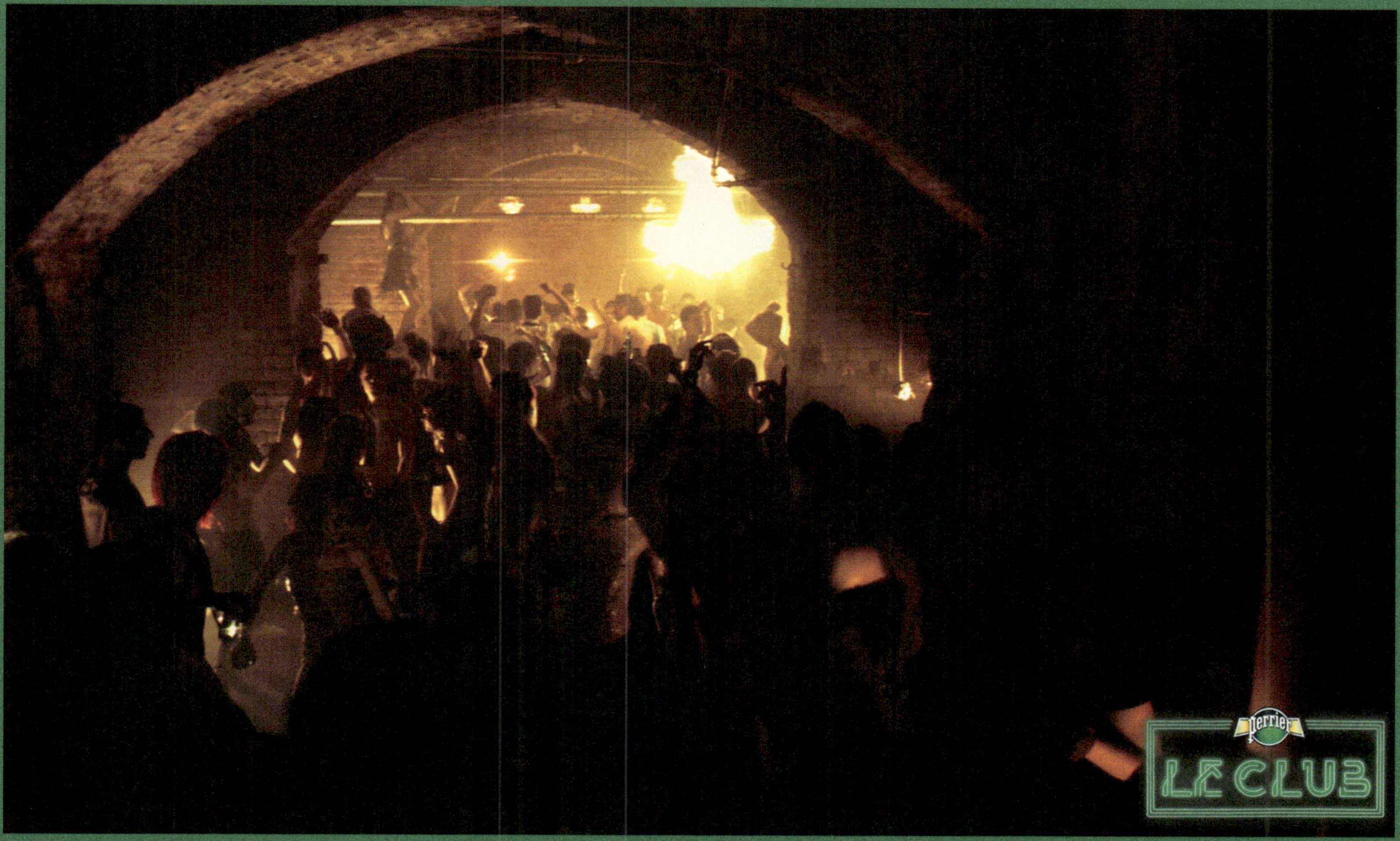

Le Club

Perrier pushes the experiment even further by launching "Le Club", a 100% digital adventure set in a nightclub where the temperature gets hotter as the number of online viewers rises.

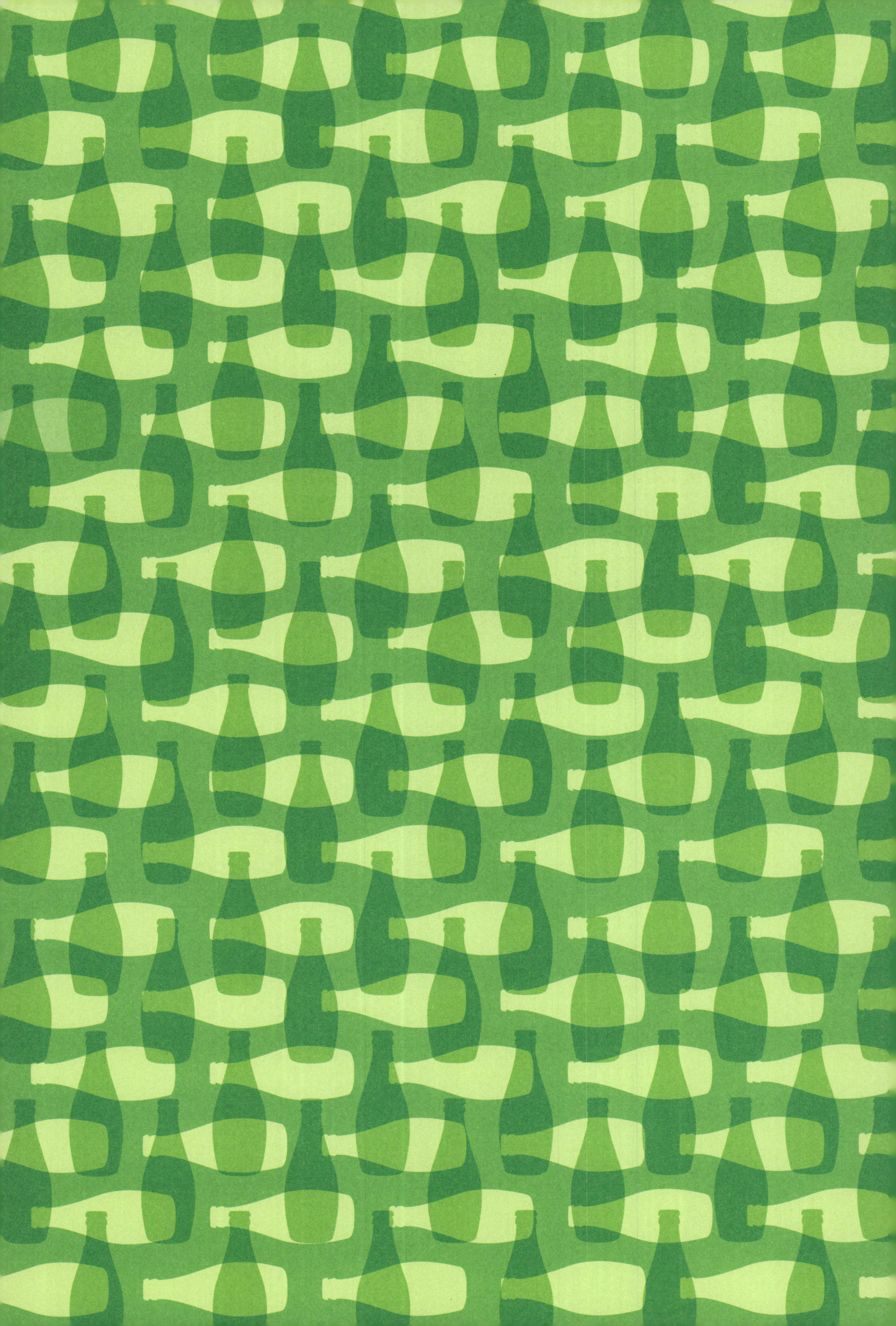

limited editions

Bottles and cans adopt a variety of guises, blending for a while with a range of different worlds, but always staying in step with the times and with the vibe and spirit of Perrier. Major names in the world of fashion and design - Sophia Wood, Agnès B, Paul & Joe – have given Perrier a signature makeover. Pin-up Dita Von Teese has featured three times on the bottle. To celebrate its 150th anniversary, Perrier is becoming a Pop Art icon with its Andy Warhol limited edition.

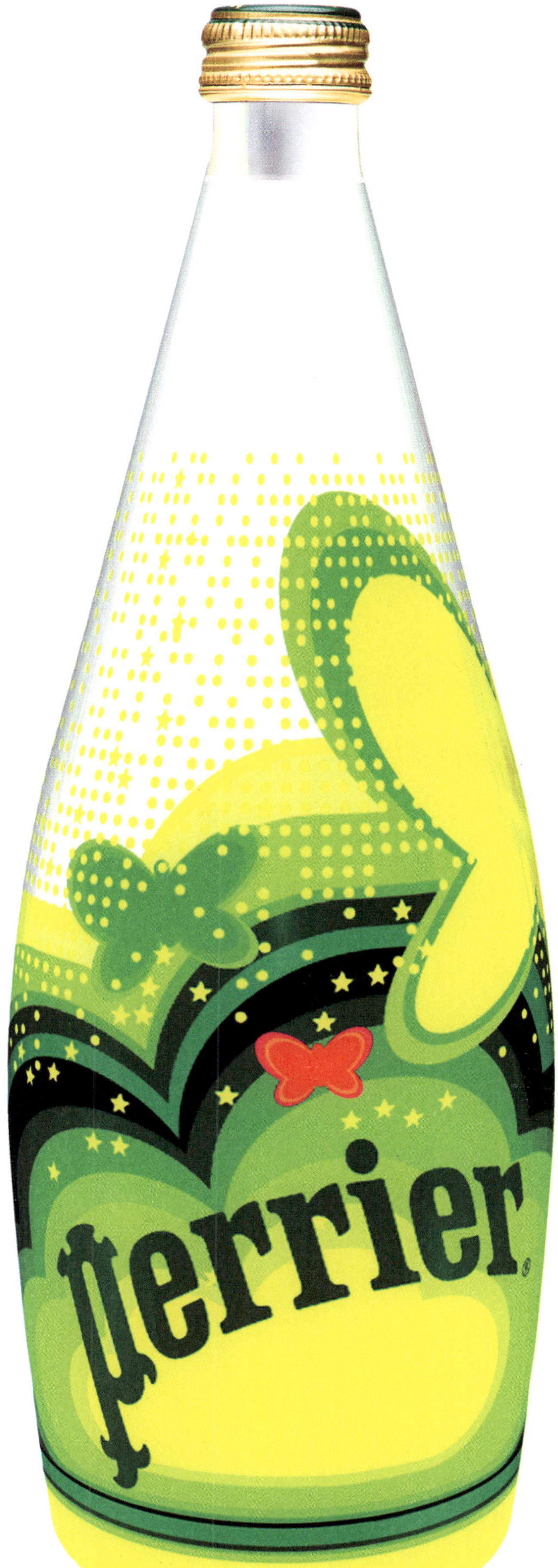
Perrier

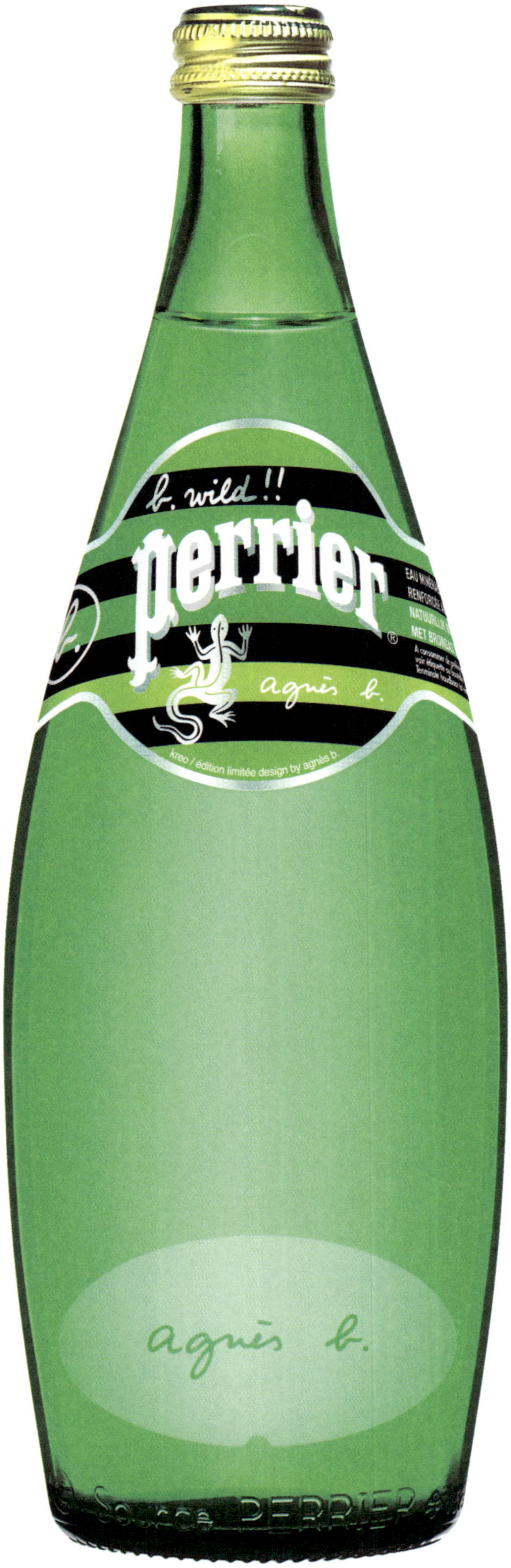
b. wild !!
perrier
agnès b.
kreo / édition limitée design by agnès b.
agnès b.
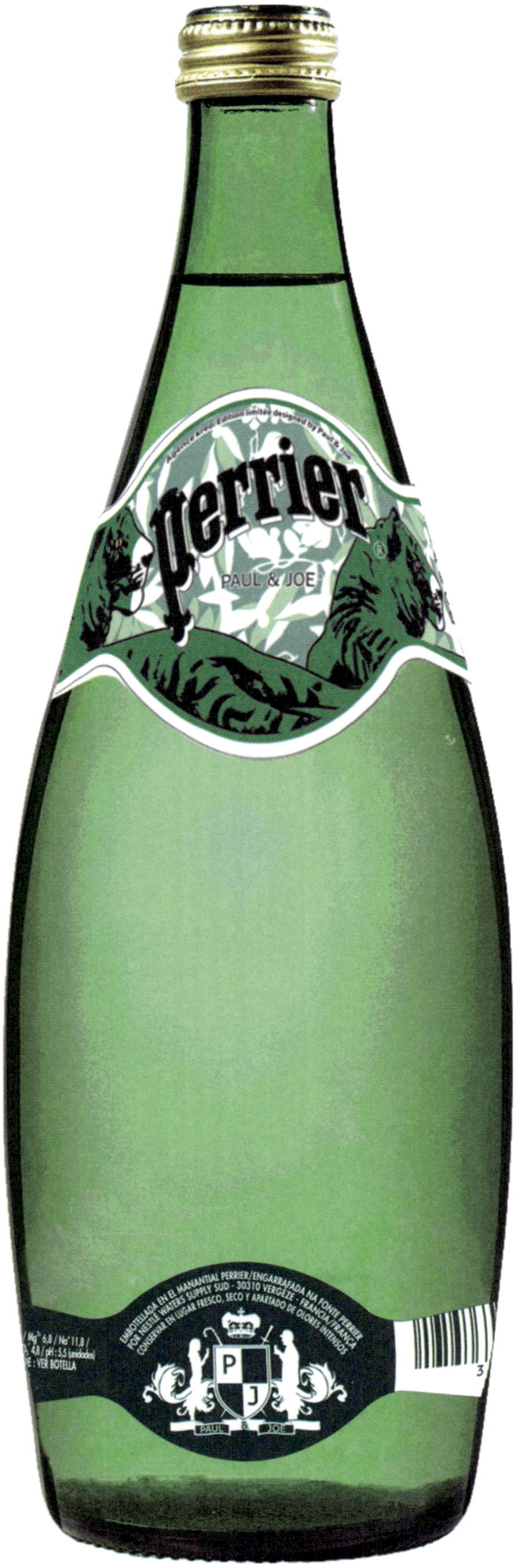
perrier
PAUL & JOE
PAUL & JOE

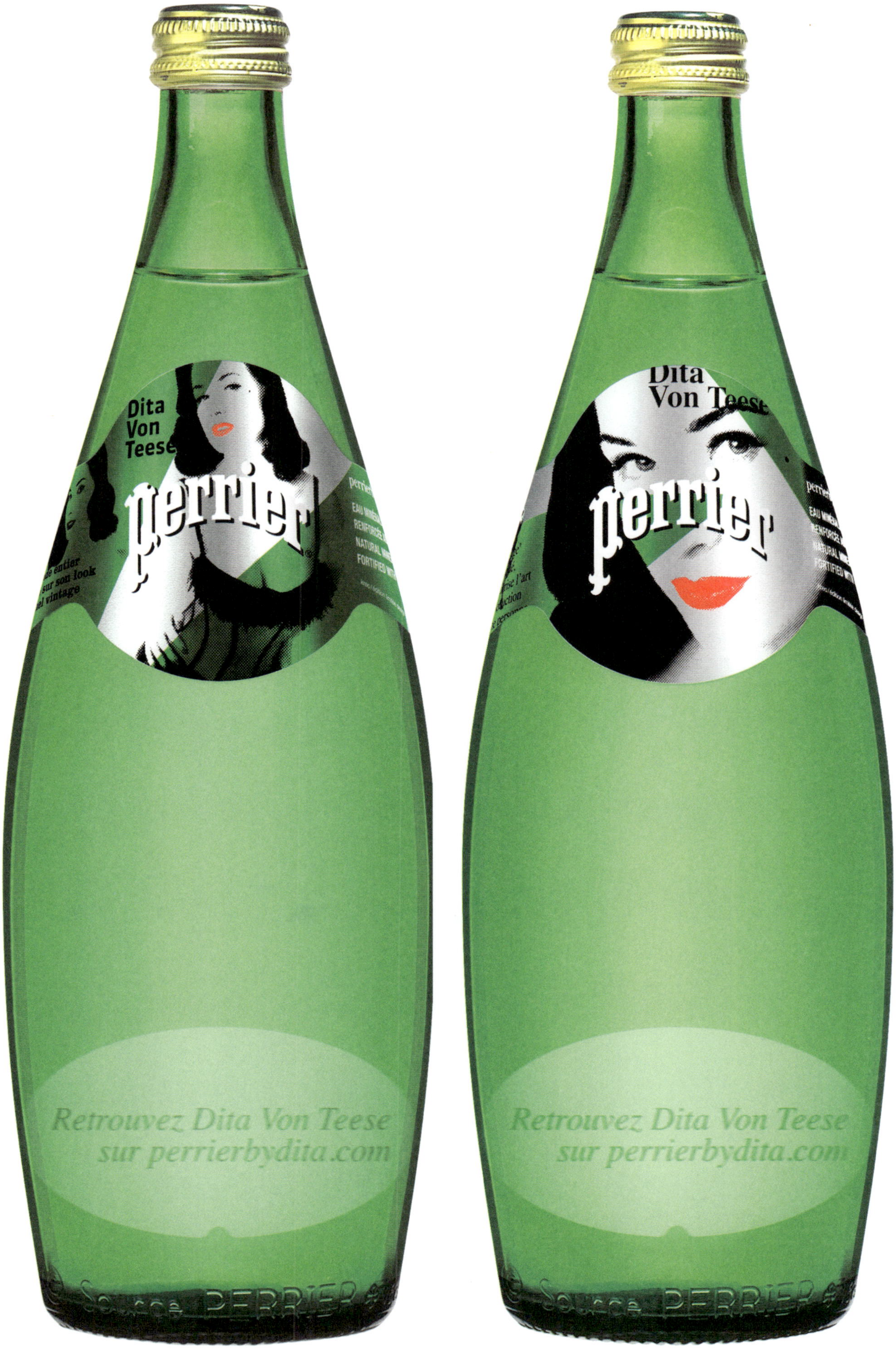
Dita
Von
Teese
perrier
Retrouvez Dita Von Teese
sur perrierbydita.com
Dita
Von Teese
perrier
Retrouvez Dita Von Teese
sur perrierbydita.com

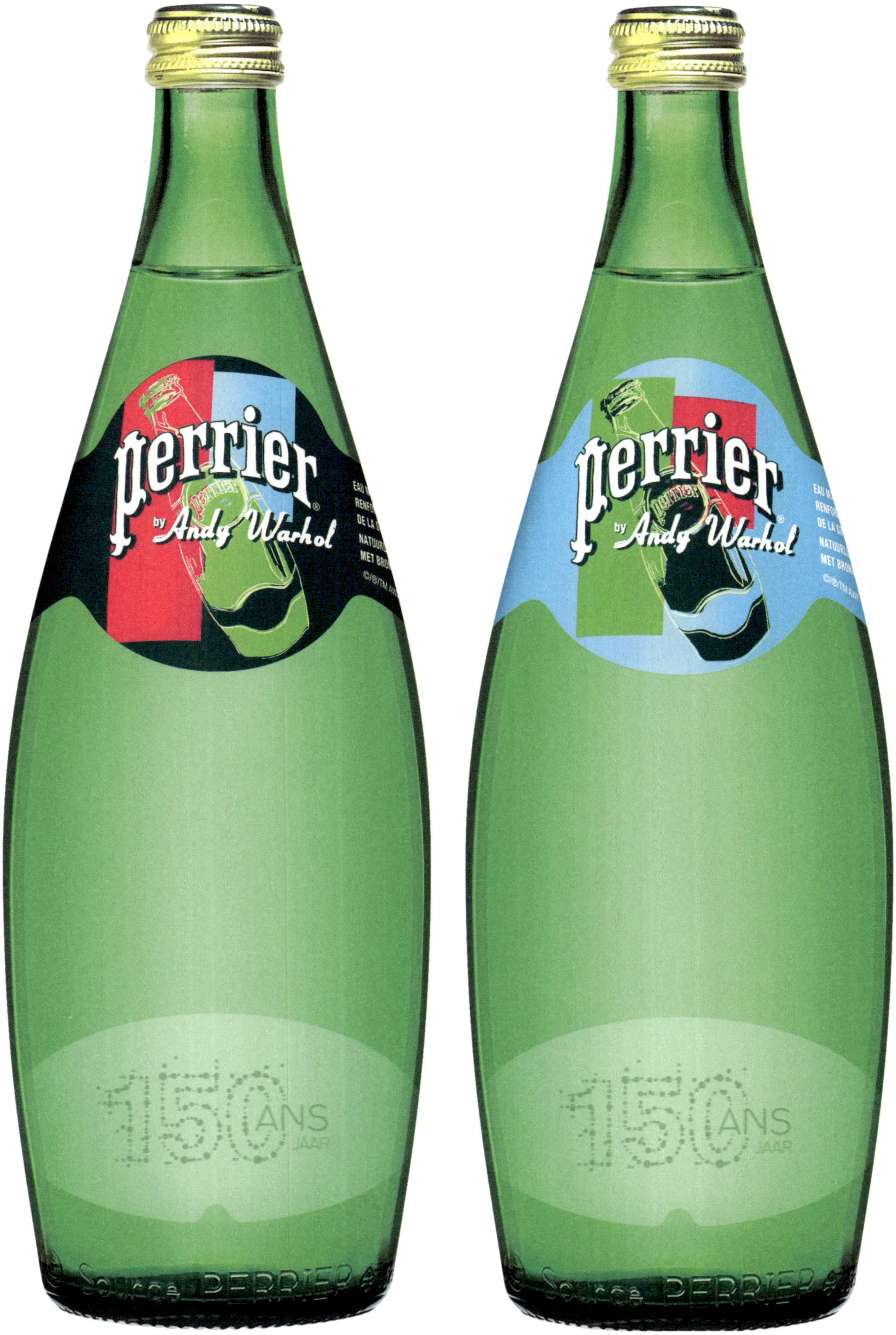
perrier
by Andy Warhol
150 ANS JAAR
Source PERRIER
perrier
by Andy Warhol
150 ANS JAAR
Source PERRIER

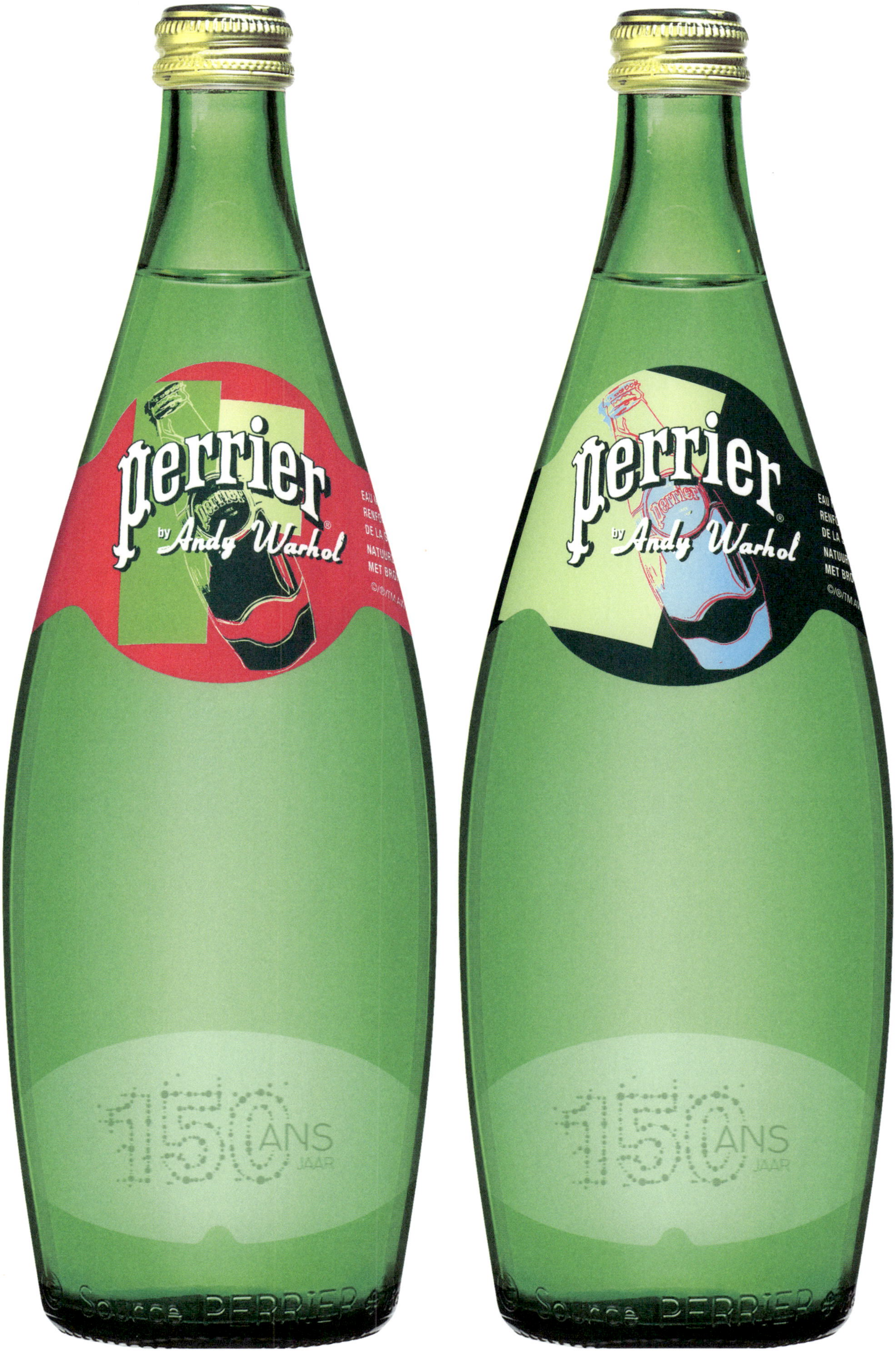
Perrier
by Andy Warhol
150 ANS JAAR
Source PERRIER
Perrier
by Andy Warhol
150 ANS JAAR
Source PERRIER

Photo credits

Pages 4-5 ©/®/TM The Andy Warhol Foundation for the Visual Arts, inc
Page 21 top © Sandrine Alouf
Page 21 bottom © Tallandier/ Rue des Archives
Page 29 © Adagp, Paris 2013
Page 35 top © Loran Dhérines/ Liquid Chef Paris
Page 35 bottom © Ogilvy/ with the kind permission of Wendy Wolf / Zohar international
Pages 41, 42, 45, 46, 47, 53, 54, 55, 57, 58, 59, 60, 63, 64,83, 84-85, 86, 87 © Adagp, Paris 2013
Page 43 © J.Dubout, www.dubout.fr
Page 61 © Kiraz
Pages 71, 72, 73 © Julien Forest
Pages 75, 76, 77, 79, 80, 81 © Jean-Claude Dewolf
Page 83 © Bibliothèque Forney/Roger-Viollet/ Adagp, Paris 2013
Pages 90-91 © Daniel Vignat
Page 93 © MGi Studio
Page 94 © MGi Studio
Page 97 © Leo Burnett London
Page 99 © Havas Worldwide Bruxelles
Pages 100-101 © Nagata Kikaku, Inc./ Takushi Yoneda/ Megumu Wada
Page 103 © Ogilvy/ vincent dixon@ask our agents / Jacques Parnel
Page 104 © Ogilvy/ vincent dixon@ask our agents
Page 105 © Ogilvy/ vincent dixon@ask our agents / Hergé/ Moulinsart 2013
Page 107 © Ogilvy/ Jean-Paul Goude / La Pac/ with the kind permission of Marie Sophie Wilson/ Viva Model Management
Page 108 © Ogilvy/ excerpt from *The Planets* directed by Ridley Scott/ RSA
Page 109 © Ogilvy/ Première Heure/
Page 111 © Ogilvy/ with the kind permission of Wendy Wolf / Zohar international
Page 112 top and bottom © Ogilvy
Page 112 centre © Ogilvy/ with the kind permission of Gabriel Marques Santos / Zohar international
Page 113 © Ogilvy/ Jean-Yves Lemoigne/ Carole Lambert
Page 115 © Ogilvy/Fighting Fish
Page 116 © Ogilvy/ with the kind permission of Dita Von Teese/ Dishell Multimedia Group
Page 117 © Ogilvy/ Moonwalk Films/ Domino Productions
Page 121 © Galerie Kreo/ Sophia Wood
Page 122 left © Galerie Kreo/ Agnès B
Page 122 right © Galerie Kreo/ Paul & Joe
Page 123 © Galerie Kreo/ Dita Von Teese
Page 124/ 125 ©/®/TM The Andy Warhol Foundation for the Visual Arts, inc
Page 127 © Jean-Philippe François

Documents held at the Perrier museum in Vergèze were photographed by François Deladerrière:
4-5,13, 15, 16, 19, 23, 25 (top and center), 27, 29, 31, 33, 39, 41, 42, 43, 45, 46, 47, 49, 50, 51, 53, 54, 55, 57, 58, 59, 60, 61, 63, 64, 65, 67, 68, 69, 71, 72, 73, 75, 76, 77, 79, 80, 81, 83,84-85, 86, 87, 88, 90-91, 97, 99, 100-101, 128.

The Dita Von Teese and Andy Warhol limited edition bottles were designed by Hartland Villa: **123, 124, 125.**

Where we have been unable, despite our best endeavours, to identify and contact photographers who do not feature in this list, we would invite them to contact the publishers.

The publishers would like to extend their warmest thanks to everybody who contributed to the preparation of this book, especially:
Team Perrier (Fabio Brusa, Émilie Lassalle, Sylvie Nelep), artists (Agnès B, Jean-Paul Goude, Kiraz, Jacques Parnel, Paul & Joe, Ridley Scott, Daniel Vignat, Dita Von Teese, Sophia Wood), photographers (Sandrine Alouf, François Deladerrière, Jean-Claude Dewolf, Loran Dhérines, Vincent Dixon, Jean-Philippe François, Jean-Yves Lemoigne), actors (Amy Bailey, Gabriel Marques Santos, Marie Sophie Wilson, Wendy Wolf), agencies (ADAGP, Leo Burnett, Carole Lambert agent, Dishell Multimedia, Domino Productions, Fighting Fish, Havas Worldwide Bruxelles, La Pac, LH Artists, MGi Studio, Moonwalk Films, Moulinsart, Nagata Kikaku inc, Ogilvy, Première Heure, Roger-Viollet, Rue des Archives, Succession Dubout, Succession Jean-Claude Forest, the Andy Warhol Foundation, Viva Model Management, Zohar international).

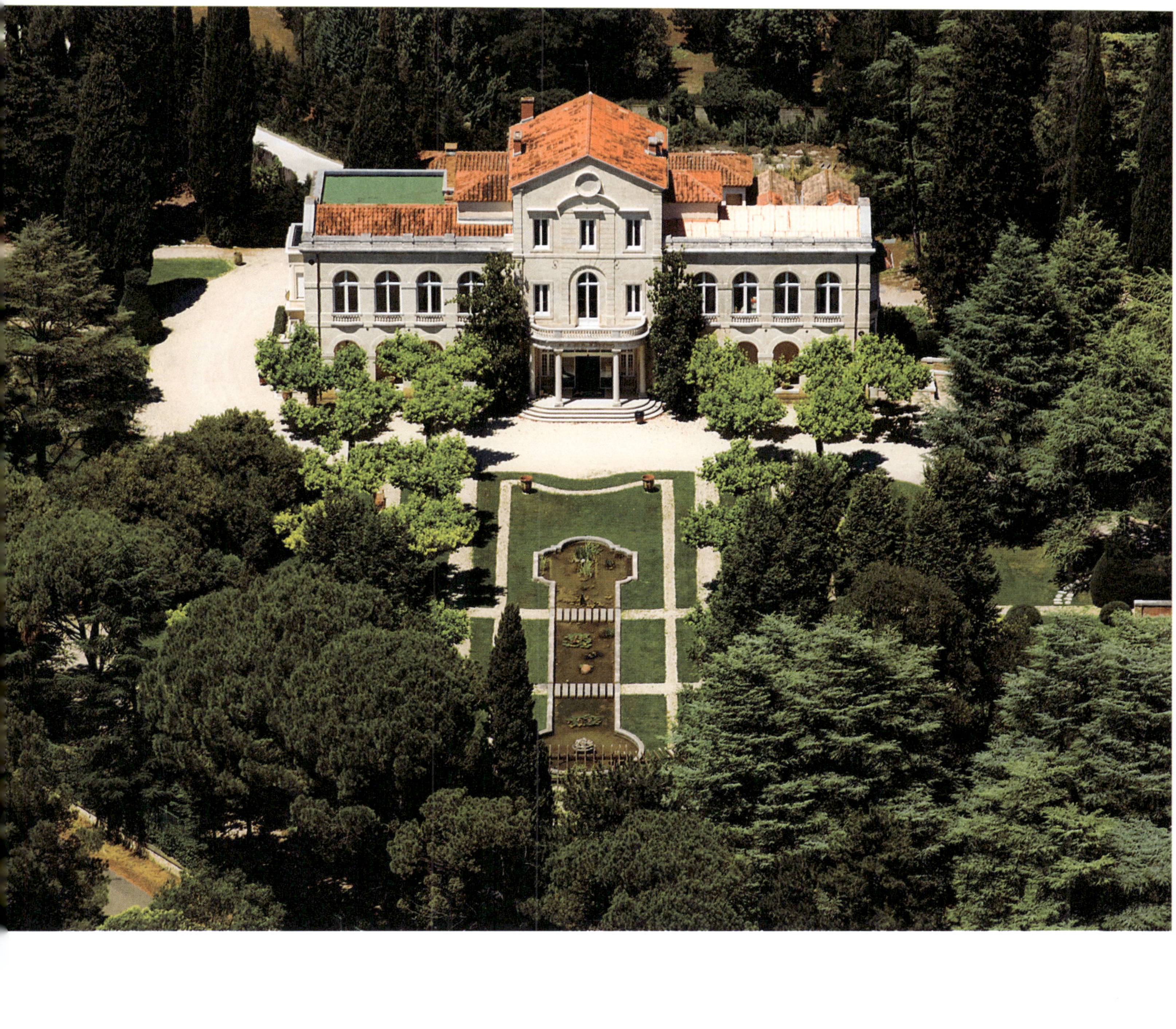

Aerial view of the Perrier castle-museum

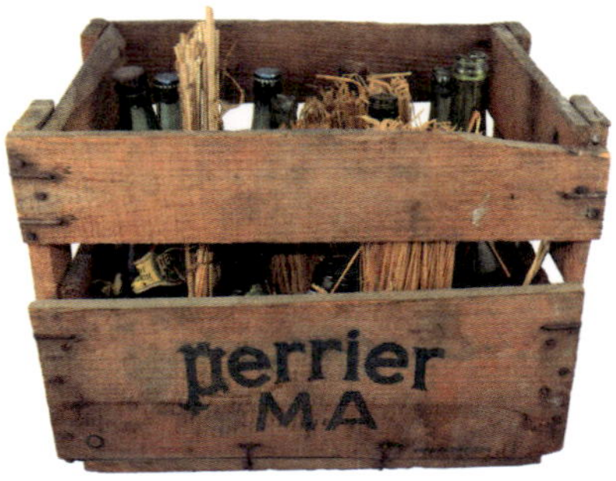

Printed in May 2013
by Grafiche Flaminia, Trevi.
Production manager
Margherita Mariano
Printed in Italy
Photoengraving Planètes Couleur,
Paris.

FSC
MIX
Papier
FSC® C007907